Nicholas of Cusa
Trinity, Freedom and Dialogue

TEXTE UND STUDIEN
ZUR EUROPÄISCHEN GEISTESGESCHICHTE

HERAUSGEGEBEN VON
IÑIGO BOCKEN, JOHANN KREUZER, KLAUS REINHARDT (†) UND
HARALD SCHWAETZER

REIHE B
BAND 13

Davide Monaco

Nicholas of Cusa: Trinity, Freedom and Dialogue

Aschendorff
Verlag

Bibliografische Information der Deutschen Bibliothek
Die Deutsche Bibliothek verzeichnet diese Publikation in der Deutschen Nationalbibliografie; detaillierte bibliografische Daten sind im Internet über <http://dnb.ddb.de> abrufbar.

www.aschendorff-buchverlag.de

Gedruckt mit freundlicher Unterstützung
der Alexander von Humboldt-Stiftung

Printed in Germany
ISSN 2365-015X

ISBN 978-3-402-15999-6
ISBN 978-3-402-16000-8 (E-Book-PDF)

To Professor Guido Mazzotta

Contents

Acknowledgements

The present work came about thanks to the support given by the *Alexander von Humboldt Foundation*, which both financed my research stay at the University of Münster, and which saw the work's completion and publication. I am most grateful to the Foundation, to its members and representatives. During the years employed in the research work which led to the drafting of the volume I incurred numerous debts of gratitude, several most profound ones. Fully mindful of the inadequacy I have in expressing my total appreciation I would like to thank Professors Francesco Tomatis, Leonardo Sileo, Giulio d'Onofrio, Francesco Piro, Thomas Leinkauf, Vincenzo Vitiello, Aniello Montano, Piero Coda, Walter Andreas Euler, Giuseppe Veltri, Werner Beierwaltes. Special thanks go to Professor Thomas Leinkauf for inviting me to the *Philosophisches Seminar* of the University of Münster and for the trouble he has gone to in publishing this volume. I thank the directors of the reviews in which some of the texts presented herein had originally appeared, together with Professors Harald Schwaetzer, Inigo Bocken and Johann Kreuzer for accepting my text in the present series. I would like to thank the *Institut für Cusanus Forschung* of the University of Trier and the *Foundation Günter Klotz und Helena Klotz-Makowiecki* for awarding this work, while still in its unpublished form entitled *Freedom and Dialogue in Cusanus' Thought*, the Helena Klotz-Makowiecki Prize, dedicated to the memory of Rudolf Haubst, for scientific research into Cusanus. It is to Prof. Guido Mazzotta who encouraged me to persevere in my philosophical pursuits by inspiring me with hope at a time of difficulty in my life, that I dedicate this text.

Key

The citations of Cusanus' works refer to the pages of the critical edition, namely *Nicolai de Cusa Opera omnia*, iussu et auctoritate Academiae Litterarum Heidelbergensis ad codicum fidem edita, Meiner, Leipzig/Hamburg 1932ff.

Apol.	*Apologia doctae ignorantiae,* II, ed. R. Klibansky, Meiner, Hamburg 1932 (2007²).
Comp.	*Compendium*, XI, 3, ed. B. Decker - K. Bormann, Meiner, Hamburg 1964.
Crib. Alk.	*Cribratio Alkorani*, VIII, ed. L. Hagemann, Meiner, Hamburg 1986.
De aequal.	*De aequalitate*, X, 1, ed. H. G. Senger, Meiner, Hamburg 2001.
De ap. theor.	*De apice theoriae*, XII, ed. R. Klibansky - H. G. Senger, Meiner, Hamburg 1982.
De beryl.	*De beryllo*, XI, 1, ed. H. G. Senger - K. Bormann, Meiner, Hamburg 1988.
De conc. cath.	*De concordantia catholica*, XIV, 1-3, ed. G. Kallen, Meiner, Hamburg 1944-1968.
De coni.	*De coniecturis*, III, ed. J. Koch - K. Bormann - G. H. Senger, Meiner, Hamburg 1972.
De dato	*De dato patris luminum*, IV, ed. P. Wilpert, Meiner, Hamburg 1959.
De Deo absc.	*De Deo abscondito*, IV, ed. P. Wilpert, Meiner, Hamburg 1959.
De docta ign.	*De docta ignorantia*, I, ed. E. Hoffmann - R. Klibansky, Meiner, Leipzig 1932.
De fil.	*De filiatione Dei*, IV, ed. P. Wilpert, Meiner, Hamburg 1959.
De gen.	*De genesi*, IV, ed. P. Wilpert, Meiner, Hamburg 1959.
De ludo	*De ludo globi*, IX, ed. G. H. Senger, Meiner, Hamburg 1998.
De pace	*De pace fidei*, VII, ed. R. Klibansky - H. Bascour, Meiner, Hamburg 1959 (1970²).
De poss.	*De possest*, XI, 2, ed. R. Steiger, Meiner, Hamburg 1973.
De princ.	*De Deo unitrino principio*, X, 2b, ed. K. Bormann - A. D. Riemann, Meiner, Hamburg 1988.
De quaer.	*De quaerendo Deum*, IV, ed. P. Wilpert, Meiner, Hamburg 1959.
De theol. compl.	*De theologicis complementis*, X, 2a, ed. A. D. Riemann - K. Bormann, Meiner, Hamburg 1994.

De ven. sap.	*De venatione sapientiae*, XII, ed. R. Klibansky - H. G. Senger, Meiner, Hamburg 1982.
De vis.	*De visione Dei*, VI, ed. A. D. Riemann, Meiner, Hamburg 2000.
De non aliud	*Directio speculantis seu de non aliud*, XIII, ed. L. Baur - P. Wilpert, Meiner, Leipzig 1944.
De sap.	*Idiota de sapientia*, V, ed. R. Steiger, Meiner, Hamburg 1983.
De mente	*Idiota de mente*, V, ed. R. Steiger, Meiner, Hamburg 1983.
De stat. exper.	*Idiota de staticis experimentis*, V, ed. L. Baur, Meiner, Hamburg 1983.

The citations of Cusanus' works are made by indicating the title abbreviation of the work, the volume in Roman numerals and, if relevant, by the edition in Arabic numerals of the *opera omnia* to which they refer, the indication (if any) of the book in Latin numerals and the chapter in Arabic numerals, and whenever available the number of the paragraph and of the pages.

Cusanus' sermons are cited by indicating the sermon number according to the new numbering of the critical edition, the reference in Roman numerals to the volume, and in Arabic numerals to the issue of the critical edition, and by an indication of the number of the paragraph and of the pages.

Preface

The underlying theme of the essays published in this volume, as the title shows, comprises the concepts of the Trinity, freedom and dialogue. These not only represent certain crucial themes of Cusanus' work, but, as we believe, they offer a possible hermeneutical key for understanding the meaning of his thought by providing an appropriate perspective for re-examining his texts and understanding his philosophy.

The Trinity is certainly one of the *Leitmotifs* of all Cusanus' thinking starting from his first sermon *In principio erat Verbum* of 1430 to his last work the *De apice theoriae* of 1464, which closes with the reference to the divine One-Trinity, as though setting a seal on all his philosophy. If, as is undeniable, Cusanus incurred a consistent debt from the speculation of Plato and the Greek Neoplatonists like Proclus, whose works he read with great perception, it is nevertheless to him that a revival of and investigation into the Christian reading of the Neoplatonic vision of the One trinitarially - and not only, are to be attributed. From Cusanus' philosophical viewpoint, without the One the Trinity would remain indescribable, ineffable, inexpressible, closed and separate in its transcendence, as shown by the aporia into which, according to Damascius, Greek henological speculation risked falling. The Trinity saves the One from his absoluteness and occultness and, although it does not cancel out his mystery, it reveals him as divine One-Trinity. In fact, if the divine Trinity was a result of Christian revelation that the Christian Platonists or Neoplatonists themselves– as for example the Church Fathers, Augustine and the masters of the school of Chartres, to quote some of Cusanus' sources – had certainly not ignored, to Cusanus goes the merit of uniting trinitarian theology with the theology of the divine names of Dionysian origin.

The re-elaboration of Platonic and Neoplatonic speculation on the One in a clearly trinitarian perspective is not the only feature of Cusanus' work. In fact at the basis of the essays presented here is the conviction founded on an analysis and textual interpretation of his works, that in his last texts he pursues his own theory on the First Principle towards an intended elaboration of his freedom. The works of the later Cusanus, that is to say those which from the *De beryllo* of 1458 arrive at the *De apice theoriae* of 1464, the year of his demise, undergo a marked reformulation of his conception of the One by focusing on the question of divine freedom. In this regard it is to be emphasised that his thought appears to be speculatively closer to that of Plotinus' than to that of Proclus' and of the other Neoplatonists, despite his attachment to them. The Neoplatonists in fact appear to think of a necessary progress of the many from the One and appear to forget the question of the origin of the First Principle, with the sole exception of Plotinus, who in contrast appears to respond to both questions through a discussion on the freedom and will of the One.

In this collection of essays an attempt is made to show both philologically and speculatively how Cusanus elaborates his conception of the One through critical dialogue with the positions held by Plato, by Proclus, by the Christian Neoplatonists such as Dionysius the Areopagite, by John Scotus Eriugena and Meister Eckhart and by several Church Fathers, through carrying out an original reappraisal of the Neoplatonic tradition. More especially with regard to Proclus as source of the idea of the *non aliud* it is to the *Commentarium in Platonis Parmenidem* that the cardinal's elaboration is first indebted, and then to the *Theologia platonica*, although being the Cardinal's last personal and original work. The cardinal elaborates his conception of the free will of the One according to a two-fold dimension: firstly in relation to the creation of the world, and then in relation to the Trinitarian generation of himself. In Cusanus' view Trinity and free will concur to define the very essence of the One, although Cusanus never overlooks the dimension of transcendence and ulteriority of the *Deus absconditus* on the very revelation of God, who inasmuch as infinite is beyond the One himself and the Trinity itself.

The theme of freedom also represents the hinge linking the different parts of the work. If freedom connotes the acting of the divine Principle, it cannot fail also to imprint the essence of his image, or, that is to say, of man. In the universal *explicatio Dei* the human *mens* plays an exclusive and privileged role: it is in fact not mere explication (unfolding), but *viva imago Dei*, or rather, inasmuch as image of infinite divine freedom, it is essentially connotated as finite and creatural freedom. Thus dialogue becomes the means through which man can operate such divine freedom in relating himself with other men, but also with God, through prayer and response to his call.

Cusanus' dialogical perspective, which he proposes as a sort of response to the question already existing in his day, namely that of the clash among the various cultures and religions, thus finds its roots in his vision of the divine and of man. If in the Trinity, the distinction among people is determined through freedom in that each is *alius* than the other, but the coessentiality of essence in that each is also *non aliud* than the other, in the same way men are able to recognise their brotherhood and communion through freedom, albeit within the sphere of the reciprocal differences and distinctions between religions, cults, cultures, and ways of living. Through freedom Trinity becomes the possible model, at the same time both speculative and practical, for dialogue. It is not by chance that in the history of Western thought Cusanus was among the first to put aside the merely denigratory and condemnatory designs against Islam and to wish for a pacific attitude of greater conciliation through theorization and implementation of a *pia inter-*

pretatio of the Koran, or rather of an interpretation directed towards recognising therein the precepts concordant with the teachings of the Gospel.

The volume closes with an investigation into several examples of dialogue, this time the historical–critical and speculative dialogue brought about by certain interpreters contemporary with Cusanus' work, especially by the Italian philosopher, Cornelio Fabbro, by the greatest Cusanus scholar living today, namely Werner Beierwaltes, and amongst those scholars concerned with the relationships between Cusanus and Leibniz. In these pages there appear yet again the familiar themes on the Trinitarian re-elaboration of the Neoplatonic vision of the One, on divine freedom and on the human *mens* as image of the creative freedom of God, as evidence of their relevance for understanding the work of the German thinker.

Part I

The Freedom of God and The Trinity

1. Cusanus and Plato's *Parmenides*

1.1 *Cusanus, Reader of Plato*

Cardinal Nicholas of Cusa (herein known and referred to as Cusanus) kept an almost complete collection of the Latin translations of the Platonic texts available in his day, and appears to have been a very careful reader.[1] Amongst the works in his possession were: *the Apology*, *Phaedo*, *Crito*, *Meno* and *Phaedrus* in Leonardo Bruni Aretino and Enrico Aristippo's Latin translations (*Codex Cusanus177*); *the Republic* in Pier Candido Decembrio's translation (*Codex Cusanus178); the Laws* in George of Trebisonda's translation, *the Apology*, *Phaedo*, *Crito*, *Meno* and *Phaedro* in Leonardo Bruni Aretino and Enrico Aristippo's Latin translations (*Codex Cusanus177*); *the Republic* in Pier Candido Decembrio's translation (*Codex Cusanus178*); *the Laws* in George of Trebisonda's translation (*Harl. 3261*); *the Letters* in Leonardo Bruni's translations; the partial translation of *the Timaeus* handed down from Chalcidius' commentary (*Harl. 2652*);[2] and, as we shall see by analysis, the first complete Latin version of the *Parmenides.*Thus it may be stated with certainty that Cusanus had a direct knowledge of Plato's dialogues, albeit in their Latin translations.

Credit goes to the Cardinal as patron and commissioner of the arts for the first Latin version of Plato's *Parmenides*. Giovanni Andrea de' Bussi in his prologue to

1 Cf. J. Hankins, *Plato in the Italian Renaissance*, Brill, Leiden 19912, pp. 163ff.; J. Marx, *Verzeichnis der Handschriften-Sammlung des Hospital zu Cues bei Bernkastel a./Mosel*, Schaar & Dathe, Trier 1905, pp. 164-169; P. O. Kristeller, *Studies in Renaissance Thought and Letters*, I, Edizioni di Storia e Letteratura, Roma 1956, pp. 35-36; H. G. Senger, *Die Exzerpte und Randnoten des Nikolaus von Kues zu den lateinischen Übersetzungen der Proclus-Schriften. Theologia Platonis-Elementatio theologica*, Winter, Heidelberg 1986, p. 24. Despite this, with the marginal notes to the Platonic texts Cusanus was somewhat sparing, cf. G. Santinello, *Glosse di mano del Cusano alla Repubblica di Platone*, in «Rinascimento», XX (1969), p. 136.

2 Cf. J. Hirschberger, *Das Platon-Bild beim Nikolaus von Kues*, in *Niccolò Cusano agli inizi del mondo moderno*, ed. G. Santinello, Sansoni, Firenze, 1970, pp. 113-135; P. O. Kristeller, *A Latin translation of Gemistos Plethon's de fato by Johannes Sophianos dedicated to Nicholas of Cusa*, in *Nicolò Cusano agli inizi del mondo moderno*, cit., pp. 190-191.

his edition of Apuleius' *Didascalicus* records that it was the Cardinal, no less, who fervently desired the translation of the Platonic dialogue.[3] On his arrival in Rome on 30 September 1458, the Cardinal commissioned George of Trebisonda (the so-called Trapezunzio) to carry out the translation, who completed it and composed the dedication to Cusanus present on the manuscript, probably between 11 January 1459 and 30 September of the same year.[4] The Cardinal received the version certainly not before the month of June when he had already concluded the *De Principio* (9 June 1459) in which constant reference to Plato is made, but without any direct citation to Plato's text, but always through Proclus' *Commentary to Plato's Parmenides.*[5] The translation of Plato's *Parmenides*, discovered by Raymond Klibansky in 1942 and contained in *Codex 6021* of the Guarnaci Library of Volterra, represents the only testimony of the first integral Latin version of the Platonic text, preceding Ficino's one by at least five years.[6] Thitherto the dialogue had been known in the West through the translation of Proclus' *Commentary to Plato's Parmenides* made by William of Moerbeke who breaks off at the end of the first hypothesis. The text was therefore known only in an indirect and incomplete form.[7]Cusanus himself who in his youthful years had already

3 Giovanni Andrea de' Bussi, *Prefazioni alle edizioni di Swynheym e Pannartz prototipografi romani*, ed. M. Miglio, Il Polifilo, Milano 1978, p. 18. In fact the *Didascalicus* is today attributed to Alcinous.

4 Cf. I. Ruocco, *Introduzione* a *Il Platone latino. Il Parmenide: Giorgio di Trebisonda e il cardinale Cusano*, ed. I. Ruocco, Olschki, Firenze 2003, p. 9. A translation that did not meet with success, seeing that only one testimony to it exists.

5 This chronology has been proposed by Monfasani as correction of the one formerly proposed by Klibansky who in contrast indicated 1450/51 as dating. Cf. J. Monfasani, *George of Trebizond: a bibliography and a study of his Rhetoric and Logic*, Leiden, Brill 1976, pp. 161-170; R. Klibansky, *Plato's Parmenides in the Middle Ages and the Renaissance. A chapter in the History of Platonic Studies*, in «Medieval and Renaissance Studies», 1 (1943), pp. 281-330. In fact, earlier, the famous historian of Platonic tradition had advanced certain doubts on this dating as between 1450/51 and the composition of the *De non aliud* there are no direct references in Cusanus' work to Plato's text. The new dating was later also accepted by Klibansky himself, cf. R. Klibansky, *Preface to* Id., *Plato's Parmenides in the Middle Ages and the Renaissance. A chapter in the History of Platonic Studies*, in *The continuity of the Platonic tradition during the Middle Ages*, Kraus, München 1981, pp. V-IX.

6 The translation is conserved in the codex *Volterranus 6021*, ff. 61r-81v. Now is published in *Il Platone latino. Il Parmenide: Giorgio di Trebisonda e il cardinale Cusano*, cit., pp. 35-84. On the recovery cf. R. Klibansky, *Plato's Parmenides in the Middle Ages and the Renaissance. A chapter in the History of Platonic Studies*, cit. On the pre-Ficinian translation of Plato's works cf. E. Garin, *Ricerche sulle traduzioni di Platone nella prima metà del sec. XV*, in *Medioevo e Rinascimento. Studi in onore di Bruno Nardi*, 2 voll., Sansoni, Firenze 1955, I, pp. 339-374.

7 The first critical edition of the Latin edition of the *Parmenides* byWilliam of Moerbeke extrapolated from Proclus' commentary to form a unique and continuous text as edited by Raymond Klibansky and Carlotta Labowsky and includes also the last book of the commentatry

made a first contact with Proclus' texts beginning from 1450-1455 had the text of Proclus'commentary at his disposal, deeply meditating on it, annotating it assiduously, and beginning from the *De Beryllo (*1458), to quote it frequently.[8] Therefore, credit goes to Cusanus if both the partial medieval version, and the direct and complete humanistic one of *The Parmenides* – just as the one of the *Meno* dating back to the 12th century[9] – were introduced into Italy.[10]

In Cusanus' work a mention of Plato's *Parmenides* first appears in the *Maria optimam partem elegit* sermon of 15 August 1446.[11] In this sermon Plato is compared with Boethius and Dionysius the Areopagite as supporter of a conception of the One understood as *necessarium*, for there to be many, and at the same time as *superexaltatum*, in that beyond the many, a vision is attributed to him of the *Unum,* essentially of Neoplatonic matrix[12]. An interpretation of Plato and of *the Parmenides* is repeated and further analysed in the *Apologia doctae ignorantiae* of 1449:

> Unde, quando Avicenna in Dei singularitatem conatur ascendere per theologiam negativam, Deum ab omni singulari et universali absolvit; sed actius ante ipsum divinus Plato in Parmenide tali modo in Deum conatus est viam pandere; quem adeo divinus Dionysius imitatus est, ut saepius Platonis verba seriatim posuisse reperiatur.[13]

of Proclus thitherto unpublished was lost in the original Greek and handed down only in the Latin version. Cf. Proclus, *Commentaire sur le Parménide de Platon. Traduction de Guillaume de Moerbeke*, 2 tt., ed. C. Steel, Brill, Leiden 1982-1985. The editions of the Greek text available of the Proclus'*Commentary on Parmenides*: Proclus, *Commentarium in Platonis Parmenidem*, in *Procli philosophi platonici opera inedita*, ed. V. Cousin, Eberhard, Paris 1820-1827 [rist. Minerva, Frankfurt am Main 1962], 617-1244; Proclus, *In Platonis Parmenidem commentaria*, III voll., ed. C. Steel, Clarendon, Oxford 2007-2009;*Proclus, Commentaire sur le Parménide de Platon*, 5 voll, eds. C. Luna - A.-Ph. Segonds, Les Belles Lettres, Paris 2007-2014.

8 An early contact with the texts is witnessed by Cusanus' own hand-written extracts contained in the present codex *Argentoratensis bibliothecae Universitatis 84* and now published in R. Haubst, *Die Thomas- und Proklos-Exzerpte des «Nicolaus Treverensis» in Codicillus Strassburg 84*, in «MFCG», 1 (1968), pp. 17-51. The first to focus attention to these extracts was E. Vansteenberghe, *Quelques lectures de jeunesse de Nicolas de Cuesd'aprèsunmanuscrit inconnu de sa bibliothèque*, in*«Archives d'Histoire Doctrinale et Littéraire du Moyen Âge»*, 3 (1928), pp. 275-284. Cusanus' knowledge of Proclus' *Commentary on the Parmenides* is attested by the marginal notes written in his hand present in the codexes *Vaticanus Latinus 3074* and *Codex Cusanus 186*, which he came into possession of during the years 1450-1455. Cf. C. Steel, *Introduction*, in Proclo, *Commentaire sur le Parménide de Platon. Traduction de Guillaume de Moerbeke*, cit., t. 1, pp. 12-17.

9 Cf. *Meno, interprete Henrico Aristippo*, ed. V. Kourdeuter, Warburg Institute, London 1940.

10 Cf. J. Hankins, *Plato in the Italian Renaissance*, cit., pp. 4-5, note 4.

11 Cf. *Sermo LXXI*, h XVII/5, n. 9, p. 427.

12 *Sermo LXXI*, h XVII/5, n. 9-11, p. 427-428.

13 *Apol.*, h II, n. 13, p. 10.

Plato's *Parmenides* is interpreted therefore, as place of origin of the negative theological approach.[14] If one takes account of a quotation from the *De Beryllo* and from Cusanus' annotations to *Codex Cusanus 186,* containing Proclus' *Commentary to the Parmenides,* it is not difficult to identify the source of this interpretation. In the *De Beryllo* (1458) Cusanus explicitly writes that:

> Recte igitur, ut Proclus recitat in commentariis Parmenidis, Plato omnia de ipso principio negat.[15]

"Divine Plato" moreover, is a recurring expression in Cusanus' texts, which is found in Proclus' text, carefully annotated, and set in the margin of the manuscript, containing the *Commentary to the Parmenides* in the Cardinal's possession.[16] The adherence of Cusanus' interpretation to Proclus' one of Plato, as father of negative theology, is confirmed and further reinforced by Cusanus' annotations to Proclus' commentary, which often pause in order to emphasize that the divine Plato has not stated anything about the One, although he has refuted all in order to ascend to him.[17] Cusanus read Plato through the optics of Neoplatonism and of Proclus and Dionysius' negative theology, and in accordance with the Proclian tradition, he attributed to Plato and to *the Parmenides* the place of origin of the negative theological approach.

14 A line of continuity between Cusanus' interpretation of the *Parmenides* and that of Proclus' has already been recognised by R. Klibansky, *Plato's Parmenides in the Middle Ages and the Renaissance*, cit., pp. 304-310. On the reading of Neoplatonic and Christian character of Plato by Cusanus cfr. J. Hirschberger, *Das Platon-Bild bei Nikolaus von Kues*, cit., pp. 113-135; W. Beierwaltes, *Das Seiende Eine. Zur neuplatonisches Interpretation der zweiten Hypothesis des platonischen Parmenides: das Beispeiel Cusanus*, in Id., *Procliana. Spätantikes Denken und seine Spuren*, Klostermann, Frankfurt am Main 2007, pp. 215-222; S. Gottlöber, *Das Prinzip der Relationalität: Grundzüge cusanischen Denkens als Parameter für Toleranz und interreligiösen Diskurs*, Thelem, Dresden 2013, pp. 141-146. On Plato and Cusanus, cf. C. Horn, *Cusanus über Platon und dessen Pythagoreismus*, in *Nicolaus von Kues in der Geschichte des Platonismus*, eds. K. Reinhardt-H. Schwaetzer, Roderer, Regensburg 2006, pp. 9-31.

15 *De Beryllo*, XI/1, n. 12, p. 15.

16 Cf. K. Bormann, *Die Exzerpte und Randnoten des Nikolaus von Kues zu den lateinischen Übersetzungen der Proclus-Schriften. Expositio in Parmenidem Platonis*, Winter, Heidelberg 1986, marg. 33: «Plato divinissimus».

17 Cf. *ibid.*, marg. 494: «plato abnegatione ad exaltatum unum ascendit»; n. 497: «plato nichil de deo affirmat»; n. 518: «plato ab uno omnia negat et deo nichil affirmat».

1.2 *De non aliud*

Plato's *Parmenides* however, presents a further aspect of interest as source of Cusanus' thought. After Cusanus had the complete text in the Latin version at his disposal, the first work in which the dialogue is quoted explicitly is the *De non aliud* of 1461-1462.[18] Starting from that moment, although Cusanus' general in-

[18] For a reconstruction of the sources and a close examination and fuller interpretation of the meaning of the non *aliud* cf. D. Monaco, Deus Trinitas. *Dio come* non altro *nel pensiero di Nicolò Cusano*, preface by Werner Beierwaltes, Città Nuova, Roma 2010. Several interesting observations regarding our work have been made by Max Rohstock; cf. M. Rohstock, *Der negative Selbstbezug des Absoluten: Untersuchungen zu Nicolaus Cusanus' Konzept des Nicht-Anderen*, De Gruyter, Berlin 2014. According to the author the idea of *non aliud* should be read under the banner of the negation and negative self-relationship of the Absolute. However, Rohstock speaking always of the Absolute and hardly ever of Trinity seems to remove Cusanus from his concrete historical habitat making him more of an idealist philosopher rather than a thinker and cardinal of the fifteenth century. For Cusanus the First Principle is the God of the medievil Christian tradition and not the Absolute of idealist philosophy. In fact Rohstock claims in several places that we stated that a negative principle would be a complete negation of Christianity by extrapolating and distorting several words of our text (*ibid.*, p. 30 note 101; p. 41, note 138; p. 44 note 150; the sentence is contained according to Rohstock in D. Monaco, *Deus Trinitas*, cit., p. 297). Yet differently from what he alleges we wrote that if nothing for Augustine of Hippo was a negative principle next to God there would be a negation of Christianity since we would have two principles and hence a relapse into gnosticism. To admit a negative principle next to God and different from him would be a negation of Christianity (D. Monaco, *Deus Trinitas*, cit., p. 297). Elsewhere Rohstock states that in our reading of the progress of Cusanus' thought we think of an Überwindung of negative theology (F. Rohstock, *Rezension von Davide Monaco, 2010, Deus Trinitas. Dio come non altro nel pensiero di Nicolò Cusano, prefazione di Werner Beierwaltes, Roma, Città Nuova*, in «Bochumer philosophisches Jahrbuch für Antike und Mittelalter» 15 (2012), p. 299). However, in our text it is possible to read explicitly: "Surpassing is understood here not as an overtaking, a mere leaving behind, a putting aside (Germ. *Ueberwindung*), but is thought of in the Latin sense of *tollere* or of the German *Aufhebung*, that is of taking in order to lead to a higher level, a suppressing-conserving. The negative theological aspiration does not disappear from Cusanus' thought, but rather by studying it closely one tries to go beyond its limits by maintaining some of its basic acquisitions: the negative-critical principle of the *docta ignorantia*, present throughout all Cusanus' speculative enquiring, is the best testimony thereof" (Cf. D. Monaco, *Deus Trinitas*, cit., p. 69, note 144). Cusanus tries to abandon the logic *of opposites* of affirmation and negation. His intention is *to go beyond* (Germ. überwinden) both positive theology and negative theology. Moreover, the *non aliud* contains a dynamic charge which differentiates it from every other form of negation, in that it reveals how through its negativity, *its act of kenosis*, God affirms himself as Trinity (*non aliud est non aliud quam non aliud*).Moreover, unlike what Rohstock states, we have never understood all Neoplatonic thought under the sign of the necessity of the One, seeing that we ourselves in fact quote Plotinus and the passages on the freedom or will of the One contained in *Enneads* VI, 8 (cf. D. Monaco, *Deus Trinitas*, cit., p. 301).

terpretation of the dialogue remains marked by Proclus and Dionysius' exegesis, Plato's *Parmenides* becomes explicitly and clearly distinguished by Proclus' commentary.[19] His influence on the genesis of the *De non aliud* and on the vision of the First Principle as *non aliud,* belonging to the later Cusanus has been mostly overlooked by the *Cusanus-Forschung*, which dwelt, and for good reasons, on Proclus and Dionysius' sources. Yet, despite the marked influence of late-ancient Neoplatonism, there exists a plausible influence of the content of the dialogue on the theology and philosophy of the later Cusanus. Seeing in fact that in the second part of the Platonic dialogue, the question posed by the old Parmenides on the relationship between the One and the many, in the development of his discourse, moves terminologically towards a scheme which mainly sees the One and the others from the One emerge as object of investigation,[20]Cusanus may have discovered in the dialogue a prefiguration of the relationship between *non aliud* and *aliud,* which is the theme of his 1461-1462 work.

On careful analysis, the One-one of the first hypothesis shows certain characteristics which appertain to Cusanus' conception of the First Principle as *non aliud,* especially as himself being identical neither to himself nor to an other, nor different either from himself or from other.[21] The One which is one, in fact is not different from itself, otherwise it would be different from the One, and therefore it would not be the One,[22] just as the *non aliud* is not *aliud,* but *non aliud* than the *non aliud.* At the same time the One of the first hypothesis is not identical to a different thing, otherwise it would no longer be the One, but rather a different thing,[23] just as the *non aliud* is not identical, but *non aliud* than the *aliud.* The

19 *De non aliud,* h XIII, c. 1, p. 3. The relationship between the *De non aliud* and Plato's *Parmenides* has often been forgotten by the *Cusanus-Forschung*: furthmore Paul Wilpert in his commentary on the work of 1952 negated the knowledge on the part of Cusanus of the Platonic dialogue. Cf. Nicolaus Cusanus, *Vom Nichtanderen*, ed. P. Wilpert, Meiner, Hamburg 1952, p. 135. To draw attention to this relationship were more especially Egil Anders Wyller and Werner Beierwaltes, whose contributions expressly dedicated to this theme we quote only: E. A. Wyller, *Zum Begriff "non aliud" bei Nicolaus Cusanus*, in *Niccolò Cusano agli inizi del mondo moderno*, cit., pp. 419-443; Id., *Nicolaus Cusanus' "De non aliud" und Platons Dialog "Parmenides"*, in *Studia Platonica*, eds.K. Döring - W. Kullmann,John Benjamins, Amsterdam 1974, pp. 239-251; W. Beierwaltes, *Das Seiende Eine. Zur neuplatonisches Interpretation der zweiten Hypothesis des platonischen Parmenides: das Beispeiel Cusanus*, cit., pp. 215-222.

20 Cf. M. Migliori, *Dialettica e verità. Commentario filosofico al "Parmenide" di Platone*, Vita e Pensiero, Milano 1990, p. 193. On Plato's *Parmenides* and his interpretations cf. F. Ferrari, *L'enigma del Parmenide*, in Plato, *Parmenide*, Bur, Milano 2004, pp. 9-161.

21 Cf. Plato, *Parm.*, 139b 4-139e 6. Cusanus therefore obtains both the first and the second hypotheses of the *Parmenides,* and not only the second as Wyller affirms. Cf. E. A. Wyller, *Zum Begriff "non aliud" bei Nicolaus Cusanus*, cit., pp. 419-443.

22 Cf. Plato, *Parm.*, 139b 7-8.

23 Cf. Plato, *Parm.*, 139b 9-13.

One of the first hypothesis, however, is neither identical to itself, otherwise it would no longer be one, but two (one and identical to one or one made identical, and one that identifies itself),[24] just as the *non aliud* is *non aliud quam non aliud.* For Plato moreover, the One of the first hypothesis is not even different from a different thing in that as the difference does not belong to the One, but rather only to what is different,[25] just so the *non aliud* is not *aliud* than *aliud.* According to Cusanus, Plato has perceived that before and beyond the other there is not an other, but rather the *Hén*, which is not-other not even than the other : the *non aliud* seems the more precise expression to call the One of the *Parmenides.*[26]In fact, its diversity or otherness is not predicated from nothing nor from the *aliud* and never *aliud* inasmuch as *non aliud.*[27]

However, although the Platonic *Hén* seems in some way close to the *non aliud,* Cusanus himself describes a subtle differentiation between the *Unum* and his idea. In its simplicity and originality the *non aliud* also precedes the One, since – the *unum* being *non aliud quam unum* – it has of the *non aliud* that which is, and not viceversa,[28] and therefore is still *aliud* in comparison with the *non aliud.*[29] The *non aliud* in its aurorality and initiality precedes the *Hén*. Cusanus however, acknowledges Plato as having approached very closely to the mystery of the *non aliud* by placing the One beyond contradiction.[30] In the *Parmenides* the Platonic *Hén* is in fact object of opposing and contradictory predications, in that in its first hypothesis, both entire being and part being are refuted, being in itself and in other, movement and stasis, sameness and otherness, similarity and dissimilarity, equality and inequality, youth and old age: opposites, which in the dimension of the finite and the determined would be patently contradictory, attribute themselves simultaneously to the One-one.[31] In placing the First Principle beyond contradiction Cusanus has a polemical intent with regard to Aristotle and all Aristotelians who, starting from the IV Book of the *Metaphysics,* retain the principle of non-contradiction as the *principium firmissimum* to which all must be subordinate.[32]

On being interpreted neoplatonically, Plato's *Parmenides* thus assumes an essential link with the fundamental problem which is at the centre of the *De non aliud.* Drawn on once more, especially through Proclus and Dionysius' speculation,

24 Cf. Plato, *Parm.*, 139d 2-e 2.

25 Cf. Plato, *Parm.*,139c 5-d 1.

26 *De non aliud*, h XIII, c. 22, pp. 52-53.

27 For a theoretical reading of the *non aliud* as a close analysis of the Platonic theme of diversity cf. F. Tomatis, *Ipseità, diversità e dia-ferenza*, in «Teoria», 1 (2006), pp. 31-35.

28 *De non aliud*, h XIII, c. 4, p. 10; *De ven. sap.*, h XII, c. 21, n. 59, p. 57.

29 *De non aliud*, h XIII, c. 4, p. 10.

30 *Ibidem.*

31 Plato, *Parm.*, 139c 4-142a 8.

32 Cf. Aristoteles, *Metaph.,* 1005a 20-1012b 31.

and then constantly examined and re-elaborated thoughout all his thinking, the question of the One which finds its apical formulation in the conception of God as *non aliud* is heavily impregnated with elements present in Plato's *Parmenides*. From this viewpoint the *non aliud* is no other than one of the most original re-formulations that the history of Western thought has ever known of the awesome question that the Neoplatonists had discerned in the most enigmatic and disturbing work of the father of philosophy.

1.3 Cusanus, Critic of Plato

Cusanus knew many of Plato's texts and took it upon himself to get them translated, but remained essentially alien to the humanistic-philological renaissance of the studies of Plato starting in the 15th century. More than the image of the "authentic Plato", or that which the Cardinal might have obtained from the direct reading of the translation of his works, Cusanus' Plato is that of Proclus and Dionysius', or a Plato re-read and interpreted through fixed structures of Neoplatonic thought. In this regard we may subscribe to a statement of the great Italian scholar Eugenio Garin according to whom: "through a need and desire to return to the text with the greatest competence possible and with greater historical precision, Cusanus remained outside the Platonic revival".[33] It is no chance happening that he did not know Greek well, nor felt the need to draw on the texts of the classical tradition in their original language. He had in fact different aims and objectives, and was disturbed by questions different from those of the humanists.

In fact, Cusanus does not read and interpret the *Parmenides,* not even superficially in keeping with the Proclian-Dionysian categories, since he re-elaborates its contents anew. Cusanus' One is not a mere reproposition of a conception of Plato's, nor much less so of the Neoplatonic Proclian-Dionysian one, as shown by the criticisms lodged by the cardinal against Plato (and therefore also, or perhaps especially, against his Neoplatonic interpreters).[34] Although all the progress of

[33] E. Garin, *Cusano e i Platonici italiani del Quattrocento*, in *Nicolò da Cusa. Relazioni tenute al convegno di Bressanone nel 1960*, ed. G. Flores d'Arcais, Sansoni, Firenze 1962, p. 88.

[34] Although Werner Beierwaltes in his authoritative studies was right to underline the affinities between Cusanus' philosophy and the Neoplatonic vision, by identifying most scrupulously the historical and speculative relationships, it nevertheless appears only right for us to stress also the differences and the originality with which Cusanus fits into the line of Neoplatonic thought at least with regard to the Proclian-Dionysian One. For Beierwaltes' decisive studies on the Neoplatonic sources of Cusanus' thinking, cf. W. Beierwaltes, *Eriugena und Cusanus*, in Id.,

Cusanus' thinking may be interpreted as an attempt to think of the One as holding the outcomes of the first hypothesis of the *Parmenides* constant as well as those of the second interpreted neoplatonically, Cusanus' conception of the Principle is considerably different from that of the Platonic and the Proclian-Dionysian conception. In other words, the Cardinal attempts to think of God as being beyond being, the One-one of the first hypothesis, and at the same time as creator of being, the One-that-is of the second hypothesis. Following Dionysius and Christian Neoplatonism in this, he does not think the absolute One as beyond being and thought, and the One as source of being and of thought, as two different and separate hypostases. He rejects the vision, held by pagan and Arab Neoplatonism, of a *creatio* thought of as emanation or procession through intermediary degrees or interposed hypostases, pertinent to ways of thinking attributed by himself to Avicenna's Neoplatonism.[35] On the contrary, for the Cardinal every single thing is fruit of the immediate creation on the part of God, without need of mediatory intervention from intermediary bodies or realities, and without the intervention of any middle zone between the One and the individual created bodies. In this original reflection and re-elaboration of the Platonic and Neoplatonic traditions, the decisive element of speculation is the conception that Cusanus has of the One, or his attributing a strongly voluntaristic character to it, thus speculatively drawing close – though he did not know their texts - to Plotinus rather than to Plato - and to Proclus or Dionysius[36].

There are two main criticisms that Cusanus lodges against the Platonic vision of the One. The first regards the trinitariety of the Principle. Plato supposedly would have only touched upon and lightly skimmed over the Trinity, without succeeding in fully understanding it[37]. The great Greek philosopher managed by ascending from the caused to the cause, going up from the sensible and visible world to the intelligible and invisible one, in order to see the Father and the Son, understanding the second as an intelligent creator and the first as God, cause of

Eriugena. Grundzüge seines Denkens, Klostermann, Frankfurt am Main 1994, pp. 266-312; Id., *Der verborgene Gott. Cusanus und Dionysius*, in Id., *Platonismus im Christentum*, Klostermann, Frankfurt am Main 1998, pp. 130-171; Id., *Theophanie. Nicolaus Cusanus und Johannes Scottus Eriugena. Eine* Retractatio, in «Philotheos», 6 (2006), pp. 153-175; Id., *Das Seiende Eine. Zur neuplatonisches Interpretation der zweiten Hypothesis des platonischen* Parmenides*: das Beispeiel Cusanus*, cit., pp. 215-222; Id., *'Centrum tocius vite'. Zur Bedeutung von Proclos' 'Theologia Platonis' im Denken des Cusanus*, in Id. *Procliana*, cit., pp. 191-214; Id., *Nicolaus Cusanus: Innovation durch Einsicht aus der Überlieferung - paradigmatisch gezeigt an seinem Denken des Einen*, in *Procliana*, cit.,pp. 165-190.

35 Cf. *De docta ign.*, h I, II, c. 4, n. 116, pp. 74-75.

36 Cf. Plotinus, *Enn.*, VI, 8.

37 Cf. *De Beryl.*, h XI/1, n. 35, pp. 39.

all and and father of this intelligence.[38] The criticism that Cusanus lodges against Plato, as against all other pagan philosophers, is that of not succeeding in reaching the vision of the Spirit, or as he himself defines it, of the principle of the connection.

> Et ob hoc omnes philosophi ad spiritum, qui est principium conexionis et est tertia persona in divinis secundum nostram perfectam theologiam, non attingerunt, licet de patre et filio plerique eleganter dixerint, maxime Platonici.[39]

The other decisive element on which Plato – just as Aristotle – grossly erred and from which all his speculative errors originated, is the attribution of an operating necessary for the One. The second criticism which Cusanus lodges against the conception of Plato's First Principle is that of starting out from a false premise, namely of attributing to the First Cause a way of acting through necessity.[40]

> Istud ignorabant tam Plato quam Aristotlem. Aperte enim uterque credidit conditorem intellectum ex necessitate naturae omnia facere, et hoc omnis eorum error secutus est .[41]

On the contrary, Cusanus' rethinking of the Platonic or Neoplatonic tradition is lodged from another presupposition, namely the attribution to God of voluntary and free acting[42]. The same possibility of holding together, albeit distinguishing between them, the first two hypotheses of Plato's *Parmenides* is founded precisely on Cusanus' vision of the action of the First as voluntary and free. The One is creator of being, albeit being at the same time beyond being in that he acts freely and voluntarily, or is conceived as holding transcendence and freedom together.

> Se ad omnem essendi modum sufficit habunde primum principium unitrinum; licet sit absolutum et superexaltatum, cum non sit principium contractum ut na-

38 Cf. *ibidem*.

39 *De Beryl.*, h XI/1, n. 42, pp. 48-49. In some passages of the *De Beryllo* Cusanus appears directed towards conceiving the same function to the Platonic soul of the world. Cf. *De Beryl.*, h XI/1, n. 35-36, p. 40. Yet, he entertains a mainly critical relationship with regard to the soul of the world, even if his attitude in this regard is not always linear. Cf. Id., *De Beryllo*, cit., n. 37, pp. 42-43. For an extensive criticism of the doctrine of the soul of the world cf. Id., *De docta ign.*, h I, II, c. 9, n. 141-150, pp. 89-96. Regarding the criticism cf. S. Mancini, *Congetture su Dio.Singolarità, finalismo, potenza nella teologia razionale di Nicola Cusano*, Mimesis, Milano 2015, pp. 29-68.

40 Cf *De Beryl.*, h XI/1, n. 68, p. 78: «Sed hoc evenit eis [scil. Plato et Aristoteles] ex malo praesupposito, quoniam necessitatem primae causae imposuerunt».

41 *De Beryl.*, h XI/1, n. 38, p. 43.

42 Cf. *De ludo*, h IX,I, n. 19, pp. 22-23.

> tura, quae ex necessitate operatur, sed sit principium ipsius naturae et ita supernaturale, liberum, quod voluntate creat omnia.[43]

Only inasmuch as the One is beyond nature is he free from it, and hence capable of deciding voluntarily to be cause of it, or not.

1.4 The Freedom of the One

> Non tamen propterea agit quasi natura seu instrumentum necessitatum per superioris imperium, sed per liberam voluntatem, quae est et essentia eius.[44]

Cusanus takes a further step in that he does not conceive the One simply as being extremely free, or as if freedom were to be thought of as a divine predicate, but thinks God himself as freedom or free will. Freedom is not a mere attribute of God, but rather that the One himself identifies himself essentially with such free will.

The German thinker does not simply repeat Proclus' interpretation of the *Parmenides*, but introduces innovations into it by re-elaborating it further according to completely non-Proclian ways. In fact, for Proclus the Principle must be nothing of all, so that he is cause of all: only by being nothing, understood as complete fullness, and not as privation or deficiency, can the One be principle of all[45].

Unlike Proclus, who saw a necessary relationship between the super-being of the One and his causality, for the Cardinal between the excellence of God and his being creator of all, there is a free and voluntary dialectic, devoid of all strict necessity: the transcendence of the divine is not the foundation or the presupposition of his creative immanence. The passage from the *hyperoché* of the First, inasmuch as beyond being to his power source of being, that is to say the possibility of keeping the two aspects distinct, even in the oneness of the One, without necessarily reducing it to the first of a series or to the cause of the great chain of being, is founded on the essential free will of God. The key to Cusanus' interpretation of Plato's *Parmenides* lies in his vision of the One as freedom or will.

In Cusanus' conception, transcendence and freedom become co-implicated circularly. Without transcendence, without the ulteriority of the One, it is not

[43] *De Beryl.*, h XI/1, n. 37, pp. 42-43.

[44] *De Beryl.*, h XI/1, n. 38, p. 44.

[45] Cf. Proclus, *Commentaire sur le Parménide de Platon. Traduction de Guillaume de Moerbeke*, cit., t. 2, p. 367, 75-77. On the theme cf. W. Beierwaltes, *Proklos. Grundzüge seiner Metaphysik*, Klostermann, Frankfurt am Main 1965, pp. 348 ff.

possible to think of the creator's freedom, his being the voluntary source of being, since he would necessarily and immediately be resolved in relationship to being. The One beyond being conserves God's freedom of entering in relationship with being and of creating or not creating. Yet, at the same time, without such freedom, without the possibilities of making himself One-that-is, the transcendence of the absolute One would be marked to remain necessarily as an unfillable gap, distance and infinite separation, leaving God in an unthinkable and unspeakable silence. Moreover, the source immanence does not destroy transcendence because also *after* the creation, after entering into relationship with being, God remains beyond his being creator, freely transcending in the relationship even the relationship itself.[46] As God voluntarily creates, albeit being transcendent, so at the same time through his very will *after* the revelation and the creation remains of himself in his mystery, ulterior and unknown with respect to his very work and his very manifestation. God not only decides freely to create, manifesting himself theophanically in creating, which is nothing other than *Dei apparitio*,[47] remaining ulterior with regard to his very being creator, but remains in his manifesting himself in the creation, giving the being the possibility of rejecting his revelation, of withdrawing, and taking the being from the created.[48]

In his elaboration of a vision of the One as free will, Cusanus does not ask himself only about divine will or freedom with regard to the creature created, about the how and why from the One the many, but – once again, more in keeping with Plotinus than with Plato, Proclus or Dionysius – thinks of God himself as the positioning of himself, as self-positioning. This theme, although it is not absent in many of Cusanus' earlier texts, finds its most complete treatment and elaboration in the Cardinal's last works.

In the trialogue *De possest* of 1460, the Cardinal goes deeply into these aspects, thanks to the idea of *possest.*[49]If every finite thing foresees a distinction between

46 Cf. *De vis.*, h VI, c. 12, n. 50, p. 43: «Sed absolutam cum te video infinitatem, cui nec nomen creatoris creantis nec creatoris creabilis competit, tunc revelate te inspicere incipio et intrare hortum deliciarum, quia nequaquam es aliquid tale, quod dici aut concipi potest, sed in infinitum super omnia talia absolute superexaltatus. Non es igitur creator, sed plus quam creator in infinitum, licet sine te nihil fiat aut fieri possit». Cf. moreover*De vis.*, h VI, c. 13, n. 51-57, pp. 44-49. Reference is made to it also in the passages in which Cusanus speaks of a freedom to create and not to create not only to the past but to the present itself, cf. *Crib. Alk.*, h VIII, II, c. 2, n. 90, p. 75.

47 Cf. *De non aliud*, h XIII, prop. XII, pp. 62-63.

48 Cf. *Comp.*, h XI/3, c. 7, n. 21, pp. 16-17: «Et sicut mens nolens se amplius ostendere, a verbi vocalis prolatione cessat, et nisi indesinenter proferat existere nequit, sic se habet creatura ad creatorem».

49 A possible source of Cusanus' *possest* may be the *Questiones disputatae de mysterio trinitatis* by Bonaventura; on the theme cf. T. Leinkauf, *Nicolaus Cusanus und Bonaventura. Zum Hinter-*

power and acting, since each creature is never at the origin of itself, it is never all that it can be, but can be other than what it is, then God, who not only is, but is at the origin of himself, in that he is power to be what he is, in that he is all what he can be, "is" *possest*, that is to say perfect coinciding of power and act. In the *possest*, original divine name thought up by Cusanus, power and being, power, acting and their linking are all one: God is perfect self-positioning, power to be what he is, or God is not only power of all things but *in primis* of himself. The *possest* indicates a theme which will be further developed in subsequent works, through the elaboration of the idea of *non aliud*, in which the two criticisms against Plato reciprocally join, namely that of not having conceived the One as free will, and that of succeeding in arriving at the Trinity. In fact the *possest* is trinitarian coincidence of three distinct moments, namely *posse*, *esse* and their joining together.

But the divine name with which Cusanus succeeds in unifying his conception of the One as free will and his vision of the Trinity is the *non aliud*, an expression already originally full of very powerful trinitarian valency. The *non aliud* not only reveals to us the freedom or will of the Principle regarding creation and the created beings – unfolding himself in his capacity to define all things[50] – but also, and above all, the still more original self-creative capacity of the Principle himself. Through the idea of *non aliud*, Cusanus manages to re-interpret perfectly the Platonic and Neoplatonic One as self-positioning and free and voluntary Trinity-positioning, thanks to the capacity to self-define himself trinitarially which is proper of, and exclusive to, the *non aliud*: «non aliud est non aliud quam non aliud».[51] God thought of as *non aliud triniter repetitum*,[52] defining himself trinitarially, knows and generates himself – according to the twofold gnosiological and ontological valency which Cusanus assigns to the definition[53] – freely and voluntarily as Trinity.

grund von Cusanus' Gottesnamen "possest", in Id., *Cusanus, Ficino, Patrizi. Formen platonischen Denkens in Renaissance*, Trafo, Berlin 2014, pp. 59-76. On the concept of possibility in Cusanus cf. T. Leinkauf, *Renovatio und unitas. Nicolaus Cusanus zwischen Tradition und Innovation. Die 'Reformation' des Möglichkeitsbegriff*, in Id., *Cusanus, Ficino, Patrizi. Formen platonischen Denkens in Renaissance*, cit., pp. 105-122; V. Vitiello, *De possest*, in *Cusanus*, cit., pp. 129-139.

50 Cf. *De non aliud*, h XIII, c. 1, p. 5: «Quid enim responderes, si quis te "quid est aliud?" interrogaret? Nonne diceres: "non aliud quam aliud"? Sic, "quid caelum?"; responderes: "non aliud quam caelum"»; D*e non aliud*, h XIII, c. 2, p. 6: «aliud enim cum sit non aliud quam aliud, utique "non aliud" praesupponit, sine quo non foret aliud».

51 The expression is repeated in several places, cf.:*De non aliud*, h XIII, c. 1, p. 4; c. 5, p. 12; prop. III, p. 61; *De ven. sap.*, h XII, c. 14, n. 40, p. 39.

52 Cf. *De non aliud*, h XIII, c. 5, p. 12.

53 An aspect which Cusanus took up again the criticism against Plato and Proclus, cf. D*e non aliud*, h XIII, c. 22, pp. 52-53: «Meministi, puto, Platonem negare quid rei definitionem attingere, quia quidditati circumponitur, uti etiam Proculus explanat. Unde non fit ita, cum ipsum "non aliud" se atque omnia definit. Non enim sic ipsum principium quidditativum definit, quasi qui lineis circumpositis triangularem determinat seu definit superficiem, sed quasi superficiem, quae

> In explicatam igitur eius definitionem intueamur, quod videlicet "non aliud" est non aliud quam non aliud; idem triniter repetitum si est primi definitio, ut vides, ipsum profecto est unitrinum et non alia ratione, quam quia se ipsum definit; non enim foret primum si se ipsum minime definiret; se autem quando definit, trinum ostendit. Ex perfectione igitur vides resultare trinitatem, quam tamen, quoniam ante aliud vides, nec numerare potes nec numerum esse affirmare, cum haec trinitas non sit aliud quam unitas, et unitas non sit aliud quam trinitas, quia tam trinitas quam unitas non sunt aliud quam simplex principium per "non aliud" significatum.[54]

For the Cardinal, the Trinity is not to be understood as the mere summing of three units, nor simple repetition of the identical, but dynamically as self-unfolding of the One, as self-relationship in which Oneness is constituted as Trinity.[55]

Yet, also in this case, the Trinity-generating of the One does not annul his transcendence regarding his own self-constituting himself as Trinity. In the *Cribratio Alkorani* Cusanus makes a fine distinction between *Deus* and *Deitas*: *Deitas* is the divine essence which in itself is neither generating nor generated, the very pure *arché* of Trinity itself.[56] Although *Deus* and *Deitas* are the same thing, they are not-other; yet, if one considers the *Deitas* one will not see any generating, whereas if

trigonus dicitur, constituat». On the double value, gnosiological and ontological, of the definition, cf. *De non aliud*, h XIII, c. 3, pp. 7-8: «Nam cum omne, quod quidem est, sit non aliud quam id ipsum, hoc utique non habet aliunde; a ‚non alio' igitur habet. Non igitur aut est aut cognoscitur esse id, quod est, nisi per ‚non aliud', quae quidem est eius causa, adaequatissima ratio scilicet sive definitio». On the *non aliud* as principle of being and of knowing, cf. *De non aliud*, h XIII, c. 3, p. 7: «Deus igitur per ‚non aliud' significatus essendi et cognoscendi omnibus principium est. Quem si quis subtrahit, nihil manet neque in re, neque in cognitione». On the theme cf. C. Rusconi, *La definicíon que se define a sí misma y a todo*, in Nicolás de Cusa, *Acerca de lo no-otro o de la definición que todo define. Nuevo texto crítico original*, intr. Span. trans by J. M. Machetta, critical text and notes by C. D'Amico - M. D'Ascenso - A. Eisenkopf - J. G. Rios - J. M. Machetta - K. Reinhardt - C. Rusconi - H. Schwaetzer, Biblios, Buenos Aires 2008, pp. 336-346.

54 *De non aliud*, h XIII, c. 5, p. 12.

55 *De non aliud*, h XIII, c. 5, p. 13: «Quando enim primum principium ipsum se definit per "non aliud" significatum, in eo definitivo motu de non alio non aliud oritur atque de non alio et non alio exohorto in non alio concluditur definitio, quae contemplans clarius, quam dici possit, intuebitur».

56 Cf. *Crib. Alk.*, h VIII, I, c. 14, n. 63-64, pp. 55-56. On the *arché* or Beginning of God in Cusanus' thought, cf.: M. Cacciari, *Filosofia e Teologia*, in *La filosofia*, vol. II, ed. P. Rossi, Utet, Torino 1995, pp. 365-421; Id., *Sul presupposto*, in «aut aut», 211-212 (1986), pp. 43-65; F. Tomatis, *Inizio e parola di Dio*, in *Dio-Trinità tra filosofi e teologi*, eds. P. Coda-M. Donà, Bompiani, Milano 2007, pp. 95-108; Id., *Libertà di sapere. Università e dialogo interculturale*, Bompiani, Milano 2009, pp. 35-38.

one considers God, one will see generating in that one will see the Father generating, which is exactly so in that He generates the Son.[57]

The same Trinity-generating indicates a more profound mystery which goes on transcending the revelation itself. As God is not immediately referable to his will and freedom, in relation to the world and to creation, so he is not de-finitively identifiable with the Trinity-generating of himself. In his freedom, God is superessential, or beyond his very essence, his free will. The self-revealing of God in the creation and in the Trinity is not complete manifestation, perfect externalisation from the divine depths, and does not annul the transcendence of God: the *Deus Trinitas*, the God revealed, does not cancel the *Deus absconditus*, but God in himself, inasmuch as infinite always remains unknowable, trascendent, ulterior, and superessential.[58] The Cardinal states that God can be understood both as Principle as well as non-Principle, and that in the latter case he is neither One, nor Triune, nor Father nor Son, nor Spirit, but incomprehensible and ineffable.[59] Also in his self-reflection and self-trinitarian constitution, God in himself, in his infiniteness, remains ulterior, real and proper *Deus absconditus*.

To conclude, we would like to recall the words of Luigi Pareyson, according to whom, «Neoplatonism is at the dawn of modern philosophy (that is to say in Humanism with Marsilio Ficino's philosophy and above all with that of Nicholas Cusanus')», especially with the «central concept of Neoplatonism which is that of God as freedom ».[60] Together with the Torinese philosopher we may say therefore

[57] Naturally, Trinity-generating is to be kept distinct from creating, which according to the Cardinal occurs through a contraction of God. For an analysis of different spheres of use of the concept of contraction, of its sources and of its developments within Cusanus' works cf. J. Hopkins, *Nicholas of Cusa's Metaphysic of Contraction,* Arthur J. Banning, Minneapolis 1983; G. d'Onofrio, *Vera Philosophia. Studies in Late Antique, Early Medieval and Renaissance Christian Thought,* Brepols, Turnhout 2008, pp. 279-300; S. Mancini, *Congetture su Dio*, cit., pp. 29-102.

[58] Cf. *De vis.*, h VI, c. 12, n. 47-50, pp. 41-43. To the *Deus absconditus* the Cardinal has dedicated a brief but very dense dialogue, *De Deo absc.*, h IV. On the theme cf. *Crib. Alk.*, h VIII, II, c. 1-2, n. 86-91, pp. 72-76; *De pace*,hVII, c. 7, n. 21, p. 20.

[59] Cf. *Crib. Alk.*, h VIII, II, c. 1, n. 87-88, pp. 73-74.

[60] Cf. L. Pareyson, *Ontologia della libertà*, Einaudi, Torino 1995, p. 7. Pareyson quotes Cusanus also in another fundamental work of his, *Verità e interpretazione.* In a passage of the text the Turinese philosopher identifies in the history of his thought two different visions with regard to the relationship between philosophy and common sense. Against the conception of a positive relationship elaborated by cardinal Cusanus – especially in his work *Idiota*, the protagonist of which is a spoon-carver far from the bookish wisdom of the erudite philosophers, from the abstract rhetoric of the orators – he opposes a negative vision elaborated by Hegel, who proclaims the most absolute opposition between philosophical thought and common sense. Cf. L. Pareyson, *Verità e interpretazione*, Mursia, Milano 1971, pp. 211-212. The other quotation is most significant with regard to the passage of negative ontology of the ineffable to the ontology of the inexhaustible and the affirmation of the revealing character of the interpretation. In the relative

that Cusanus represents an essential cornerstone for the passage of the conception of the One as freedom of Neoplatonic origin, elaborated *in primis* by Plotinus, for the design of modern thought, and remained for the most part incomplete – except for a minority trend – for elaborating a philosophy of freedom.[61]

notes, Pareyson quotes as testimony of his affirmations Schelling and Cusanus, pointing out the resipiscence of the latter – testified by the Cardinal's very words in his very last work the *De apice theoriae* (1464) – regarding the idea contained in his first works that the truth can be gathered incomprehensibly in the shadow of darkness. A mystical-negative position which Cusanus starting from the *Idiota* (1450), was to re-elaborate in favour of a vision which insists mostly on revealing the infinite and inexhaustible character of truth. I became interested in this development of Cusanus' thought and of its consequences in D. Monaco, Deus Trinitas. *Dio come* non altro *nel pensiero di Nicolò Cusano*, cit., pp. 67-162; Id., *Dalla* coincidentia oppositorum *al non aliud: la caccia cusaniana all'infinito*, in *A caccia dell'Infinito. L'Umano e il Divino nell'opera di Nicola Cusano*, ed. C. Catà, Aracne, Roma 2010, 103-116. On Cusanus and Schelling cf. A. Franz, *Möglichkeit und Wirklichkeit als Grundprinzipien neuzeitlichen Wirklichkeitverständnisses bei Nikolaus von Kues und F.W.J. Schelling*, in *Nicolaus Cusanus und der deutsche Idealismus*, eds. K. Reinhardt- H. Schwaetzer,Roderer, Regensburg 2007, pp. 41-58; H. Schwaetzer, *Zur Cusanus-Rezeption im Deutschen Idealismus*, in «Litterae Cusanae», 3 (2003), pp. 24-26; Id., *Die intellektuelle Anschauung als methodisches Prinzip einer naturwissenschaftlichen "scientia aenigmatica": Anmerkungen zur Konzeption von Wissenschaft bei Cusanus und im Deutschen Idealismus*, in «MFCG», 29 (2005), pp. 247-261; Id., *"Visio intellectualis" – Cusanus und Schelling. Eine systematische Annäherung*, in *Nicolaus Cusanus und der deutsche Idealismus*, cit., pp. 87-102; P. Ziche, *"der Punkt sey der Kreis in seinem Chaos". Cusanische Kreisbildlichkeit und Schellingsche Möglichkeitsstrukturen&Spuren von Cusanus im Idealismus*, in *Nicolaus Cusanus und der deutsche Idealismus*, cit., pp. 59-86; H. Schwaetzer, *Ein unbekannter Bekannter – Die Rezeption des Nikolaus von Kues bei Schelling*, in *Nicolaus Cusanus: ein bewundernswerter historischer Brennpunkt. Philosophische Tradition und wissenschaftliche Rezeption*, eds. K. Reinhardt- H. Schwaetzer, Roderer, Regensburg 2008, pp. 167-188; F. Tomatis, *Cusano e l'ultimo Schelling*, in *Cusano*, ed. D. Monaco, «Il Pensiero», 1-2 (2009), pp. 75-114; K. Zeyer, *Neuplatonismusrezeption im Umfeld der deutschen Idealisten. Eine Recherche mit Blick auf Schelling und Cusanus*, in «Verbum» 14 (2012), pp. 61-81.

61 On Pareyson and Neoplatonism cf. C. Ciancio, *Introduzione al convegno*, in «Annuario Filosofico, 20 (2004), pp. 33-37. For an accurate reconstruction and close examination of the ontology of freedom elaborated by the most recent Pareyson, cf. F. Tomatis, *Ontologia del male. L'ermeneutica del male*, Città Nuova, Roma 1995. On these themes cf. G. Riconda, *Tradizione e avventura*, SEI, Torino 2001; Id., *Tradizione e pensiero*, Edizioni dell'Orso, Torino 2009; C. Ciancio, *Libertà e dono dell'essere*, Marietti, Torino 2009.

2. *Non aliud*: Neoplatonic, Patristic and Medieval Sources

2.1 Proclus and Dionysius the Areopagite

The relationship between Proclus' thought and that of Cusanus' has been object of considerable authoritative research. Especially significant, for evaluating the historical and theoretical relationship between the two thinkers, were the study and edition of the Cardinal's copious marginal annotations on the writings of Proclus[62]. Cusanus' acceptance of the philosophy of the Athenian diadochos may be

[62] For the edition of the marginal notes cf.: H. G. Senger, *Die Exzerpte und Randnoten des Nikolaus von Kues zu den lateinischen Übersetzungen der Proclus-Schriften. Theologia Platonis-Elementatio theologica*, cit.; K. Bormann, *Die Exzerpte und Randnoten des Nikolaus von Kues zu den lateinischen Übersetzungen der Proclus-Schriften. Expositio in Parmenidem Platonis*, cit. On the relationship between Proclus' thought and that of Cusanus' cf.: E. Vansteenberghe, *Le cardinal Nicolas de Cues (1401-1464). L'action – la pensée*, Champion, Paris 1920 [rist. Minerva, Frankfurt am Main 1963], pp. 436-438; E. Vansteenberghe, *Quelques lectures de jeunesse de Nicolas de Cues d'après un manuscrit inconnu de sa bibliothèque*, cit.,pp. 275-284; R. Klibansky, *Ein Proklos-Fund und seine Bedeutung*, Winter, Heidelberg 1929, pp. 25-29; R. Klibansky, *Plato's Parmenides in the Middle Ages and the Renaissance. A chapter in the History of Platonic Studies*, cit., pp. 304-310; R. Haubst, *Die Thomas- und Proklos-Exzerpte des "Nicolaus Treverensis"*, cit., pp. 17-51; W. Beierwaltes, *Philosophische Marginalien zu Proklos-Texten*, «Philosophische Rundschau», 11 (1963), pp. 49-90; Id., *Cusanus und Proclus. Zum neuplatonischen Ursprung des non-aliud, Cusanusund Proclus*; G. Santinello, *Proclo nel pensiero del Cusano*, in Id., *Saggi sull' «umanesimo» di Proclo*, Pàtron, Bologna 1966, pp. 15-50; S. Otto, *Language dialectique et silence hiérophanique. L'horizon de la métaphysique chez Proclus, Cusanus et Hegel*, in «Archivio di Filosofia», 1 (1975), pp. 105-114; H. G. Senger, *Die Exzerpte und Randnoten des Nikolaus von Kues zu den lateinischen Übersetzungen der Proclus-Schriften. Theologia Platonis-Elementatio theologica*, cit., pp. 11-42; K. Kremer, *Gott- in Allem Alles, in Nichts Nichts. Bedeutung und Herkunft dieser Lehre des Nikolaus von Kues*, in «MFCG», 17 (1986), pp. 188-219; C. Riccati, *La presenza di Proclo tra Neoplatonismo arabizzante e tradizione dionisiana (Bertoldo di Moosburg e Niccolò Cusano), Concordia discors. Studi su Niccolò Cusano e l'umanesimo europeo offerti a Giovanni Santinello*, in ed. G. Piaia, Antenore, Padova 1993, pp. 23-38; K. Flasch, *Nikolaus von Kues. Geschichte einer Entwicklung*, Klostermann, Frankfurt am Main 1998, pp. 500-516; K. Bormann, *Affirmation und Negation. Der Parmenides-Kommentar des Proklos in Nikolaus von Kues' Schrift Tu quis es*, in «Theologische Quartalschrift», 181 (2001), pp. 84-96; C. D'Amico, *Nicolaus von Kues als Leser von Proklos*, in *Nicolaus von Kues in der Geschichte des Platonismus*, cit., pp. 33-64; W. Beierwaltes, *Das Seiende Eine. Zur neuplatonisches Interpretation der zweiten Hypothesis des platonischen Parmenides: das Beispeiel Cusanus*,in Id., *Procliana*, cit., pp. 215-222; W. Beierwaltes, *"Centrum tocius vite". Zur Bedeutung von Proklos' Theologia Platonis im Denken des Cusanus*, cit., pp. 191-214; C. D'Amico, *La presencia de Proclo*, in *Acerca de lo no-otro o de la definición que todo define. Nuevo texto crítico original*, cit., pp. 359-369; S. Gottlöber, *Das Prinzip der Relationalität:*

schematically subdivided into three main moments: a first phase, connected to the discovery of certain Proclian extracts contained in *Codex Argentoratensis 84* ,which attest to a knowledge, albeit limited, of Proclus' thought by the young Cusanus[63]; a second phase, connected to the acquisition, occurring between 1450 and 1455 of the Latin translation by William of Moerbeke of the *Commentarium in Platonis Parmenidem*[64]; and a third phase, marked by his reading of the *Theologia Platonica* translated by Pietro Balbo[65].

The third moment of the reception of Proclus' thought opens with the acquisition, during the years of the writing up of the *De non aliud*, of the Latin translation of the *Theologia Platonica,* made by Pietro Balbo and commissioned by the Cardinal himself. On the basis of several marginal annotations to the text, some interpreters have tried to identify in Proclus' work the place of origin or of inspiration of the idea of the *non aliud.* Yet, even earlier than the *Theologia Platonica,* the conception of the First Principle that acts as foundation to the idea of *non aliud* must be set in relation to Proclus' vision of the *Hén,* contained in the *Commentarium in Platonis Parmenidem,* studied closely by the Cardinal with a threefold painstaking work of marginal annotations, from the years 1450-1455[66]. The two works, although very close – albeit central in both is the interpretation of the text considered as "sacred" *par excellence* by the Neoplatonists, Plato's *Parmenides* - examine two different aspects of Proclus' thought, while the *Theologia Platonica* analyzes more diffusely the *próodos* of the One, that is to say the divine orders deriving therefrom[67],while the commentary, especially Books VI and VII,

Grundzüge cusanischen Denkens als Parameter für Toleranz und interreligiösen Diskurs, cit., pp. 146-150.

63 As anticipated, the extracts contained in the *Codex Argentoratensis bibliothecae Universitatis 84* were published by R. Haubst, *Die Thomas- und Proklos-Exzerpte des «Nicolaus Treverensis» in Codicillus Strassburg 84*, cit., pp. 17-51.

64 On the dating proposed cf. C. Steel, *Introduction*, in Proclus, *Commentaire sur le Parménide de Platon*, cit., t. 1, p. 12-17. Cusanus read and annotated Proclus'text first in the modern-day codex *Vaticanus latinus 3074* and then in that which was to become his personal copy, the *Codex Cusanus 186*. Cf. J. Marx, *Verzeichnis der Handschriften-Sammlung des Hospital zu Cues bei Bernkastel a./Mosel*,cit., p. 173; K. Bormann, *Die Exzerpte und Randnoten des Nikolaus von Kues zu den lateinischen Übersetzungen der Proclus-Schriften. Expositio in Parmenidem Platonis*, cit.,pp. 17-51.

65 Cusanus read and copiously annotated the Latin translation of the *Theologia Platonica* in the present-day *Codex Cusanus 185*. Cf. J. Marx, *Verzeichnis der Handschriften-Sammlung des Hospital zu Cues bei Bernkastel a./Mosel*,cit., p. 172.

66 A triple scansion in the annotations is witnessed by the differences in style and colour among them. Cf. R. Klibansky, *Ein Proklos-Fund und seine Bedeutung*, cit., pp. 27-28.

67 With the exception of the second book dedicated to One-one. Cf. M. Abbate, *Il divino tra unità e molteplicità: saggio sulla Teologia Platonica di Proclo*, Edizioni dell'Orso, Alessandria 2008, pp. 165-183.

represents a compact in-depth interpretation of the first hypothesis of the second part of the Platonic dialogue dedicated to the *Hèn ei Hén* in a sort of hymn of negations to the One. The conception of the First Principle as *non aliud* has a close link with Proclus' henology. It is witnessed, on the one hand, by two interlocutors of the tetralogue, namely Giovanni Andrea de Bussi and Pietro Balbo Pisano, both presented as two excellent connoisseurs of Proclus[68], and on the other the passages in which Cusanus compares his own speculation with that of the Athenian diadochos'[69] and *a fortiori*, the points of *koinonía* between the two visions of the *arché*. Cusanus himself, in Chapter XXI, explicitly affirms the closeness between Proclus' conception of the *Hén* and his own idea of the *non aliud*[70]. For a clear understanding of the fundamental structure of Proclus' vision of the *Hén* with which the Cardinal compared himself, by meditating on it, accepting it, and, at the same time, differentiating his own conception from that of the Athenian diadochos is in the *Commentarium in Platonis Parmenidem, to* which we must turn.

Proclus repeatedly emphasised that in its simplicity the *Hén* transcends all opposition – *exaltatum est propter semplicitatem ab omni oppositione*[71] – a role that it shares with Cusanus' conception of God. The idea of God's transcendence regarding all opposition – which might have had its definitive source in Proclus through the extract of his youth of Book VI of the *Commentarium in Platonis Parmenidem* contained in the *Codex Argentoratensis 84,* in which one reads «in omni enim oppositione necessarium est unum exaltatum esse ab ambobus oppositis»[72] – finds its *akmé* in the *non aliud,* unique hunting ground for divine wisdom in which no form of opposition exists and beyond which, to search for God, who is *ante omnem oppositorum differentiam*, would be futile[73].

In following the Neoplatonic exegesis of Plato's *Parmenides*, Proclus transforms into hypostases the hypotheses of the long discourse which occupies all the second part of the dialogue and takes on the series of negations which distinguish the first deduction of Plato's first hypothesis, the *Hèn ei Hén*, as negations of the *Unum superexaltatum*, which in its *hyperoché* is superior to every possible predication[74]. In

[68] Cf. *De non aliud*, h XIII, c. 1, p. 3.

[69] Cf. *De non aliud*, c. XIX-XXIV, pp. 47-56.

[70] Cf. *De non aliud*, c. XIX, p. 48.

[71] Cf. Proclus, *Commentaire sur le Parménide de Platon. Traduction de Guillaume de Moerbeke*, cit., t. 2, pp. 366, 79; 378, 25; 403, 16 ff.; 406, 13; 466, 70s.

[72] Cf. Haubst, *Die Thomas- und Proklos-Exzerpte des "Nicolaus Treverensis"*, cit., p. 27.

[73] Cf. *De ven sap.*, c. 14, n. 40-41, pp. 40-41.

[74] Cf. Proclus, *Commentaire sur le Parménide de Platon. Traduction de Guillaume de Moerbeke*, cit., t. 2, p. 371, 95-04. All the negations are retranscribed in the margin by Cusanus in gloss 447. Regarding samenness and otherness he writes: «*quod neque idem neque alterum*» (cf. K. Bormann, *Die Exzerpte und Randnoten des Nikolaus von Kues zu den lateinischen Übersetzungen der Proclus-Schriften. Expositio in Parmenidem Platonis*, cit., marg. 447). On the *Hén* neither same

taking up the *Parmenides ad litteram* once more, the Athenian diadochos writes: «puta quod neque idem sibi ipsi neque alterum sibi ipsi, neque idem aliis neque alterum ab aliis»[75] – a passage duly annotated by Cusanus in gloss 486: «neque idem sibi ipsi, neque alterum sibi ipsi neque idem alijs neque alterum ab hijs»[76]– reaffirming that Proclus' First Principle, just as previously that of Plato's and subsequently Cusanus', is neither identical to itself nor to other than itself. Neither sameness nor otherness is certainly not predicate of the *arché* in that, as Proclus writes, «le unum neque idem est neque alterum»[77], the *Hén* is therefore neither sameness nor otherness, in that it is – as Cusanus annotates in the margin of another passage of Proclus' commentary – «supra ydemptitatem et alteritatem»[78], metaphysically before sameness and otherness which exist only after it and beginning from it. The points of contact between the two thinkers do not stop here: by denying the otherness of the *Hén* Proclus arrives at the affirmation «unum enim est solum, aliud autem nichil»[79], remarkably close to Cusanus' idea of *non aliud.*

How can the *Hén* transcend all if it is not-other than it?[80] The answer to this question perceptively posed by Proclus throws new light on the closeness between the two conceptions of the First Principle: the *Hén* is not transcendent for the fact of being other than all – since in its otherness it would not in fact transcend all being, which is precisely such in that it is identical to itself and other than the other – but «non secundum alteritatem le separatum habet hoc et exaltatum preeminens omnibus, sed secundum aliam indisseribilem supereminentiam, et non qualem alteritas exibet entibus»; words underlined in the margin by Cusanus: «unum superexaltatum non secundum alteritatem sed supereminenciam»[81]. The *Hén* cannot be "other than all" – just as the *non aliud* is never *aliud*, but transcends

nor other than self cf. Proclus, *Commentaire sur le Parménide de Platon. Traduction de Guillaume de Moerbeke*, cit., t. 2, pp. 442-456.

75 Proclus, *Commentaire sur le Parménide de Platon. Traduction de Guillaume de Moerbeke*, cit., t. 2, p. 387, 3 ff.

76 Cf. K. Bormann, *Die Exzerpte und Randnoten des Nikolaus von Kues zu den lateinischen Übersetzungen der Proclus-Schriften. Expositio in Parmenidem Platonis*, cit., marg. 486.

77 Proclus, *Commentaire sur le Parménide de Platon. Traduction de Guillaume de Moerbeke*, cit., t. 2, p. 341, 39-40. Cf. moreover: *ibid.*, pp. 367, 77 ff; 378, 25; 403, 16 ff; 406, 13; 466, 70 f.

78 K. Bormann, *Die Exzerpte und Randnoten des Nikolaus von Kues zu den lateinischen Übersetzungen der Proclus-Schriften. Expositio in Parmenidem Platonis*, cit., marg. 567. The annotation is marginal to the Proclus' passage: «[...] le vnum autem ens ydemptitatem et alteritatem, a quibus exaltatum est le vnum ipsum» (Proclus, *Commentaire sur le Parménide de Platon. Traduction de Guillaume de Moerbeke*, cit., t. 2, p. 454, 93s).

79 Cf. Proclus, *Commentaire sur le Parménide de Platon. Traduction de Guillaume de Moerbeke*, cit., t. 2, p. 446, 37.

80 Cf. *ivi*, p. 450, 70s.

81 K. Bormann, *Die Exzerpte und Randnoten des Nikolaus von Kues zu den lateinischen Übersetzungen der Proclus-Schriften. Expositio in Parmenidem Platonis*, cit., marg. 567.

all the *aliud,* being *non aliud* – otherwise precisely inasmuch as being other would participate of the otherness which determines the sameness of every other being existing among the others. Unlike Plotinus, who in the *Ennead* repeatedly thinks of the *Hén* as *pánton héteron*[82], Proclus understands the First Principle as *oudenòs héteron, a nullo alterum*[83], thus bringing to fulfilment the tiresome search for retaining the difference of the *primum principium* from all, and by transfiguring the idea of transcendence, no longer understood as otherness or difference, but rather as eminence or excellence.The root of the idea of *non aliud* might now be found completely in a close study of the transcendence of the *Hén* of the *Commentarium in Platonis Parmenidem* if, as the Cardinal affirms, through the Abbot Giovanni Andrea Vigevio the expression *non aliud* represents a clarification first of Plato's idea and then of Proclus' of the non-otherness of the Principle from all the other[84].

According to the sense of the term "nothing" and that of "negation", outlined by the diadochos of Athens in his work, the *negatio* is no longer understood as mere *stéresis* with regard to the affirmation, but rather as excellence, fullness, excess in regard to it and, at the same time, as generating principle of the same[85]. To think of the *arché* as *non ens,* to deny being to the First Principle is not to affirm its non-existence or a shortcoming of it, but its *supersubstantialitatem,* its "being" before and beyond being itself. In the same way the negation applied to otherness

82 Plotinus, *Enn.*, V 3, 11, 18; V 4, 1, 6; V 6, 3, 6; VI 7, 42, 13; VI 9, 1, 37. Next to these passages on the One as *pánton héteron* should be set also the passages in which Plotinus excludes every otherness from the One or intends it as non-different in itself (Plotinus, *Enn.*, V 6, 4, 4; V 6, 5, 11; VI, 7, 41, 14 ff ; VI 8, 9, 13; VI 8, 10, 25; VI 8, 12, 23 f; VI 8, 15, 26; VI 8, 21, 32 f; VI 9, 8, 32) being able to think it precisely for this as absolute difference. These passages represent a significant premonitary speculative sign of the idea of the First Principle as *non aliud,* even if they remain historically uninfluential in that Cusanus did not know Plotinus' *Enneads* except through what is reported by Eusebius in the *De preparatione evangelica* taking up Numenius, cf. E. Vansteenberghe, *Le cardinal Nicolas de Cues (1401-1464). L'action – la pensée*, cit., p. 432. Cf. moreover: E. Garin, *Medioevo e Rinascimento. Studi e ricerche*, Laterza, Roma-Bari 1954, p. 228.

83 Proclus, *Commentaire sur le Parménide de Platon. Traduction de Guillaume de Moerbeke*, cit., t. 2, p. 450, 58. The entire Proclian page in question however is laden with possible seminal expressions of Proclus' conception of the *non aliud*: «*A nullo est alterum*» (K. Bormann, *Die Exzerpte und Randnoten des Nikolaus von Kues zu den lateinischen Übersetzungen der Proclus-Schriften. Expositio in Parmenidem Platonis*, cit., marg. 51); «*Nullatenus ergo alterum est le unum*» (*ibid.*, 67). Cf. inoltre Proclus, *Théologie Platonicienne*, vol. 2, ed. H. Saffrey – L.G. Westerink, Les Belles Lettres, Paris 1974, II, 12, pp. 66-73:*oudè héteron tôn állon*. On the theme cf. W. Beierwaltes, *Identität und Differenz*, Vittorio Klostermann, Frankfurt am Main 1980, pp. 41-42.

84 Cf. *De non aliud*, h XIII, c. XXII, p. 52.

85 Cf. Proclus, *Commentaire sur le Parménide de Platon. Traduction de Guillaume de Moerbeke*, cit., t. 2, p. 365, 86 ff: 366, 43 ff ; 392, 46 ff; 413, 33 ff; 470, 98 ff. Cf. moreover the Cusanus' corresponding marginal notes contained in K. Bormann, *Die Exzerpte und Randnoten des Nikolaus von Kues zu den lateinischen Übersetzungen der Proclus-Schriften. Expositio in Parmenidem Platonis*, cit., margg. 432, 436, 439, 498, 499, 520, 585.

does not indicate a shortcoming, but rather expresses the being *supra alteritatem*, the excellence of the *principium* with regard to all other which descends from it. Cusanus is a faithful disciple of the Athenian diadochos: the negation of otherness does not indicate a shortcoming, as if the Principle required something, but rather his predominance above all the other of which he is generating and constituting principle. If otherness is in itself negation, shortcoming, the negation of otherness is therefore *negatio negationis*, pure affirmation, index of the transcendence, infinity and incommensurability of the First Principle[86].

Paradoxically, inasmuch as nothing of all, the *Hén* is at the same time cause of all, and inasmuch as cause of all must be nothing of all. «Omnia igitur quaecumque abnegantur ab uno, ex ipso procedunt. Oportet enim ipsum nichil esse omnium, ut sint omnia ab ipso»[87]: With these words Proclus expresses the contemporary affiliation of immanence and transcendence of the Principle taken afresh and repeatedly examined by Cusanus until his final re-elaboration in the idea of *non aliud* which is, at the same time, *non aliud* than the *aliud* and negation of the *aliud*, inasmuch as not *aliud*. According to this dialectic of negation, Proclus' conception is further examined in the idea of the *Hén* as *non multa* which,

86 On the theme of the *negatio negationis* rather than to Proclus Cusanus' conception appears more akin to that of Eckhart's. On the need to remove also the same negations cf. Proclus, *Commentaire sur le Parménide de Platon. Traduction de Guillaume de Moerbeke*, cit., t. 2, pp. 518, 72-85; 519, 00-521, 63. On the theme cf. W. Beierwaltes, *Proklos. Grundzüge seiner Metaphysik*, cit., pp. 395-398. On the *negatio negationis* in Proclus cf. T. Khobusch, *Negative theologie als praktische Metaphysik*, in *Théologie négative*, ed. M.M. Olivetti, CEDAM, Padova 2002, pp. 185-200; C. Steel, *Beyond the Principle of contradiction? Proclus' Parmenides and the Origin of Negative Theologie*, in *Die Logik der Transzendentalen. Festschrift für Jan A. Aertsen zum 65. Geburtstag*, ed. M. Pickavé, de Gruyter, Berlin 2003, pp. 581-599;M. Abbate, *Il divino tra unità e molteplicità: saggio sulla Teologia Platonica di Proclo*, cit., pp. 176-179. For the *negatio negationis* in Eckart's Latin cf.: Meister Eckhart, *Expositio sancti Evangelii secundum Iohannem*, n. 207.556, in Id., *Die lateinischen Werke*, vol. III, eds. K. Christ - B. Decker - J. Koch - H. Fischer, A. Zimmermann, Kohlhammer, Stuttgart 1994, pp. 485-486; 174-175; Id. *Expositio libri Sapientiae*, n. 148, in Id., *Die lateinischen Werke*, vol. II, eds. J. Koch - H. Fischer - K. Weiss, Kohlhammer, Stuttgart 1992, pp. 485-486; Id., *Prologi in Opus tripartitum*, nn.12.13, in Id., *Die lateinischen Werke*, vol. I.1, ed. K. Weiss, Kohlhammer, Stuttgart 1965, pp. 156-159; Id., *Expositio libri Genesis*, nn. 25-27, in Id., *Die lateinischen Werke*, vol. I.1, cit., pp. 204-205; Id., *Expositio libri Exodi*, 74, in Id., *Die lateinischen Werke*, vol. II, ed. K. Weiss, Kohlhammer, Stuttgart 1954, pp. 76-78. On the theme, cf. W. Beierwaltes, *Platonismus im Christentum*, cit., pp. 112 ff., 122 f.; On the *negatio negationis* in Eckhart cf. S. Grotz, *Negationen des Absoluten. Meister Eckhart. Cusanus. Hegel*, Meiner, Hamburg 2009, pp. 20-24.

87 Proclus, *Commentaire sur le Parménide de Platon. Traduction de Guillaume de Moerbeke*, cit., t. 2, p. 367, 75 ff. Cf. furthermore: Proclus, *Commentaire sur le Parménide de Platon. Traduction de Guillaume de Moerbeke*, cit., t. 2, p. 517, 43; p. 391, 34; K. Bormann, *Die Exzerpte und Randnoten des Nikolaus von Kues zu den lateinischen Übersetzungen der Proclus-Schriften. Expositio in Parmenidem Platonis*, cit., marg. 440.

inasmuch as such, is at the same time negation of the many and their generating principle – significant forerunner of the idea of *non aliud* which the Cardinal has not failed to emphasize[88].

Reassuming and synthesising his conception of the First Principle, closely studied and ascensively elaborated in the commentary to the *Parmenides,* Proclus in a page of the *Theologia Platonica*, expresses the *Hén* through the idea of *non multa*, setting it above sameness and difference, and understanding it as negation of the many and *simul* their generating principle. Cusanus' corresponding marginal annotation «pro non aliud» would not be limitedly understood as reference to the words of Proclus' text correlated to it spatially– «nam simile passum est idem. Sicut et dissimile passum alterum» – but to all the passage of the *Theologia Platonica* in question, which perhaps represents the speculative moment of the very close proximity between Proclus' conception of the *Hén* and Cusanus' idea of *non aliud*[89]. Together with it, glosses 143, 175 and 208 should also be considered: in the marginal annotation 143 Cusanus writes «unum est nichil aliud quam unum»[90], an expression which, with almost imperceptible variations, is found *ad litteram* in the text of the work of 1461-1462[91]; in note 175, next to Proclus' text «nam quod per se bonum est et quod nichil aliud est: si moveatur a bonitate destituetur»[92], Cusanus annotates «nichil aliud»[93]; in note 208 of Proclus' text «Hoc autem nichil aliud est quam quod exstremissimum in hijs que sunt et est id quod per se est, ac nichil aliud quam id quod est»[94] is underlined with the marginal retranscription, the expression «nichil aliud»[95].

88 Proclus, *Commentaire sur le Parménide de Platon. Traduction de Guillaume de Moerbeke*, cit., t. 2, p. 379, 47 ff.; K. Bormann, *Die Exzerpte und Randnoten des Nikolaus von Kues zu den lateinischen Übersetzungen der Proclus-Schriften. Expositio in Parmenidem Platonis*, cit., marg. 468. Cf. inoltre Proclus, *Commentaire sur le Parménide de Platon. Traduction de Guillaume de Moerbeke*, cit., t. 2, p. 391, 34; Proclus, *Théologie Platonicienne*, cit., II, 5, pp. 37-38; II, 7, pp. 43-53; II, 8, pp. 51-57. On the name "One" as simple negation of the many and on the First Principle as A-pollôn, cf. Plotinus, *Enn.*,V 5, 6, 26 ff.

89 Cf. Proclus, *Théologie Platonicienne*, cit., II, 12, pp. 66-73; H. G. Senger, *Die Exzerpte und Randnoten des Nikolaus von Kues zu den lateinischen Übersetzungen der Proclus-Schriften. Theologia Platonis-Elementatio theologica*, marg. 190.

90 H. G. Senger, *Die Exzerpte und Randnoten des Nikolaus von Kues zu den lateinischen Übersetzungen der Proclus-Schriften. Theologia Platonis-Elementatio theologica*, cit., marg. 143.

91 Cf. *De non aliud*, h XIII, c. 4, p. 10.

92 Proclus, *Théologie Platonicienne*, cit., II, 7, pp. 43-53.

93 H. G. Senger, *Die Exzerpte und Randnoten des Nikolaus von Kues zu den lateinischen Übersetzungen der Proclus-Schriften. Theologia Platonis-Elementatio theologica*, cit., marg. 175.

94 Proclus, *Théologie Platonicienne*, vol. 3, ed. H. Saffrey – L.G. Westerink, Les Belles Lettres, Paris 1978, III, 9, pp. 34-40.

95 H. G. Senger, *Die Exzerpte und Randnoten des Nikolaus von Kues zu den lateinischen Übersetzungen der Proclus-Schriften. Theologia Platonis-Elementatio theologica*, cit., marg. 208.

Based on the above-mentioned marginal notes[96], a considerable part of the *Cusanusforschung* sets out to identify in Proclus' work the place of origin or of inspiration of the idea of *non aliud*[97] the interpretation hypothesis. Although almost unanimously accepted or supported by the interpreters, yet if focused on more attentively, reveals at least some area of doubt. According to the data we possess, the dating of the *De non aliud* should be set between the second half of 1461 and the first half of 1462, especially before 18 January 1462, while the translation of the *Theologia Platonica* was concluded by Pietro Balbo on 22 March 1462, thus, just following the drawing up of the *Directio*. Moreover in the *De non aliud* it is clearly stated in several places that the translation of the *Theologia Platonica* by Pietro Balbo, who is one of the interlocutors of the dialogue, is in progress at the moment[98]. Naturally, on the basis of his close relationship with the translator and as commissioner of the translation, Cusanus could have had access to an unfinished draft of his, which would explain why the the Cardinal is invited during the tetralogue to discuss the contents of the *Theologia Platonica*[99].

From a philosophical-speculative viewpoint or examination of the glosses we are led to conclusions compatible with those which the historico-philological analysis appears to bring about. The re-reading of Cusanus' annotations and of Proclus' correspective text brings us to at least two orders of considerations. Firstly – as shown by annotation 208 in which Proclus is speaking of the "first mixed" which together with the "limit" and the "non-limit" proceeds from the *Hén* – the

96 To them Senger adds the less significant marginal gloss 159, in which the Cardinal annotates «*unum quod est. non est aliquid eorum que sunt/ sed a quo omnia quod sunt existunt*». Cf. H. G. Senger, *Die Exzerpte und Randnoten des Nikolaus von Kues zu den lateinischen Übersetzungen der Proclus-Schriften. Theologia Platonis-Elementatio theologica*, cit., marg. 159.

97 Vansteenberghe believes that through the margin notation 143 Proclus gives the Cardinal the first idea on *non aliud*, cf. E. Vansteenberghe, *Le cardinal Nicolas de Cues (1401-1464). L'action – la pensée*, cit., pp. 436-438; according to Klibansky the *non aliud* taken from Proclus, cf. R. Klibansky, *Plato's Parmenides in the Middle Ages and the Renaissance. A chapter in the History of Platonic Studies*, in *The continuity of the Platonic tradition during the Middle Ages*, cit., p. VII; for Senger through the reading of *Theologia Platonica* Cusano arrives at his idea of *non aliud*, cf. H. G. Senger, *Die Exzerpte und Randnoten des Nikolaus von Kues zu den lateinischen Übersetzungen der Proclus-Schriften. Theologia Platonis-Elementatio theologica*, cit., pp. 25-26; according to D'Amico reading *Theologia Platonica* not only inspired the *non aliud*, but also gave the defining formula of «*non aliud quam*», cf. C. D'Amico, *Nicolaus von Kues als Leser von Proklos*, cit., pp. pp.33-64.On much more caution is based, and according to us more convincing is Beierwaltes, who highlights the close relationship between the idea of *non aliud* and the Cusianian reading of *Theologia* Platonica claiming that the Cardinal read Proclus' text in the light of his conception of *non* aliud, namely that it had given a cue, depth and vigour to a such conception cf. W. Beierwaltes, *Cusanusund Proclus.Zum neuplatonischen Ursprung des non-aliud*, cit., p. 137.

98 *De non aliud*, h XIII, c. 1, p. 3; c. 19, 47.

99 Cf. *De non aliud*, h XIII, c. 20, pp. 47-49.

diadochos of Athens utilizes the expression in different contexts, and not only when he deals with the One. Secondly, the expression – as shown by annotations 143, 175 and 208 – does not possess a separate existence and an autonomous meaning as, in contrast, it has in the Cardinal's thought. In the *Theologia Platonica* the *non aliud* does not have the relevance which, in contrast Cusanus attributes to it. It is he who extrapolates the expression in Proclus' affirmations in which it plays only a secondary role. One might suppose that the Cardinal re-reads the *Theologia Platonica* in the light of his idea of *non aliud* and – going beyond Proclus's interpretation – finds a reconfirmation of his conception in the text [100].

In the *Commentarium in Platonis Parmenidem*, in the development of its fortunate interpretation of the first hypothesis of the Platonic dialogue relating to the One-one, Proclus goes directly into the theme of the negation regarding the theological discourse on the Principle. The careful and close conceptual examination of the Neoplatonic philosopher aims *in primis* to disclose the *communis opinio* according to which the affirmation would be of a higher status with regard to the negation, in that the former would indicate a certain way of being and the presence of a form, while the second would indicate a privation. This is true in fact not for the negation in itself, but only for one of its multiple meanings, or that which it conceives in relation to the beings, to the things endowed with form[101]. To a more refined and more philosophically marked analysis the negation reveals a much more complex semantic spectrum formed by a plurality of significances constituted on the basis of his paradigmatic model represented by the non-being: as the non-being is a *pollachòs legómenon*, expressed in many ways, so the negation, which has its *exemplar* in it, will have a plurality of meanings which differ amongst themselves[102].

> Quoniam autem multis modis le non ens, hoc quidem ut melius ente, hoc autem ut enti coordinatum, hoc autem ut priuatio entis, palam utique quod triplices et negationum species considerabimus, hanc quidem supra affirmationem, hanc autem ab affirmatione deficientem, hanc autem adequantem aliqualiter ad affirmationem[103].

[100] On this Cusanus' wonted way of operating with regard to Proclus' text cf. G. Santinello, *Proclo nel pensiero del Cusano,* in Id., *Saggi sull' «umanesimo» di Proclo*, cit., pp. 15-50

[101] Cf. Proclus, *Commentaire sur le Parménide de Platon. Traduction de Guillaume de Moerbeke*, cit., t. 2, pp. 364-365, 72sgg.

[102] The idea of being is the paradigm of the affirmation, and the non-being of the negations is taken up again in a marginal note by Cusanus, cf. K. Bormann, *Die Exzerpte und Randnoten des Nikolaus von Kues zu den lateinischen Übersetzungen der Proclus-Schriften. Expositio in Parmenidem Platonis*, cit., marg. 431: «Ens affirmationis exemplar, non ens negacionis».

[103] Proclus, *Commentaire sur le Parménide de Platon. Traduction de Guillaume de Moerbeke*, cit., t. 2, p. 365, 86-91. The passage is annotated by Cusanus, cf. K. Bormann, *Die Exzerpte und Rand-*

Proclus identifies at least three distinct fundamental meanings of not-being: one according to which it is superior to being, another for which it is coordinated with being, and a third in conformity with which it is inferior to being. Consequently, also three corresponding meanings of the negation will be given: according to which one is superior to the affirmation, another for which it is corresponding to it, and a third one in accordance with which it is inferior. The identification of a meaning of a sense of the not-being beyond being, on which a conception is modelled of the negation beyond the affirmation, grants confuting the idea commonly accepted of the absolute superiority of affirmation over negation:

> Non ergo monoydaliter affirmatio semper negatione melior, sed aliquando et secundum habet ordinem, quando negatio dicit illud non ens quod est ultra ens[104].

The theological *intentio* of Proclus' conceptual analysis immediately emerges. Since in contrast to the negations the affirmations aim to grasp and express some form or other regarding the First Principle which is beyond form, it will be more convenient to talk negatively rather than affirmatively. While the affirmations indicate in fact something definite, the negations possess an indefinite value, so that their use will be more appropriate for indicating the unlimited, incomprehensible and uncircumscribable causality of the One[105].

What sense do the negations assume when they are applied to the One *epékeina tês ousías*? The negations relating to the One-one can indicate neither the something which even if it may be accepted by the First has not been accepted, nor something that could be accepted by him, as if he were not worthy of accepting it[106].

noten des Nikolaus von Kues zu den lateinischen Übersetzungen der Proclus-Schriften. Expositio in Parmenidem Platonis, marg. 432: «nota tripliciter dici non ens et ita negationem. Nam sicut non ens dicitur quia supra ens. Ita et negatio supra affirmacionem».

104 Proclus, *Commentaire sur le Parménide de Platon. Traduction de Guillaume de Moerbeke*, cit., t. 2, p. 365, 91-93.

105 Cf. Proclus, *Commentaire sur le Parménide de Platon. Traduction de Guillaume de Moerbeke*, cit., t. 2, pp. 365, 02 -366, 14. Proclus' words, «incomprehensibilem igitur et incircumterminabilem vnius causam conuenientius est exprimere per negationes», are underlined by Cusanus with the marginal annotation: «nota quomodo negationes in diuinis praeferunt affirmationibus». Cf. K. Bormann, *Die Exzerpte und Randnoten des Nikolaus von Kues zu den lateinischen Übersetzungen der Proclus-Schriften. Expositio in Parmenidem Platonis*, cit., marg. 434. The idea that the affirmations refer to the definite, while the negations to the indefinite is expressly present also in the propositions on the *non aliud* which accompany the tetralogue, cf. *De non aliud*, h XIII, prop. XV, p. 63: «Negationes igitur dirigunt visum mentis in quid, affirmationes autem in tale quid».

106 Cf. Proclus, *Commentaire sur le Parménide de Platon. Traduction de Guillaume de Moerbeke*, cit., t. 2, p. 366, 22 ff.

> Sed si mi oportet breviter dicere quod uidetur, sicut le unum causa est totorum, sic et negationes cause affirmationum sunt. Vnde et quecumque affirmauit secunda, sicut prediximus, ypothesis, tanta negauit prima. Omnia enim affirmatiua illa procedunt ex hiis negatiuis, et omnium causa le unum, ut ante omnia ens. Sicut enim incorporea ens anima corpus produxit, ut intellectus uelut inanimatus ens – qui non est anima – animam substituit, sic le unum immultiplicatum ens omnem multitudinem substituit et innumeratum ens numerum et infiguratum ens figuram, et in aliis similiter. Nichil enim est eorum que substituit[107].

As the Soul, albeit being embodied, has produced the bodies, and the Intellect beyond the Soul has produced the souls, so the One, although without multiplicity, number and figure, has generated every multiplicity, number, figure and all things. Starting from the presupposition that the cause is not identified with its caused objects, and therefore the Principle is none of the things that it produces, the negations are applied to the One not to indicate a privation, but because by generating all things it is not, he is not identified with anything. As the One is nothing of all, *omnium nihil*, precisely because he is cause of all, *omnium causa*, so *abnegationes sunt matres affirmationum*[108] in that they indicate the same fecundity of the Principle, his being active generative power, creative of all that which is negated of him. The negations are applied to the One, therefore, precisely to affirm his transcending causality with regard to that which is negated of him.

> Si igitur omnia affirmatiue cognoscimus, illud abnegatiue ab unoquoque omnium insinuamus, et ita hec species negationis generatiua est affirmationum, puta quod infiguratum de uno non est tale quale quod materie, quod secundum priuationem consideratur figure, sed quod generat et producit eum qui secundum figuram ordinem[109].

[107] Proclus, *Commentaire sur le Parménide de Platon. Traduction de Guillaume de Moerbeke*, cit., t. 2, p. 366, 43-45. The passage is marked and glossed in the margin by the Cardinal: «Conclusio. Sicut vnum causa totorum. Sic negationes cause affirmacionum et bene exponit et exemplum ponit, sicut incorporea anima corpus producit et inanimealis intellectus animam. Sic vnum immultiplicatum multitudinem». Cf. K. Bormann, *Die Exzerpte und Randnoten des Nikolaus von Kues zu den lateinischen Übersetzungen der Proclus-Schriften. Expositio in Parmenidem Platonis*, cit., marg. 436.

[108] Cf. Proclus, *Commentaire sur le Parménide de Platon. Traduction de Guillaume de Moerbeke*, cit., t. 2, p. 411, 55. The expression is recopied in the margin by Cusanus: «Abnegationes matres affirmacionum». K. Bormann, *Die Exzerpte und Randnoten des Nikolaus von Kues zu den lateinischen Übersetzungen der Proclus-Schriften. Expositio in Parmenidem Platonis*, cit., marg. 520.

[109] Proclus, *Commentaire sur le Parménide de Platon. Traduction de Guillaume de Moerbeke*, cit., t. 2, p. 367, 53-58. Cf. K. Bormann, *Die Exzerpte und Randnoten des Nikolaus von Kues zu den*

If in the case of the material the negations indicate a shortcoming, a mere *stéresis* or *privatio*, and thus are inferior to the affirmations, in the case of the One they indicate the transcendence, the eminence of the cause, and for this are superior to the affirmations, «in uno autem cause insinuant supereminentiam, et huius meliores sunt affirmationibus»[110]. Proclus identifies a sense of the negation according to which it, rather than being merely an affirmation of reversed meaning, and therefore its ontological symmetrical and specular correlation, the affirmation is considered as transcendent in that it is creative, generating principle, mirror of the One's excellence and of his poietic and source capacity. In synthesising and glossing Proclus' commentary the Cardinal of Kues writes: «negaciones de deo non sunt priuaciones sed dicuntur excellentiam ab affirmationibus exaltate»[111], in that – Cusanus always annotates – «abnegatio generatio affirmationis»[112].

The German thinker, now at the height of his ecclesiastical career and of his speculative journeying, closely studies and improves on Proclus' interpretation of Plato's *Parmenides* by re-elaborating - in the light of the Christian gospel and theology and of his own theoretical perspectives - the idea of *non aliud*, profound, radical and original verification, and vertiginous reformulation of the conception of negation and of the First Principle contained in Proclus' work[113]. The *De non aliud* begins – as most of Cusanus' texts – with the analysis of a problem that seems exclusively gnosiological. In dialogue with the Aristotelian Ferdinando Martins de Roritz, his personal doctor, forming part of his entourage in Rome, the Cardinal asks himself about what it is that permits knowledge. The reply – of markedly Aristotelian taste – is the definition.

lateinischen Übersetzungen der Proclus-Schriften. Expositio in Parmenidem Platonis, cit., marg. 437: «In materia negationes deteriores sunt quia sunt priuaciones».

110 Proclus, *Commentaire sur le Parménide de Platon. Traduction de Guillaume de Moerbeke*, cit., t. 2, p. 367, 63-64.

111 K. Bormann, *Die Exzerpte und Randnoten des Nikolaus von Kues zu den lateinischen Übersetzungen der Proclus-Schriften. Expositio in Parmenidem Platonis*, cit., marg. 498. And still in the subsequent annotation: «Oportet non priuacionis sed excellentie significatum». Cf. K. Bormann, *Die Exzerpte und Randnoten des Nikolaus von Kues zu den lateinischen Übersetzungen der Proclus-Schriften. Expositio in Parmenidem Platonis*, cit., marg. 499.

112 K. Bormann, *Die Exzerpte und Randnoten des Nikolaus von Kues zu den lateinischen Übersetzungen der Proclus-Schriften. Expositio in Parmenidem Platonis*, cit., marg. 585.

113 On the theme cf. W. Beierwaltes, *Cusanusund Proclus. Zum neuplatonischen Ursprung des non-aliud*, in *Nicolò Cusano agli inizi del mondo moderno*, cit., pp. 138-140.

> Nicolaus: Abs te igitur in primis quaero: quid est quod nos apprime facit scire? Ferdinandus: Definitio[114]. Sed unde dicitur definitio? Ferdinandus: A definiendo, quia omnia definit[115].

What, however, defines all things?

> Nicolaus: Nihil cognitu facilius. Quid enim responderes, si quis te "quid est aliud?" interrogaret? Nonne diceres: "non aliud quam aliud"? Sic, "quid caelum?"; responderes: "non aliud quam caelum". Ferdinandus: Utique veraciter sic respondere possem de omnibus, quae a me definiri expeterentur[116].

Cusanus starts out from Aristotle, but in order to directly follow on a path quite other than peripatetic: while the Aristotelian definition is composed of at least two predicates, that is by the indication of the nearest genre and of the specific difference[117], that of Cusanus' has its fulcrum, its essential pivot in the *non aliud.* If the *definitio* of Aristotelian matrix sets its objective within the most comprehensive persepective of the genre in order later to determine it and distinguish it through the indication of its specific difference, that of Cusanus' – in a way only formally analogous to the first – is structured according to a double movement. *In primis* it sets the object within the completely indefinite perspective of the *aliud* in order then, through the power of negation given by the *non*, to bring the object back to itself as if detaching it from the perspective of the totally indeterminate and revealing it for what it is[118]. *Aliud est non aliud quam aliud, caelum est non aliud quam caelum* and so on. Every thing is defined through the indication of its own being, *non aliud* than itself, or by acquiring its own "sameness", a sort of non-static self-referential identity, but constitutively dynamic and omnicorrelative which has already set it since ever before in rapport not only on a horizontal plane with every possible *aliud*, but above all on a vertical one, with the intranscendible transcendence of the Principle expressed by the *non aliud*[119].

114 *De non aliud*, h XIII, c. 1, pp. 3-4.

115 *De non aliud*, h XIII, c. 1, p. 4.

116 *De non aliud*, h XIII, c. 1, p. 5.

117 Aristoteles, *Analytica posteriora*; II, 3, 90 b 30ff. Cf furthermore *Topica*, I, 5, 101b, 38; 8, 103 b 15; VI 1, 139 a 28-29; 6, 143 b 8-9. Thomas refers to Aristotle cf. Thomas Aquinas, *In duodecim libros Metaphysicorum Aristotelis expositio*, VII, 3, 1328, eds. M. R. Cathala – R. M. Spiazzi, Marietti, Torino 1950, p. 329: «Unde videtur, quod sola ratio speciei, quae ex genere et differentiis constituitur, sit definitio».

118 On the *non aliud* as principle of the definition cf. S. Dangelmayr, *Gotteserkenntnis und Gottesbegriff in den philosophischen Schriften des Nikolaus von Kues*, Anton Hain, Meisenheim am Glan 1969, pp. 246-248.

119 Cf. F. Tomatis, *Ipseità, diversità e dia-ferenza*, in «Teoria», XXVI/1 (2006), pp. 31-35.

Since according to the Cardinal «oratio seu ratio est definitio»[120] the definition is not only the main instrument of knowledge, but links together two distinct dimensions, albeit closely correlated to each other, one logical and one ontological. According to the logico-gnosiological meaning it is the necessary condition for the perfect knowledge of something determinate as such. According to its ontological-metaphysical dimension it is the constitutive principle of the entity of all things and of each thing[121]. The definition is the means *par excellence* of knowledge since it is proposition or reason that determines ontologically the thing defined by limiting it before all other things[122]. The *non aliud* not only gives the being-known, but the very being itself to the thing, determining not only the logical-gnosiological form of the bodies, but their very constitutive and ontological structure. Cusanus disassociates himself from the Platonic conception contained in the *VII Letter* according to which the definition does not directly draw the essence, the *quid*, the "what thing" of the thing defined[123]:

[120] *De non aliud*, h XIII, c. 1, p. 4. Cf. Aristoteles, *Metaphysica*, 1034b 20. Latin Translation of *lógos* of Bessarion: *oratio*; of William of Moerbecke: *ratio* (Cf. Nicolás de Cusa, *Acerca de lo no-otro o de la definición que todo define*, cit., p. 28 note). Cusanus studied closely Aristotle's *Metaphysics*, thanks to Bassarion's translation.Cf. R. Haubst, *Die Christologie des Nikolaus von Kues*, Herder, Freiburg im Breisgau 1956, p. 19. In a passage of *Compendium* Cusanus writes: «Oratio enim est rei designatio seu definitio» (*Comp.*, h. XI/3, c. 9, n. 25, p. 21).

[121] Cf. C. Rusconi, *La definicíon que se define a sí misma y a todo*, cit., pp. 336-346.

[122] Already for Aristotle the definition has a substantial value, in fact there is the definition only of the substances and it is the notion of the essence, cf. Aristoteles, *Metaphysica*, 1031a 1; 1031a 12. In a passage on the *Super Dyonisium de divinis nominibus*, Albertus Magnus taking up Book IV of Aristotle's *Metaphysics* writes : «Dicendum quod sicut dicit philosophus IV Metaphysicorum ratio quam significat nomen est diffinitio. Unde idem est quod importatur in nomine rei et diffinitione eius. Diffinitio autem esplica quod in nomine implicite continetur» (cf. Albertus Magnus, *Super Dionysium de divinis nominibus*, ed. P. Simon, in Id., *Opera omnia*, t. XXXVII, Pars I, Aschendorff, Münster 1972, c. 13, n. 27, p. 448). In a marginal gloss to the passage in question the Cardinal himself annotates the words: «Ratio quam signat nomen est diffinitio», cf. L. Baur, *Nicolaus Cusanus und Pseudo Dionysius im Lichte der Zitate und Randbemerkungen des Cusanus*, Winter, Heidelberg, 1941, marg. 584. Aristotle is taken up again by Thomas, cf. Thomas Aquinas, *Summa theologiae*, I, q. 13, a. 1, in Id., *Opera omnia iussu Leonis XIII P.M. edita*, ed. cura et studio Fratrum Ordinis Praedicatorum, IV, Tip. Polyglotta, Roma 1888, p. 139: «Ratio, quam significat nomen, est definitio».

[123] Plato, *Epist.*, VII, 342b-344d.

> Meministi, puto, Platonem negare quid rei definitionem attingere, quia quidditati circumponitur, uti etiam Proculus explanat. Unde non fit ita, cum ipsum "non aliud" se atque omnia definit. Non enim sic ipsum principium quidditativum definit, quasi qui lineis circumpositis triangularem determinat seu definit superficiem, sed quasi superficiem, quae trigonus dicitur, constituat[124].

According to the cardinal's interpretation, the *non aliud*, unlike Plato's definition, inasmuch as quiddative principle, and the definition based on it do not encompass the *quid* of the thing, as if they limited the surface of the thing from outside, but by defining it they constitute it from within.

On the basis of its *virtus definiendi*, that is of its poietic and source capacity, the hunting ground of the *non aliud* is the only one in which the negation does not oppose the affirmation, since it, unlike every other name, does not oppose that which according to the logic of the finite supported by the principle of the non-contradiction should be its opposite, that is the *aliud*, but precedes it and defines it: «aliud enim cum sit non aliud quam aliud, utique "non aliud" praesupponit, sine quo non foret aliud»[125].The *non aliud* is not a simple *negatio* which opposes the *affirmatio*, and certainly does not indicate *stéresis* or *exclusio* – which would entail a shortcoming of the One – nor refers in an oversimplified way to a body which has, even if perfectly and completely, as a property, the complete absence of otherness, nor is it a mere *negatio negationis*[126], a negation of the negativity of the

[124] *De non aliud*, h XIII, c. 22, p. 52. The Proclian reference is to Proclus, *Commentaire sur le Parménide de Platon. Traduction de Guillaume de Moerbeke*, cit., t. 2, pp. 295-296. Cf. moreover the Cusanus' corresponding marginal annotation contained in K. Bormann, *Die Exzerpte und Randnoten des Nikolaus von Kues zu den lateinischen Übersetzungen der Proclus-Schriften. Expositio in Parmenidem Platonis*, cit., marg. 351.

[125] *De non aliud*, h XIII, c. 2, p. 6.

[126] If the *negatio negationis* is understood in the Proclian-Dionysian sense, or as the more exterior act of the thought which goes beyond itself and thus tries to arrive at a tangent with the non-thinkable Principle, the Cusanus' conception is *radicitu* different from it, in contrast the Cardinal's vision shows itself nearer to the Eckhartian idea of *negatio negationis* according to which it is to be set in relationship to the expression of *Es* 3, 14 "ego sum qui sum" in which case it assumes the sense in first place of a pure affirmation which excludes from God any type of negativity (also of the negative enunciation), and secondly of reflexive referring of the Principle himself in himself who perseveres in himself to burst forth in order to give himself to the light.The substantial difference between the two genres of *negatio negationis* is therefore that in the first case it leads inasmuch as fulfilment of the thought to the surpassing of any thought and of any enunciation, and in the second place it is no longer a proposition regarding the being of the Principle like any other proposition regarding objectable beings, but is instead self-enunciation of the Principle himself inasmuch as pure affirmation of himself.Cf. on the theme W. Beierwaltes, *Proklos. Grundzüge seiner Metaphysik*, cit., pp. 395-398. Starting from this differentiation Cusanus' words contained are understood in the *Propositio XIV* of the work, cf. *De non aliud*, prop. XIV, p. 63:

finite, of the otherness that always constitutes it, but rather is a pure expression of the infinite and free causality of the Principle.

> Ferdinandus: Visne dicere "non aliud" affirmationem esse vel negationem vel eius generis tale? Nicolaus: Nequaquam, sed ante omnia talia.

The *non aliud* is neither negation nor affirmation, but «videtur ante omnem positionem atque ablationem»[127] in that it is their very generating principle which cannot be understood either by means of the one or by means of the other.

> Sequor te, pater, quantum valeo, mihique videtur certissimum "non aliud" nec affirmatione negationeve aut alio quolibet modo comprehendi[128].

Re-elaborating Proclus' interpretation of Plato's first hypothesis of *Parmenides* and analysing the generative and creative capacity of the First Principle, the speculation of the Cardinal of Kues reaches its highest point by arriving at the idea of *non aliud*, revelation of the excellence and of the source capacity of the One with regard to every thing:

> per hoc enim video "non aliud" talia omnia antecedere, quia ipsa definit, et ipsa alia esse, cum "non aliud" antecedat[129].

To search for God in other fields is a waste of effort, since outside this affirmation the negation is opposed, while God is before every difference of opposites in that – as Cusanus writes, taking up Dionysius – «ipsi nihil contrarium»[130].

> Extra hunc campum negatio affirmationi opponitur, ut immortale mortali, incorruptibile corruptibili; et ita de omnibus, solum li non aliud excepto. Quaerere igitur deum in aliis campis, ubi non reperitur, vacua venatio est. Non enim est Deus, qui alicui opponitur, cum sit ante omnem oppositorum differentiam[131].

«Et qui Deum videt ante affirmationem et negationem, ille Deum videt in affirmationibus, quae de ipso per nos fiunt, non esse negativam, quae affirmatur, sed affirmationis affirmationem».

127 *De non aliud*, h XIII, c. 4, p. 9.

128 *De non aliud*, h XIII, c. 4, p. 9.

129 Cf. *De non aliud*, h XIII, c. 2, p. 6.

130 *De non aliud*, h XIII, c. XIV, p. 35. La citation is taken from Ps. Dionysius Areopagita, *De divinis nominibus*, VI, 2, in Id., *Corpus Dionysiacum*, vol I, ed. B.R. Suchla, De Gruyter, Berlin 1990, pp. 191-192.

131 Cf. *De ven. sap.*, h XII, c. 14, n. 41, pp. 40-41.

Thanks to his direct knowledge of the Latin translations and holding the differences constant– first amongst all the conception issuing from the Christian revelation of a trinitarian God, personal and endowed with thought who freely creates the world far differently from Proclus' idea of the One who in his absolute austerity and solitude excludes every form of a relational nature, thought and will[132] – Cusanus' tireless and untiring hunt for the First Principle is intrinsically guided by several profound traces of Proclus' which make of the diadochos of Athens - thanks also to the mediation of Dionysius, who re-elaborates many of Proclus' doctrines in the light of the Christian gospel - one of the preferred sources for understanding the genesis and the elaboration of that *apex theoriae* constituted by the idea of *non aliud*. Whether Cusanus read it prior to, or whether he read after the draft of the *De non aliud*, just as the *Commentarium in Platonis Parmenidem* the *Theologia Platonis* reveals a close link with Cusanus' vision of the First Principle as *non aliud*, index of a profound speculative *koinonía* between the Cardinal, Vicar of the Pope in Rome, and the diadochos of the school of Athens.

Considered the *theologus kat'exochén*, Dionysius is one of the thinkers who has more effectively influenced the Cardinal's speculation directly and lastingly, exerting throughout his philosophical-theological journeying a profound and decisive influence on the fundamental structures of his thought[133]. From his first sermons

[132] Cusanus was fully aware of the differences: suffice it to think of the marginal annotation 152 to the *Theologia Platonica* in which he writes «*Ostendit PLATONEM principalem causam ponere supra intellectum*». Cf. H. G. Senger, *Die Exzerpte und Randnoten des Nikolaus von Kues zu den lateinischen Übersetzungen der Proclus-Schriften. Theologia Platonis-Elementatio theologica*, cit., marg. 152. On the differences between Proclus' system and Cusanus' cf.: W. Beierwaltes, *Cusanusund Proclus. Zum neuplatonischen Ursprung des non-aliud*, cit., pp. 137-140; Id., *"Centrum tocius vite". Zur Bedeutung von Proklos' Theologia Platonis im Denken des Cusanus*, cit., pp. 191-214.

[133] On the influence of Dionysius' thought on that of Cusanus' cf: E. Vansteenberghe, *Le cardinal Nicolas de Cues (1401-1464). L'action – la pensée*, cit., pp. 413-416; L. Baur, *Nicolaus Cusanus und Pseudo Dionysius im Lichte der Zitate und Randbemerkungen des Cusanus*, cit., pp. 9-17; W. Beierwaltes, *Der verborgene Gott. Cusanus und Dionysius*, in Id., *Platonismus im Christentum*, cit., pp.130-171;W. J. Hoye, *Die mystische Theologie des Nicolaus Cusanus*, Herder, Freiburg 2004;W. J. Hoye, *Die Grenze des Wissens. Nikolaus von Kues in Auseinandersetzung mit der mystischen Theologie des Dionysius Areopagita*, in *Nicolaus von Kues in der Geschichte des Platonismus*, cit., pp. 87-101; C. D'Amico, *La docta ignorancia y la tiniebla del inconoscimiento: Nicolás de Cusa y Pseudo Dionisio Areopagita*, in *Memoria y silencio en la filosofía medieval*, ed. C. Ruta, Jorge Baudino, Buenos Aires 2006, pp. 225-235; J. G. Ríos, *Presencia del Pseudo Dionisio Areopagita en el De non aliud de Nicolás de Cusa*, in Nicolás de Cusa, *Acerca de lo no-otro o de la definición que todo define*, cit., pp. 347-358; A. Hubert, *Influencia del Pseudo Dionisio en Nicolás de Cusa*, in «Teología y Vida», 4 (2007), pp. 425-438; G. Zedania, *Von Einheit zu Pluralität. Nikolaus von Kues als Interpret der Schriften des Dionysius Pseudo-Areopagita*, Suedwestdeutscher Verlag für Hochschulschriften,Saarbrücken 2009; P. Casarella, *Cusanus on Dionysius*, in *Re-thinking Dionysius the Areopagite*, eds. S. Coakley – C.M. Stang, Blackwell, Chichester 2009 pp. 137-148; L.

to his final works the citations of Dionysius follow each other progressively until they reach their *akmé*, and not only quantitatively, in the works of his maturity including the *De non aliud* and the *De venatione sapientiae*[134]. The exceptional importance of Dionysian thought in the genesis and the development of Cusanus' speculation is attested by the huge collection of Latin translations and commentaries of the *Corpus Dionysianum* possessed by the Cardinal, who in his library could count – in addition to an exemplar in Greek of the writings of the Areopagite which he came into possession of during his journey to Constantinople of 1437/38 – on the main medieval Latin translations, especially the versions of Hilduin, of Johannes Scotus, of Johannes Saracenus, of Tommaso Gallo, Abbot of Vercelli (which regards only some extracts) and of Robert Grosseteste[135]. Yet the translation most utilized by the Cardinal was the one brought to completion by his friend and humanist Ambrogio Traversari, General of the Order of the Camaldolesi in 1436 and which was probably available to him from 1438[136]. Apart from the numerous Latin translations – indications of a more than evident interest in the Dionysian work – are to be mentioned the commentaries to the *Corpus dionysianum* possessed and cited by Cusanus: the commentaries by Hugh of Saint Victor and by Roberto Grossatesta, contained in the same codexes of Cusanus' of

Dupré, *The Mystical Theology of Cusanus's De visione dei*, in *"videre et videri coincidunt". Theorien des Sehens in der ersten Hälfte des 15. Jahrhunderts*, eds. W. C. Schneider – H. Schwaetzer – M. de Mey - I. Bocken, Aschendorff, Münster 2011, pp. 45-66; S. Gottlöber, *Das Prinzip der Relationalität: Grundzüge cusanischen Denkens als Parameter für Toleranz und interreligiösen Diskurs*, cit., pp. 151-155; V. Ranff, *Mystische Theologie und Gottes-Gedanke bei Pseudo-Dionysius und Nikolaus von Kues*, in «MFCG», 33 (2012), pp. 19-36; V. Ranff, *Mit Dionysius gegen Wenck*, in *Die Modernitäten des Nikolaus von Kues*, in T. Müller – M. Vollet (eds.), Transcript, Bielefeld 2013, pp. 43-56; M. H. van der Meer, *Divus Dionysius: Jean Gerson, Nicholas of Cusa, and the Interpretation of Pseudo-Dionysius's Mystical Theology* , in «Viator», 2 (2013), 323-342.

134 L. Baur, *Nicolaus Cusanus und Pseudo Dionysius im Lichte der Zitate und Randbemerkungen des Cusanus*, cit., p. 9-17.

135 Of Cusanus' possession of an exemplar in Greek there remains a testimony in a letter of his dated 14 September 1453 to the Abbot of Tagernsee. Cf. E. Vansteenberghe, *Autour de la docte ignorance. Une controverse sur la Théologie mystique au XV siècle*, Aschendorff, Münster 1915, ep. 5, p. 116. On the translations possessed by the Cardinal cf. L. Baur, *Nicolaus Cusanus und Pseudo Dionysius im Lichte der Zitate und Randbemerkungen des Cusanus*, cit., p. 10.

136 Traversari's translation is contained in the *Codex Cusanus 43*, the other medieval translations, together with the commentaries in the *Codex Cusanus 44* and *45*. Cf. J. Marx, *Verzeichnis der Handschriften-Sammlung des Hospital zu Cues bei Bernkastel a./Mosel*, cit., pp. 38-42. On the translations of the *corpus dionysianum* and their utilisation by the Cardinal cf. L. Baur, *Nicolaus Cusanus und Pseudo Dionysius im Lichte der Zitate und Randbemerkungen des Cusanus*, cit., pp. 9-17. The Latin translations of the *Corpus dionysianum* having come down to us in all thirteen including that of Traversari, are now published in *Dionysiaca. Recueil donnant l'ensemble des traductions latines des ouvrage attribués au Denis de l'Aréopage*, 2 voll.,ed. P. Chevallier, Desclée de Brouwer, Paris 1937-1950.

the Latin medieval translations, of Albertus Magnus, received in 1453 and copiously glossed by the Cardinal, of Maximus the Confessor, quoted in the *Apologia*, and of Thomas Aquinas, quoted in the *De venatione sapientiae*[137].

Dionysius, applying to the same objective the opposite conclusions of the first and second hypotheses of Plato's *Parmenides* thitherto radically held separate from Greek-pagan Neoplatonism, if setting aside Porphyry's comment[138], is for Cusanus the inevitable *prius* of his every attempt to express the inexpressible, and to gather the ungatherable *secretum* of the One, overwhelming beginning, inexhaustible source, and elusive end, of Cusanus' tireless pursuit of the divine and one of his highest theoretical peaks, namely the *non aliud.*

Cusanus reads the Dionysian work in the light of the *non aliud* searching for a confirmation of his idea in the pages of the *theologorum maximus*[139]. A further confirmation is given by the long Dionysian anthology contained in Chapter XIV of the *De non aliud*, aiming to show through a series of citations from Traversari's

[137] Hugh of Saint Victor's commentary utilizes Johannes Scotus's translation, while that of Roberta Grosseteste accompanies the translation of the same. The commentaries by Albertus are contained in the*Codex Cusanus 96* (cf. J. Marx, *Verzeichnis der Handschriften-Sammlung des Hospital zu Cues bei Bernkastel a./Mosel*, cit., pp. 97-98); on the commentaries cf. L. Baur, *Nicolaus Cusanus und Pseudo Dionysius im Lichte der Zitate und Randbemerkungen des Cusanus*, cit., pp. 9-17, in which are also published Albertus' numerous marginal annotations (*ibid.*, pp. 93-113). The commentary by Thomas, as Albertus utilizes the translation of Johannes Saracenus cf. *ibid.*, p. 16. The citation is in *De ven. sap.*, h XII, c. 33, p. 94. On the quotation of Maximus the Confessor cf. *Apol.*, h II, pp. 20-21.

[138] Fundamental on Porphyry and his interpretation of the *Parmenides* is P. Hadot's study, which also includes the edition of the commentary to the *Parmenides* attributed by the scholar to the philosopher from Tyre cf. P. Hadot, *Porphyre et Victorinus*, 2 voll., Études Augustiniennes, Paris 1968. The attribution of the anonymous *Commentary to the Parmenides* to Porphyry is not accepted by all scholars. Indeed regarding the authorship of the anonymous *Commentary to the Parmenides* a lively discussion is raging amongst scholars who have adopted a wide variety of positions. For a synthesis of these positions and their relative authors, cf. R. Chiaradonna, *Nota su Partecipazione e atto d'essere nel neoplatonismo: l'anonimo* Commento al Parmenide, in «Studia graeco-arabica», 2 (2012), pp. 87-97, in part. p. 87-88 note 2.

[139] An attitude not alien to the Cardinal if one thinks for example that the idea of God as *oppositio oppositorum sine oppositione* comes from Cusanus attributed to Dionysius – both in *Apol.*, h II, p. 15, and in *De non aliud*, h XIII, c. 19, p. 47 – without it being possible to find any direct reference in the Dionisyan text. Cf. L. Baur, *Nicolaus Cusanus und Pseudo Dionysius im Lichte der Zitate und Randbemerkungen des Cusanus*, cit., p. 51. The doctrine of the *oppositio oppositorum sine oppositione* has become one of the topoi of Cusanus'interpretation by Werner Beierwaltes, on the theme of which cf. W. Beierwaltes, *Deus oppositio oppositorum. Nicolaus Cusanus, De visione Dei XIII*, in «Salzburger Jahrbuch für Philosophie», 8 (1964), pp. 175-185; Id., *Eriugena und Cusanus*, in Id. *Eriugena. Grundzüge seines Denkens*, cit., pp. 266-312; Id., *Mystische Elemente im Denken des Cusanus*, in *Deutsche Mystik im abendländischen Zusammenhang. Neu erschlossene Texte, neue methodische Ansätze, neue theoretische Konzepte*, eds. W. Haug - W. Schneider-Lastin, Niemeyer, Tübingen 2000, pp. 425-448.

Latin translation of the *Corpus dionysianum* that the *theologus* in his most profound theological speculations has expressed the *non aliud* as nothing other than *multifariam et multis modis*[140]. Cusanus may thus compare the new formulation of the divine *arché* with the *auctoritas* of Dionysius and show the closeness of the Dionysian theological conception to his new formulation of the First Principle[141].

In truth, unlike what we have seen in Plato and Proclus, in the *De divinis nominibus* otherness is not denied, but rather it is explicitly affirmed as a positive predicate of God : the *aliud* – together with the *idem*[142] – thus becomes one of the intelligible divine names aimed to emphasize the inexorable giving himself of the divine in making himself freely *pánta en pâsin*[143] for the salvation of all, albeit continuing unmoving in himself in his own *identitas supraessentialis*[144]. Cusanus himself does not fail to underline the: «*Verum Dionysius ille Areopagita dicebat etiam Deum alterum dici*»[145]. In another passage of the same chapter, which emphasizes the absolute transcendence of the divine One, God is even more emphatically referred to by the expression *pánton héteron*, different or other from all[146]. The positive affirmation of divine otherness is however, to be taken up in its context, or that of affirmative theology and of the search for intelligible divine names which never represent God in his essence, but rather try to express his creative and providential work in his more general determinations, the Principle inasmuch as *aitía toû eînai*, the divine in his relationship to the world, and in his being creator. The names of God represent the universal subsisting realities which make possible the existence of the beings hierarchically arranged, the models of the things which ex-

140 *De non aliud*, h XIII, c. 14, pp. 29-38. The Latin translation quotes does not coincide perfectly with that contained in the *Codex Cusanus 43*. It is possible therefore, that in Rome Cusanus had available a copy of the same translation different from the one possessed by his library in Kues (cf. J. G. Ríos, *Presencia del Pseudo Dionisio Areopagita en el De non aliud de Nicolás de Cusa*, in Nicolás de Cusa, *Acerca de lo no-otro o de la definición que todo define. Nuevo texto crítico original*, cit., pp. 347-358). On the Dionysian anthology that occupies the whole of the long chapter XIV of the work cf.; L. Baur, *Nicolaus Cusanus und Pseudo Dionysius im Lichte der Zitate und Randbemerkungen des Cusanus*, cit., pp. 24-25; K. Flasch, *Nicolaus von Kues. Geschichte einer Entwicklung*, cit., pp. 569-570; M. von Perger, *Nichts Anderes – Ein Fund des Cusanus auf der Namensuche für das erste Prinzip aller Dinge*, in «Internationale Zeitschrift für Philosophie» 2 (2004), pp. 114-139; J. G. Ríos, *Presencia del Pseudo Dionisio Areopagita en el De non aliud de Nicolás de Cusa*, cit., pp. 347-358.

141 Cf. *De non aliud*, h XIII, c. 15-17, pp. 38-43.

142 Cf. Ps. Dionysius Areopagita, *De divinis nominibus*, IX, 4, cit., pp. 209-210,.

143 *1 Cor* 15, 28.

144 Cf. Ps. Dionysius Areopagita, *De divinis nominibus*, IX, 5, cit., pp. 210-211.

145 *De non aliud*, h XIII, c. 22, p. 52.

146 Expression we have already seen present in Plotinus (cf. Plotinus, *Enn.*, V 3, 11, 18; V 4, 1, 6; V 6, 3, 6; VI 7, 42, 13; VI 9, 1, 37).

ist and their properties[147]. The *De divinis nominibus* therefore, analyzes the divine *próodos*, the divine procession through which God communicates himself, albeit remaining in his *moné*, unknowable in himself and beyond all. Negative theology committed to safeguarding and closely examining the *chorís theoû*, in its function of perfect counterbalancing and in its superiority regarding the affirmative – although it always remains inadequate for a perfect and complete expression of the divine unity in itself – must duly deny all the predicates of God attributed to him by positive theology, including that of *aliud.* The Cardinal can therefore refer to Dionysius the negation of the *aliud,* although in the last vertiginous chapter of the *Mystica Theologia* – in which all the positive determinations of the divinity are finely and regularly denied up to the *negatio negationis*, until the negation of the very negations –this expression is not literally immediately retraceable. The very name of *Hén*, which represents the *akmé* of the *katáphasis theoû*, closing the Dionisyan search for the divine names, apophatically must be, and is, definitely negated[148].

Cusanus thinks of the One beyond the being of negative theology by closely examining the supersubstantial One of Dionysius, but at the same time does not release it from the One which is one, and which, inasmuch as it is coordinated with multiplicity, is cause of the latter, although he further examines this aspect of it. The vertiginous result is the *non aliud* which at the same time tries to express the paradoxicality of an immanence which does not annul transcendence and of a transcendence which does not negate immanence absolutely, that is the central mystery of the Christian re-velation of the *Deus incarnatus et simul absconditus.* The paradoxical conception of the simultaneous immanence and transcendence of God, which is a foundation element of Cusanus' theology right from his first work of speculation, the *De docta ignorantia*, is brought to terminological and conceptual perfection by means of the idea of *non aliud* which, inasmuch as such is *non aliud* than the *aliud* and negation of it by succeeding in expressing in a single expression its coincidental doubleness, the two faces of a single two-faced Janus. The dialectic of "in" and "beyond", of being cause of all and, at the same time, beyond all on the part of the *arché* represents one of the reliable supporting

147 On the Biblical and Platonic origin of the divine names cf.: S. Lilla, *Dionigi Areopagita e il platonismo cristiano*, Morcelliana, Brescia 2005; E. Corsini, *Il trattato* De divinis nominibus *dello Pseudo Dionigi Areopagitae i commenti neoplatonici al Parmenide*, Giappichelli, Torino 1962, pp. 75-111; E. Bellini, *Introduzione alla lettura del corpus dionisiano*, in D. Areopagita, *Tutte le opere*, eds. P Scazzoso and E. Bellini, Rusconi, Milano 1981, pp. 23-38.

148 On the One as divine name cf. Ps. Dionysius Areopagita, *De divinis nominibus*, XIII, 2-3, cit., pp. 227-230. On the negation of the One cf. Ps. Dionysius Areopagita, *De mystica theologia*, V, in Id., *Corpus Dionysiacum*, vol. II, ed. G. Heil – A. M. Ritter, De Gruyter, Berlin 1991, pp. 149-150.

pillars of the speculative link between Dionysius' thought and that of Cusanus', and finds in the *De non aliud* an elegant in-depth study and perfect accomplishment[149].

2.2 The Patristic and Neoplatonic-Medieval Origins

In his first sermon handed down to us, *In principio erat Verbum* (1430), Cusanus' thought significantly concentrates on the exegesis of the Prologue of John's Gospel, and we are plunged into the abysses of the Beginning that may be retraced in the famous first verse: *In principio erat Verbum, et Verbum erat apud Deum, et Deus erat Verbum*. Listening attentively to John's text we are present at the first auroral sign of the formulation of the *non aliud*.

> "Consubstantialis" enim est "Patri" Filius, quia <tres personae unus Deus>. Quidquid Deo convenit, omnibus personis aequaliter convenit. Quamquam "alius Pater, alius Filius, alius Spiritus", non tamen alterius essentiae est Pater, nec aliud est Pater, aliud Filius, aliud Spiritus Sanctus, quia <Pater, Filii et Spiritus Sancti una est essentia, coaequalis Gloria, aeterna maiestatis>.[150]

In order to comprehend the contrast between *alius* and *aliud* present in Cusanus' first reflection on the Trinity we must go back to his sources, to the early Christian thinking, to the far from simple task of the Fathers to clarify and defend the Christian truth, or better its mystery, through a philosophico-theological terminology inevitably modelled on that of Greek-pagan philosophy. Earlier Tertullian in his work fundamental from the point of view of Trinity theology *Adversus Praexean* – a supporter of "patripassionism" according to which the Father was born in the Virgin and the Father suffered – refers to the distinction, which is not division,

149 On the theme cf.: J. Stallmach, *Das Nichtandere als Begriff des Absoluten*, in *Universitas. Dienst an Wahrheit und Leben. Festschrift für Bischof Dr. Albert* Stohr, vol. I, ed. Ludwig Lenhart, Grünewald, Mainz 1960, 329-355; W. Beierwaltes, *Der verborgene Gott. Cusanus und Dionysius*, in Id., *Platonismus im Christentum*, cit., pp. 130-171;M. Álvarez-Gómez, *Die verborgene Gegenwart des Unendlichen bei Nikolaus von Kues*, Anton Pustet, München 1968, pp. 179-199; J. Stallmach, *Immanenz und Transzendenz im Denken des Cusanus*, in *Transzendenz. Zu einem Grundwort der klassischen Metaphysik*, eds. L. Honnefelder - W. Schüssler, Schöningh, München 1992, pp. 183-192; T. Leinkauf, *Nicolaus Cusanus. Eine Einführung*, Aschendorff, Münster 2006, pp. 143-153.

150 *Sermo I*, h. XVI/1, n. 10, p. 9. Cf. D. Monaco, Deus Trinitas, cit., pp. 192-193; F. Resch, *Triunitas*, Aschendorff, Münster 2014, pp. 41-52.

among the Trinity persons through the use of the *alius*: «Ecce enim dico alium esse Patrem et alium Filium et alium Spiritum»[151]. In Epistle 101 *Ad Cledonium* by Gregorius Nazianzenus, written against the theses of Apollinaris of Laodicea, we find the first use in a trinitarian context of the negation of the *aliud*, as opposed to the affirmation of the *alius*[152]. It was to be Augustine, author in the West of the most profound and complete reflection on the Trinity of the epoch, to affirm the distinction of the persons and the unity of the substance through the antithetical use of *alius* and *aliud*. In the *De anima et eius origine*, in contrasting modalism, he writes: «alius est quidam Verbum Dei Filius, sed non est aliud: hoc est alia persona, sed non diversa natura»[153]. In the *De Civitate Dei*, in referring to the Spirit Augustine states: «Alius est autem quam Pater et Filius, quia nec Pater est nec Filius; sed alius dixi, non aliud, quia et hoc pariter simplex pariterque incommutabile bonum est et coaeternum»[154].

The distinction between *alius* and *aliud* in its various forms spands all Western theological reflection. Anselm writes in the *Monologion*:

> Ecce enim, cum sic impossibile sit eundem esse eum qui gignite eum qui gignitur, atque eundem esse parentem et prolem, ut necesse sit alium esse genitorem, alium genitum, et alium esse patrem, alium filium: sic tamen necesse est idem esse illum qui gignit et illum qui gignitur, necnon parentem et prolem, ut impossibile sit aliud esse genitorem quam quod est genitus, aliud esse patrem quam quod filius.[155]

Thomas in his *Summa theologiae* quoting Gregorius Nazianzenus's already mentioned epistle states: «Ibi [scil. in Trinitate] enim alius et alius dicimus, ut non subsistentias confundamus, non aliud autem et aliud»[156]. Eckhart in the *Expositio sancti Evangelii secundum Iohannem* distinguishes – in a passage which the Cardinal does not fail to quote[157] – the other according to the person, the *alius* from the other according to nature, the *aliud*: «Filius est enim qui fit alius in persona, non

[151] Tertullianus, *Adversus Praxeam*, ed. A. Kroymann, IX, 1, in Id., *Opera montanistica*, eds. A Gerlo et alii, Brepols, Turnhout 1954, p. 1168.

[152] Gregorius Nazianzenus, *Epistula 101*, in PG 37, 180 B.

[153] Aurelius Augustinus, *De anima et eius origine*, II, 5, in PL 44, 500.

[154] Aurelius Augustinus, *De civitate Dei*, vol. II, eds. B. Dombart – A. Kalb, Brepols, Turnhout 1955, p. 330, XI, 10.

[155] Anselmus Cantuariensis, *Monologion*, XLIII, in Id., *Opera omnia*, ed. F. S. Schmitt, Fromman-Holzboog, Stuttgart-Bad Cannstatt, 1968, t. I, vol. II, pp. 59-60.

[156] Thomas Aquinas, *Summa theologiae*, III, q. 2, art. 3, in Id., *Opera omnia iussu Leonis XIII P.M. edita*, ed. cura et studio Fratrum Ordinis Praedicatorum, XI, Tip. Polyglotta, Roma 1903, p. 30.

[157] Cf. *Sermo CXL*, h. XVIII/ 1, p. 91.

aliud in natura»[158]. A distinction which continually returns in the commentary to the Gospel of John by the Domenican master[159]. For Eckhart it is a question of thinking radically of the disconcerting declaration of John's Christ «Ego et Pater unum sumus» (*Jn* 10, 30), holding together the one thing alone of the neuter *unum*, expressing the sameness of the substance, and the plurality of the *sumus*, indicating the distinction between the persons[160]. Cusanus himself taking up John's expression again writes «Pater et Filius sunt unum quamvis non unus»[161].

The idea of *non aliud* plunges its roots into the reflection on the Trinity, especially in the expression of the *homoousía* of the three divine persons, distinct but not different: the living unity of the Trinity requires the distinction of the person, the otherness of the Son from the Father, and of both from the Spirit, yet at the same time this otherness must be negated in its substantiality, otherwise we would not have God, but three separate divinities. Through the idea of *non aliud* Cusanus tries to express the incomprehensible mystery of the *homooúsion*, of the consubstantial; such reflection is inspired by the opening verses of John's Gospel, abyssal and profound beginning of all authentically Christian thinking in which such distinct indistinction is affirmed as eternally present *en archê*, *in principio*. The *non aliud* expresses therefore the consubstantiality of the three Trinity persons, albeit in their being distinct, and tries to indicate the more hidden side of the Trinity and of the Christian God, by reserving their mystery. The distinction between the three presupposes their consubstantiality eternally *in principio*, their relationship of non-otherness, and the consubstantiality presupposes the distinction. If they were not consubstantial they would in fact be different, and not distinct, and they would be separate substances, three and not one. At the same time if they were not distinct we would have only a lifeless sameness of self to self, and not an authentic relationship of freedom or love.

In his extraordinary expertise regarding ancient and medieval thought, Cusanus includes, in fact, also the direct reading of Book I of the *Periphyseon* of the

158 Meister Eckhart, *Expositio sancti Evangelii secundum Iohannem*, n. 5, in Id., *Die lateinischen Werke*, vol. III, eds. K. Christ - B. Decker - J. Koch - H. Fischer - A. Zimmermann, Kohlhammer, Stuttgart 1994, p. 7. The *Expositio sancti Evangelii secundum Iohannem* by Eckhart has come down to us in two manuscripts: one of Berlin and the other of Cusanus' own property, the *Codex Cusanus 21*, which was composed about 1444 and contains almost all the Latin writings of the Dominican master. Cf. H. Denifle, *Das Cusanische Exemplar lateinischer Schriften Eckharts in Cues*, in «Archiv fuer Literatur- und Kirchengeschichte des Mittelalters», 2 (1986), pp. 673-687.

159 Cf. Meister Eckhart, *Expositio sancti Evangelii secundum Iohannem*, nn. 16.57.133.161.362.477.479, in Id., *Die lateinischen Werke*, vol. III, cit., p. 14; pp. 47-48; pp. 114; p. 132; pp. 307-308: p. 410; pp. 411-412.

160 Cf. *Ibid.*, n. 362, pp. 307-308.

161 *Sermo XI*, v. XVI/3, n. 4, p. 225.

Irish philosopher and theologian, as borne out by his marginal notes contained in the *Codex Additivus 11035* of the British Museum; the notes identified by R. Klibansky in 1935 were transcribed and published by J. Koch in 1963[162]. Familiarity with the thought of the Carolingian theologian do not stop, however, only at the first book. Cusanus in fact studied and annotated the other books of Eriugena's *magnum opus* through the *excerpta* contained in the *Clavis physicae* by Honorius Augustodunensis in the version conserved in the *Cod. lat. 6734* of the Bibliothèque Nationale of Paris[163]. To this must be added the frequentation of the *Omelia sul Prologo di Giovanni*, evidenced by the long quotation – under the name of Origen – contained in the text of the sermon *Verbum caro factum est* of the year 1438[164].

The possibility of an influence from Eriugenian thought on the later Cusanus' own conception of God as *non aliud* must therefore be taken seriously into consideration, not only for the presence in the *Directio* of doctrines which could go back to Johannes Scotus, but rather to trace a possible influence of the reading of the Eriugenian texts on the very origin and genesis of the idea and conception of the n*on aliud*[165]. Among Cusanus' marginal notes to the *Periphyseon* we find the

[162] Cf. J. Koch, *Kritisches Verzeichnis der Londoner Handschriften aus dem Besitz des Nikolaus von Kues*, in «MFCG», 3 (1963), pp. 86-100.

[163] Cusanus' authorship of the glosses has been recognised by M.-T. D'Alverny, *Le cosmos symbolique du XIIe siècle*, in «Archives d'Histoire Doctrinale et Littéraire du Moyen Age», 20 (1953), pp. 31-81; have now been published by P. Lucentini, *Le annotazioni di Nicola Cusano alla Clavis Physicae*, in Id., *Platonismo medievale. Contributi per la storia dell'eriugenismo*, La Nuova Italia, Firenze 1979, pp. 77-109. Honorius' work is now available in the earlier quoted edition: Honorius Augustodunensis, *Clavis physicae*, ed. P. Lucentini, Edizioni di Storia e Letteratura, Roma 1974. On the theme, cf. D. F. Duclow, *Coinciding in the Margins: Cusanus Glosses Eriugena*, in *Eriugena – Cusanus*, eds. A. Kijewska - R. Majeran - H. Schwaetzer, KUL, Lublin 2011, pp. 83-103.

[164] Cf. *Sermo XIX*, h. XVI/2, p. 294. Cf. Iohannes Scotus Eriugena, *Omelia super Prologum Iohannis*, 6, 30, in Jean Scot, *Homélie sur le Prologue de Jean*, ed. É. Jeauneau, Cerf, Paris 1969, p. 230. On the theme, cf. K. Reinhardt, *Die Auslegung des Johannesprologs bei Johannes Scottus Eriugena und Nikolaus von Kues*, in *Eriugena – Cusanus*, cit., pp. 104-116.

[165] In favour of Johannes Scotus Eriugena as decisive source of the idea of the *non aliud* cf. M. Rohstock, *Der negative Selbstbezug des Absoluten: Untersuchungen zu Nicolaus Cusanus' Konzept des Nicht-Anderen*, De Gruyter, Berlin 2014, pp. 132-189. On Johannes Scotus Eriugena's influence on Cusanus cf..: E. Vansteenberghe, *Le cardinal Nicolas de Cues (1401-1464). L'action – la pensée*, cit., pp. 416-417; D. F. Duclow, *Pseudo Dionysius, John Scotus Eriugena, Nicholas of Cusa. An approach to Hermeneutic of Divine Name*, in «International Philosophical Quarterly», XII (1972), pp. 260-278; C. Riccati, *Eriugena e Cusano: due concezioni del mondo come esplicazione della natura intellettuale*, in «Memorie dell'Accademia delle scienze di Torino», I (1976-77), pp. 85-161; Id., «Processio» et «Explicatio»: *la doctrine de la création chez Jean Scote et Nicolas de Cues*, Bibliopolis, Napoli 1983; D. Moran, *The philosophy of Johannes Scottus Eriugena. A Study on Idealism in the Middle Ages*, Cambridge University Press, Cambridge 1989, pp. 279-282;

absolute negation of otherness and of diversity in God. At the end of Book I of his fundamental work Johannes Scotus writes that «Vbi enim est uera et aeterna et insolubilis per se ipsam simplicitas ibi aliud-et-aliud et multumdiversorumque fieri impossibile est»[166], a passage annotated by Cusanus with the words: «In deo non est aliud et diversum»[167]. Cusanus was also able to find in Johannes Scotus the negation of otherness in God, possible embryonic origin – holding the differences constant, and the powerful and original development imprinted on this doctrine by the later Cusanus – of his conception of God as *non aliud*.

Another moment of the Eriugenian text which aroused the Cardinal's interest and potentially close to his idea of *non aliud* might well be the passage annotated by him in the margin with the words «verba mirabilia» present in Honorius's *Clavis physicae*[168]. With the words of Book III of the *Periphyseon*, Honorius states that:

> Omne enim quod intelligitur et sentitur nichil aliud est nisi non apparentis apparitio, occulti manifestatio, negati affirmatio, incomprehensibilis comprehensio, ineffabilis fatus, inacessibilis accessus, inintelligibilis intellectus, incorporalis corpus, superessentialis essentia, informis forma, inmensurabilis mensura, innumerabilis numerus, carentis pondere pondus, spiritualis incrassatio, invisibilis visibilitas, illocalis localitas, carentis tempore temporalitas, infiniti diffinitio, incircumscripti circumscriptio, et cetera que puro intellectu et cogitantur et perspiciuntur, et que

D. Moran, *Pantheism from John Scottus Eriugena to Nicholas of Cusa*, in «American Catholic Philosophical Quarterly», 1 (1990), pp. 131-152; J.L.C. Alonso, *Teofanía y Concordia. Leyendo a Escoto Eriúgena y Nicolás de Cusa*, in *Coincidencia de Opuestos y Concordia. Los Caminos del Pensamiento en Nicolás de Cusa*, vol. II, eds. J. M. André - M. Álvarez-Gómez, Ed. Sociedad Castellano-Leonesa de Filosofia, Salamanca 2002, pp. 107-131; A. Kijewska, *Divine Non-Being in Eriugena and Cusanus*, «Philotheos», 2 (2002), pp. 155-167; O. F. Bauchwitz, *Nicolás de Cusa y Escoto Eriúgena: aportes para una metafísica más allá de la ontoteología*, in J. M. Machetta-C. D'Amico, (eds.), *El problema del conocimiento en Nicolás de Cusa: genealogía y proyección*, Biblos, Buenos Aires 2005, pp. 41-48; W. Beierwaltes, *Eriugena und Cusanus*, in Id., *Eriugena. Gründzuge seines Denkens*, cit., pp. 266-312; Id., *Theophanie. Nicolaus Cusanus und Johannes Scottus Eriugena. Eine Retractatio*, cit., pp. 153-175; A. Kijewska, *Conception of Intellect in Eriugena and Cusanus*, in *Nicolaus Cusanus: ein bewundernswerter historischer Brennpunkt. Philosophische Tradition und wissenschaftliche Rezeption*, Eds. K. Reinhardt – H. Schwaetzer, Roderer, Regensburg 2008, pp. 11-20; A. Kijewska - R. Majeran - H. Schwaetzer (eds.), *Eriugena – Cusanus*, cit., pp. 83-230.

166 Iohannes Scotus Eriugena, *Periphyseon (De divisione naturae)*, Liber I, ed. É. Jeauneau, Brepols, Turnhout 1996, p. 105, 3289.

167 J. Koch, *Kritisches Verzeichnis der Londoner Handschriften aus dem Besitz des Nikolaus von Kues*, cit., p. 99.

168 P. Lucentini, *Le annotazioni di Nicola Cusano alla Clavis Physicae*, cit., p. 99, note 76.

memorie sinibus capi nesciunt et mentis aciem fugiunt.[169]

In the text quoted in correspondence to a clear formulation of the doctrine – of Dionysian origin, but developed in depth by the Eriugenian system–of the world as *Dei apparitio* or *theophanía*, which is taken up by Cusanus himself and re-elaborated in the *Directio* on the underlying theme of the idea of *non aliud*, we find the expression *nichil aliud est nisi* so close to the locution "*non est aliud quam*" fundamental in Cusanus' conception. Likewise the linguistic form is to be emphasised in which Johannes Scotus expresses himself, that is through a series of paradoxical negative affirmations so similar to Cusanus' taste for paradox and paradoxical expression, from which also the expression *non aliud* does not escape. To all this, and probably also to much more, Cusanus' marginal annotation «*verba mirabilia*» refers[170].

Apart from the name of the Carolingian theologian, another important medieval thinker might have had a possible influence on the conception of the First Principle as *non aliud* of the later Cusanus, namely Meister Eckhart[171]. To the Cardinal's library we owe the transmission of almost all the texts of the Latin Eckhart, little known both by his contemporaries and in subsequent centuries, many of which would have been lost had it not been for his passion for the Thuringian thinker. Cusanus knew his more important Latin works, having read and annotated them copiously, beginning from 1444 – the year of the dating of the codex –

169 Honorius Augustodunensis, *Clavis physicae*, cit., 128, 12-23. The passages is found in Iohannes Scotus Eriugena, *Periphyseon (De divisione naturae)*, Liber III, ed. É. Jeauneau, Brepols, Turnhout 1999, p. 22, 589.

170 For an interpretation of the passage cf. W. Beierwaltes, *Theophanie. Nicolaus Cusanus und Johannes Scottus Eriugena. Eine Retractatio*, cit., pp. 153-175.

171 Another source might be identified in Thierry of Chartres, who utilises the concept of *nichil aliud* in his speculation on the Trinity; cf. F. Resch, *Triunitas. Die Trinitätspeculation de Nikolaus von Kues*, Aschendorff, Münster 2014, p. 36 n. 153. Cf. Theodoricus Carnotensis, *Tractatusde sex dierum operibus*, 38, in *Commentaries on Boethius by Thierry of Chartres and his School*, ed. N. M. Häring, Pontifical Institute of Mediaeval Studies, Toronto 1971, p. 571, 69; Id., *Glosa super Boethii librum De Trinitate*, V, 18, in *Commentaries on Boethius by Thierry of Chartres and his School*, cit.., p. 297, 44. On Thierry of Chartres' influence on Cusanus cf.W. Beierwaltes, *Einheit und Gleichheit. Eine Fragestellung im Platonismus von Chartres und ihre Rezeption durch Nicolaus Cusanus*, in Id., *Denken des Einen. Studien zum Neuplatonismus und dessen Wirkungsgeschichte*, Klostermann, Frankfurt am Main 1985, pp. 368-384; E. Reinhardt, *Gemeinsamkeiten und Unterschiede in der trinitarischen Terminologie bei Thierry von Chartres und Nikolaus von Kues*, in-*Eriugena – Cusanus*, cit., pp. 231-248; C. M. Rusconi, *Commentator Boethii* De Trinitate[...] ingenio clarissimus. *Die Kommentare des Thierry von Chartres zu De Trinitate des Boethius als Quellen des Cusanus*, in «MFCG», 33 (2012), pp. 247-290; D. Albertson, *Mathematical Theologies. Nicholas of Cusa and the Legacy of Thierry of Chartres*, Oxford University, Oxford 2014.

in *Codex Cusanus 21* of his library[172]. To the courageous and impassioned defence of the Domenican master are dedicated some of the pages of the *Apologia doctae ignorantiae*, mark of appraisal and considerable regard for his thought in view of the papal bull *In agro dominico* dated 27 March 1329 which attacked some of his works, declaring them as heretical[173]. The influence of Eckhart's thought on Cusanus', amply present throughout the whole progress of the cardinal's thinking, is attested right from his youthful days and has been carefully examined several times by the *Cusanus-Forschung*[174].

172 For the edition of the marginal notes to the *Codex Cusanus 21* cf. S. Frost, *Nikolaus von Kues und Meister Eckhart. Rezeption im Spiegel der Marginalien zum Opus Tripartitum Meister Eckharts*, Aschendorff, Münster 2006. On the discovery and the importance of Cusanus' codex for the transmission of the Latin Eckhart cf. H. Denifle, *Das cusanische Exemplar lateinischer Schriften Eckharts in Cues*, cit.

173 Cf. *Apol.*, h. II, pp. 24ff.

174 On Eckhart's influence on Cusanus cf.: E. Vansteenberghe, *Le cardinal Nicolas de Cues (1401-1464). L'action – la pensée*, cit., pp. 246-429; E. Hoffmann, *Gottesschau bei Meister Eckhart und Nikolaus von Kues*, in *Festschrift Heinrich Zangger*, ed. J. Dettling, Rascher, Zürich 1935, II, pp. 1033-1045; H. Wackerzapp, *Der Einfluss Meister Eckharts auf die ersten philosophischen Schriften des Nikolau von Kues*, Aschendorff, Münster 1962; J. Koch, *Nikolaus von Kues und Meister Eckhart. Randbemerkungen zu zwei in der Schrift «de coinecturis» gegebenen Problem*, in «MFCG», 4 (1964), pp. 164-173; R. Haubst, *Nikolaus von Kues als Interpreter und Verteidiger Meister Eckharts*, in *Freiheit und Gelassenheit: Meister Eckhart heute*, ed. U. Kern, Kaiser, München 1980, pp. 75-96; B. Mojsisch, *Nichts und Negation. Meister Eckhart und Nikolaus von Kues*, in *Historia Philosophiae Medii Aevi. Studien zur Geschichte der Philosophie des Mittelalters*, 2 voll., eds. B. Mojsisch - O. Pluta, John Benjamins, Amsterdam 1991, vol. II, pp. 675-693; M. Thurner, *Die Philosophie der Gabe bei Meister Eckhart und Nikolaus Cusanus*, in Id. (ed.), *Nicolaus Cusanus zwischen Deutschland und Italien*, Akademie, Berlin 2002, pp. 153-184; G. Steer, *Die Predigten des Nikolaus von Kues im Vergleich mit dem Predigtenwerk von Meister Eckhart*, in «MFCG», 30 (2005), pp. 145-169; M.-A. Vannier, (ed.), *La naissance de Dieu dans l'âme chez Eckhart et Nicolas de Cues*, Cerf, Paris 2006; F. D. Duclow, *Masters of Learned Ignorance: Eriugena, Eckhart, Cusanus*, Ashgate, Aldershot 2006; L. Dupré, *The question of pantheism from Eckhart Cusanus*, in *Cusanus. The legacy of learned ignorance*, ed. P. J. Casarella, The Catholic University of America, Washington 2006, pp. 74-88; C. Ruta, *Ein verborgen Wort. Memoria y Gottesgeburt en Meister Eckhart (Predigtzyklus 101-104)*, in *Memoria y silencio en la filosofía medieval*, cit., pp. 143-169; H. Schwaetzer, *"Mens" y "Memoria". El maestro Eckhart en el espejo del Cusano*, in *Memoria y silencio en la filosofía medieval*, cit., pp. 171-180; K. Reinhardt, *El nacimento de Dios en el alma según Nicolás de Cusa*, in *Memoria y silencio en la filosofía medieval*, cit., pp. 181-190; M.-A. Vannier, *Hat Nikolaus von Kues die Predigten 101 bis 104 von Eckhart gelesen?*, in *Das europäische Erbe im Denken des Nikolaus von Kues*, eds. H. Schwaetzer –K. Zeyer, Aschendorff, Münster 2008, pp. 303-314; *La Trinité chez Eckhart et Nicolas de Cues*, ed. M.A. Vannier, Cerf, Paris 2009;M. A. Vannier (ed.), *La création et l'anthropologie chez Eckhart et Nicolas de Cues*, Cerf, Paris 2011; H. Schwaetzer - G. Steer (eds.), *Meister Eckhart und Nikolaus von Kues*, Kohlhammer, Stuttgart 2011; H. Schwaetzer – M. A. Vannier (eds.), *Zum Subjektbegriff bei Meister Eckhart und Niklaus von Kues*, Aschendorff, Münster 2011; H. Schwaetzer – M.A. Vannier (eds.), *Zum Intellektverständnis bei Meister Eckhart und Nikolaus*, Aschendorff, Münster 2012;

In Sermo XXIX, *Deus Unus est*[175], wherein is presented a brief, yet profound synthesis of Eckhart's perceptive henological conception of the divine, Cusanus came across several expressions, duly underlined by him, which could prove interesting from the viewpoint of a genealogy of the *non aliud*, if not for their direct and immediate influence on the genesis of Cusanus' expression, then at least to show a line of continuity among the great Platonic and Neoplatonic, Greek and Christian, ancient and medieval speculation – according to the direction given by Plato, Proclus, Dionysius, Johannes Scotus and Meister Eckhart – and the conception of the *non aliud* of the Cardinal of Kues. In the sermon is present the negation of all otherness in God – which we have seen being proper to the whole Neoplatonic conception of the One – expressed with the words «In deo enim non est aliud», which, as is attested by marginal note 314, have been underlined by Cusanus[176]. The expression could therefore reveal a vital thread which connects the highest Neoplatonic speculation, in keeping with the above-mentioned line of continuity, and which would result in the original and vertiginous conception of the One-God as *non aliud* of the thinker of Kues. For further proof of the thesis another Eckhartian passage is also underlined by the Cardinal in note 304 – «Deus tuus deus unus est, quasi nihil aliud est vere unum», which presents a formulation relating to the One very close to Cusanus' idea of *non aliud* and in which the significant expression *nihil aliud est*[177] recurs.

The closeness between Eckhart's conception and Cusanus' does not stop here: the idea of *non aliud* appears to be further anticipated in the Eckhartian vision whereby God in order to be One and true God is absolutely indistinct one and, at the same time, precisely because of his indistinctness from all distinct, a con-

A. Speer, *Zwei Versuche, Gott zu denken: Meister Eckhart und Nicolaus Cusanus*, in «MFCG», 33 (2012), pp. 169-194; E. Brient, *Meister Eckhart's Influence on Nicholas of Cusa: A Survey of the Literature*, in *A Companion to Meister Eckhart*, ed. J. M. Hackett, Brill, Leiden 2013, pp. 553-586; H. Schwaetzer – M.A. Vannier (eds.), *Der Bildbegriff bei Meister Eckhart und Nikolaus von Kues*, Aschendorff, Münster 2015; S. Gottlöber, *Das Prinzip der Relationalität: Grundzüge cusanischen Denkens als Parameter für Toleranz und interreligiösen Diskurs*, cit., pp. 156-165. More specifically on the relationship of Eckhartian thought with Cusanus' conception of the *non aliud* cf.: P. Wilpert, *Anmerkungen*,in Nikolaus von Kues, *Vom Nichtanderen*, Meiner, Hamburg 1952, pp. 148-149; E. A. Wyller, *Zum Begriff "non aliud" bei Nicolaus Cusanus*, in G. Santinello (ed.), *Niccolò Cusano agli inizi del mondo moderno*, cit., pp. 437-438; R. Haubst, *Nikolaus von Kues als Interpreter und Verteidiger Meister Eckharts*, cit., pp. 75-78; B. Mojsisch, *Meister Eckhart. Analogie, Univozität und Einheit*, Meiner, Hamburg 1984, pp. 92-95; W. Beierwaltes, *Identität und Differenz*, cit., pp. 97-104, p. 114.

175 Cf. Meister Eckhart, *Sermo XXIX*, in Id., *Lateinischen Werke*, vol. IV, eds. E. Benz – B. Decker – J. Koch, Kohlhammer, Stuttgart 1956, pp. 263-270.

176 Cf. S. Frost, *Nikolaus von Kues und Meister Eckhart. Rezeption im Spiegel der Marginalien zum Opus Tripartitum Meister Eckharts*, cit., marg. 314.

177 *Ibid.*, marg. 304.

ception present on several times in the texts of the Domenican master – including the quoted sermon *Deus Unus est* – always duly underlined or annotated in the margin by the Cardinal[178]. Eckhart's idea according to which *Deus sua indistinctione distinguitur*[179] reveals an extraordinary closeness to Cusanus' idea of the First Principle in the *Directio*, which inasmuch as *non aliud*, absolute negation of otherness in itself, is *non aliud* than all. Eckhart, in his philosophical, theological and mystical search for the One-God, had at that time finely re-elaborated the Neoplatonic conception first of Proclus' and then of Dionysius', of the simultaneous and paradoxical transcendence and immanence of the First Principle which Cusanus was to bring to conceptual and terminological perfection in his new idea of *non aliud.* The points of contact between the philosophies of the two German thinkers become closer also on the ontological plane, since the Eckhartian henological conception, just as Cusanus' also reflects on the being of the created, which in participating in divine indistinction is indistinct in itself, and the more it is indistinct the more it is distinguished from the other indistinct distinct[180], just as every thing, thanks to its participation in the divine principle, being *non aliud* which itself is distinct in its singleness from every other, which in its turn, is Not-Other than itself. The conception of Eckhart's One represents a significant and authoritative precedent which the Cardinal himself was mindful of, and to which he had paid much attention in the readings of the Thuringian master[181].

[178] Cf. Meister Eckhart, *Sermo II*, n. 7, in Id., *Lateinischen Werke*, vol. IV, cit., p. 9; Id., *Sermo IV*, n. 28, in Id., *Lateinischen Werke*, vol. IV, cit., p. 27; Id., *Sermo X*, n. 98. 100, in Id., *Lateinischen Werke*, vol. IV, cit., p. 98, p. 100; Id., *Sermo XIX*, n. 198, in Id., *Lateinischen Werke*, vol. IV, cit., p. 182; Id., *Sermo XXIX*, n. 298, in Id., *Lateinischen Werke*, vol. IV, cit., p. 264; Id., *Sermo XXX*, n. 344, in Id., *Lateinischen Werke*, vol. IV, cit., p. 298; Id., *Sermo XXXVII*, n. 375, in Id., *Lateinischen Werke*, vol. IV, cit., pp. 320-321; Id., *Sermo XLIV*, n. 438, in Id., *Lateinischen Werke*, vol. IV, cit., pp. 367-368; Id., *Sermo LV*, n. 540, in Id., *Lateinischen Werke*, vol. IV, cit., pp. 453-454; Id., *Expositio sancti Evangelii secundum Iohannem*, n. 562, in Id., *Lateinischen Werke*, vol. III, cit., p. 489; Id. *Expositio libri Sapientiae*, n. 144. 154, in Id., *Die lateinischen Werke*, cit., p. 481, p. 489; Id., *Expositio libri Exodi*, n. 117, in Id., *Die lateinischen Werke*, vol. II, cit., p.112. For Cusanus' marginal annotations cf.: S. Frost, *Nikolaus von Kues und Meister Eckhart. Rezeption im Spiegel der Marginalien zum Opus Tripartitum Meister Eckharts*, cit. margg. 35, 152, 154, 155, 301, 340, 396.

[179] Id. *Expositio libri Sapientiae*, n. 154, in Id., *Lateiniscen Werke*, vol. II, cit., p. 489. An annotated marginal expression by Cusanus, cf. S. Frost, *Nikolaus von Kues und Meister Eckhart. Rezeption im Spiegel der Marginalien zum Opus Tripartitum Meister Eckharts*, cit., marg. 35.

[180] Cf. Meister Eckhart, *Sermo III*, n. 317, in Id., *Lateinischen Werke*, vol. IV, cit., pp. 278. An annotated passage by Cusanus, cf. S. Frost, *Nikolaus von Kues und Meister Eckhart. Rezeption im Spiegel der Marginalien zum Opus Tripartitum Meister Eckharts*, cit., marg. 325.

[181] On the relationship between this doctrine and the idea of *non aliud* cf.: B. Mojsisch, *Meister Eckhart. Analogie, Univozität und Einheit*, Meiner, Hamburg 1984, pp. 92-95; W. Beierwaltes, *Identität und Differenz*, cit., pp. 97-104. For another medieval source of *non aluid*, that relating to the debate on the transcendentals, cf. D. Monaco, Deus Trinitas, cit., pp. 43-43. On medieval

In conclusion, it is possible to show that Cusanus knew how to conjugate together a speculative trinitarian tradition, which made use of the negation of the *aliud* in contrast with the affirmation of the *alius* to express the consubstantiality of the three divine persons, distinct but not different, and a line of Neoplatonic speculation, first Greek and then Christian – long known and examined by Cusanus – who employs the negation of the *aliud* in his own conception of the One, and which the Cardinal is in some way heir to, and the greatest interpreter of - through the vertiginous and extremely deep, abyssal idea of - the *non aliud.*

3. The Why of Creation: The Freedom of God

The progress of Cusanus' thought - at least starting from what may be considered his first great work of speculation, the *De docta ignorantia*, up to his final philosophical-theological effort, the *De apice theoriae* – is all marked by a single leitmotif, namely the attempt to think the One as beyond being and at the same time as cause of holding together the teachings of the Christian Neoplatonic tradition, namely the first and second hypothesis of the Platonic *Parmenides*. Research which in Cusanus' work becomes a tireless search for the name of God to be understood not in the Dionysian sense– where divine names indicate the precise series of predicable attributes of the creative and providential work of God in his more general determinations identified as beginning from the text of the Scriptures and of Plato's *Parmenides* Rather it is to be understood as fields, enigmatic images, roads and symbolic paths, in order to ascend to the divine. Beginning with the creation and in particular from the structures of his thought and knowledge – on the basis of the particular ontological statute of the *mens* understood unlike the rest of the created beings not as a simple *explicatio Dei* but as *viva imago Dei* – the Cardinal, thanks to their elaboration, attempts to reach the divine mystery through a scholarly re-elaboration of positive and negative theology.[182]

In Cusanus' work beginning at least from the *De Visione Dei* (1453) – although there is no shortage of useful hints also in his previous works – a thematization is seen as well as a close study of the question of divine freedom and of the voluntaristic character of the First Principle and of its action which finds its apex

theories of transcendentals cf. L. Sileo, *L'esordio della teologia universitaria: i maestri secolari della prima metà del Duecento*, in G. d'Onofrio (dir.), *Storia della teologia nel medioevo*, II, Piemme, Casale Monferrato 1996, pp. 603-644.

182 On the differences between the divine names of the Dionysian tradition and those of Cusanus cf. D. Monaco, Deus Trinitas, cit., pp. 241-243.

in Cusanus' final speculation, and more especially in the *De Beryllo* (1458), in the *De possest* (1460), in the *Cribratio Alkorani* (1460-1461), in the *De non aliud* (1461-1462), in the *De VenationeSapientiae* (1462-1463), in the *Compendium* (1463-1464) and in the *De Apice Theoriae* (1464)[183].

Reinterpreting the Biblical passage of *Psalm*115, 3 according to which God «omnia, quaecumque voluit, fecit»,[184] Cusanus criticises Plato and Aristotle as being guilty of not having understood that the First Principle does not operate *ex necessitate naturae*, but *per liberam voluntatem*.[185]According to the Cardinal the Principle does not act through compulsion from some form of necessity, but according to will, freely and gratuitously. He is principle of nature although being supernatural, beyond nature, free from it, and it is precisely because he creates freely and voluntarily that he, although being principle of nature is absolute, unfettered, free, transcendent with regard to it.[186]The possibility of applying the outcomes of the first two hypotheses of Plato's *Parminides*, of conceiving the One at the same time as cause of being and beyond it, is founded on the conception of the essential freedom of the action of the First Principle. The One is creator of being, albeit being *simul* beyond being in that he acts freely and of his own free will. There emerges a first aspect of Cusanus' conception of freedom, namely the essential link of co-implication between transcendence and freedom; without transcendence one in fact could not consider the relationship the One establishes with the many as free, but it would be merely the first of a series, and also at the same

183 On the theme cf. P. Moffitt Watts, *Nicolaus Cusanus. A fifteenth-century vision of man*, Brill, Leiden 1982; G. Santinello, *Novità nel pensiero del tardo Cusano*, in En kai plēthos*: Einheit und Vielheit. Festschrift für Karl Bormann zum 65. Geburtstag*, eds. L. Hagemann – R. Glei, Würzburg 1993, pp. 161-173; G. von Bredow, *Nachdenken mit Nikolaus von Kues über das Wesen der Freiheit*, in En kai plēthos*: Einheit und Vielheit. Festschrift für Karl Bormann zum 65. Geburtstag*, eds. L. Hagemann – R. Glei, Würzburg 1993, pp. 56-76.

184 Cf. also *Sal* 135, 6: «Omnia, quaecumque voluit, Dominus fecit in caelo et in terra, in mari et in omnibus abyssi».

185 Cf *De beryl.*, h XI/1, n. 38, p. 43: «Aperte enim uterque [scil. Plato et Aristoteles] credidit conditorem intellectum ex necessitate naturae omnia facere, et hoc omnis eorum error secutus est». The same criticism against Plato and Aristotle is repeated in *De beryl.*, h XI/1, n. 67-68, pp. 77-78: «Postquam Anaxagoras vidit intellectum esse principium et causam rerum et in motis dubiis alias causas quam intellectum assignaret, tam per Platonem in Phaedone quam Aristotelem in Metaphysica reprehenditur, quasi voluerit quod intellectus sit principium universi et non singulorum. Miratus sum de ipsis principibus philosophorum, cum ipsi in hoc viderent Anaxagoram reprehensibilem et de principio secum concordarent, cur ipsi alias rationes indagarunt et in eo, in quo Anaxagoram arguebant, similiter errasse reperiuntur. Sed hoc evenit eis ex malo praesupposito, quoniam necessitatem primae causae imposuerunt».

186 Cf. *De beryl.*, h XI/1, n. 37, pp. 42-43: «Se ad omnem essendi modum sufficit habunde primum principium unitrinum; licet sit absolutum et superexaltatum, cum non sit principium contractum ut natura, quae ex necessitate operatur, sed sit principium ipsius naturae et ita supernaturale, liberum, quod voluntate creat omnia».

time, without freedom. The One would not effectively transcend the multiplicity, but would be forced to be an inexorable cause of it, and hence in both cases would be included in the large chain of being and perfectly determined. The *leitmotif* of Neoplatonic speculation according to which the One-God is *omnia in omnibus* although *omnium nihil* finds a definite realisation, close examination and re-elaboration thanks to Cusanus' conception of the essential freedom or voluntariness of the One.[187]

> Illud autem principium, cum non necessitaretur ab alio, quia principium, ante quod non est aliud principium, liberum fuit et est creare et non creare, quemadmodum intellectualis natura libera est in suis operationibus.[188]

According to the Cardinal God was free to create as not to create.[189] His freedom is choice, an authentic decision which in order to be really such, spontaneous and free, must presuppose its opposite, or an alternative between possible ones of which one is the negation, the opposite of the other. Likewise it must be emphasized that according to Cusanus God not only "was", but "is" free to create and not to create, that is that God remains free also after creation. The Principle persists in his furtherness with respect to being even in relation with it, also in the relationship that he himself establishes. Divine freedom is not circumscribed to the past act otherwise it would be limited, whereas God is not forced by anything not even by his own decision, nor by his past. God remains free to create or not to create also after creating and also after choosing to create. The divine freedom to create and not to create does not simply mean his possibility of de-creating, since that would further limit the divine freedom, and would fix it to his past decision. On the contrary God not only can change the present by changing the decision already made, but can bring it about that his very choice has never been, and that the past has never been. God can decide not only about the present and the future, but also about the past, about his own past, otherwise his omnipotence would be

[187] On the dialectic of immanence and transcendence in Cusanus' thought and on his sources cf. J. Stallmach, *Das Nichtandere als Begriff des Absoluten*, in *Universitas. Dienst an Wahrheit und Leben. Festschrift für Bischof Dr. Albert* Stohr, cit., 329-355. W. Beierwaltes, *Deus oppositio oppositorum. Nicolaus Cusanus, De visione Dei XIII*, in «Salzburger Jahrbuch für Philosophie», 8 (1964), pp. 175-185; M. Álvarez-Gómez, *Die verborgene Gegenwart des Unendlichen bei Nikolaus von Kues*, cit., pp. 179-199. W. Beierwaltes, *Identität und Differenz als Prinzip des cusanischen Denkens*, in Id., *Identität und Differenz*, cit., pp. 105-143; K. Kremer, *Gott – in allem alles, in nichts nichts. Bedeutung und Herkunft dieser Lehrer des Nikolaus von Kues*, in «MFCG» 17 (1986), pp. 188-219.

[188] *Crib. Alk.*,h VIII, II, c. 2, n. 90, p. 75.

[189] Cf. moreover *De ven. sap.*, h XII, c. 27, n. 82, p. 78: «Sed quia ipsa mensa eterna libera ad creandum et non creandum vel sic vel aliter, suam omnipotentiam, ut voluit, intra se ab aeterno determinavit».

limited.

Thus, the freedom of God seems on the one hand – being unfettered from all, even from his past, and from himself – pure will, and yet on the other hand still limited to an alternative one of that between creating and not creating, or choosing between two possibilities, between two terms which would appear as pre-existing God's choice. Yet according to Cusanus'conception in God's essence will and reason coincide[190] and such essential coincidence signifies on the one hand that God's will is not unseeing, is not fruit of eventuality, is not arbitrary, in that it is not disconnected from reason, from knowledge and, at the same time, that the alternative between the possibles does not precede God's choice, or that he does not decide between two possibilities pre-existing his choice, but that paradoxically his freedom is together at the same time choice between possibilities and the beginning of these possibilities themselves. The alternative between creating and not creating does not precede divine freedom, but it is God himself who simultaneously with his decision institutes it. The coincidence of will and reason means that there are not two possibilities that God knows before choosing – as it would be if God were reason before will – nor that God chooses between them without knowing – as it would be if God were will before reason – but rather that in God knowledge and decision coincide perfectly. God therefore is not only free to create or not to create, but he is not even forced by the alternative in that it does not precede God, but God precedes it.

According to the Cardinal God created himself to manifest himself: the creation is fruit of the divine intention of revealing himself. In joining together the declaration of Paul of *Romans 1, 20*[191] with the Neoplatonic-Christian doctrine of the *theophaniae* Cusanus conceives the world as no other than *Dei apparitio.*[192] God created the world in order to manifest himself, yet that does not mean that he is forced or needs to manifest himself, but rather that God decides freely and voluntarily and the same intention of communicating himself is fruit of his own

[190] Cf. *De beryl.*, h XI/1, n. 38, p. 44: «Bene vidit Aristoteles in Metaphysica, quomodo omnia in principio primo sunt ipsum; sed non attendit voluntatem eius non esse aliud a ratione eius et essentia»; *De non aliud,* h XIII, c. 9, p. 20: «Voluntas igitur, quae ante aliud "non aliud" cernitur, non est alia a ratione, neque sapientia». On the identity between *ratio* and*voluntas* cf. moreover *De beryl.*, h XI/1, n. 17, p. 21: «Voluntas autem, quae est ipsa ratio in primo intellectu».

[191] «Invisibilia enim ipsius a creatura mundi per ea, quae facta sunt, intellecta conspiciuntur».

[192] On Cusanus' conception of the world as *Dei apparitio* and his sources cf.: C. Riccati, «Processio» et «Explicatio»: la doctrine de la création chez Jean Scote et Nicolas de Cues, Bibliopolis, Napoli 1983; W. Beierwaltes, *Eriugena und Cusanus*, in Id., *Eriugena. Gründzuge seines Denkens*, cit., pp. 266-312; *Theophanie. Nicolaus Cusanus und Johannes Scottus Eriugena. Eine* Retractatio, cit., pp. 153-175.

free choice.[193] For the German thinker God is not only free or otherwise to reveal himself, but even being manifested in his creating may decide not to concede his manifestation any further, denying being to the creature and to creation itself of which his theophanic intent is essential root.[194] God not only decides freely to reveal himself, but reserves the possibility of withdrawing himself, no longer conceding his manifestation and taking away his very being from creating and from creation.

The world therefore has no foundation other than the freedom of God. Creation is dependent on a gratuitous act, on the voluntary decision of God, whose freedom is the unfounded foundation of the world. To the question on the why of creation one cannot, according to the Cardinal, say that: «voluntas Dei est libera, et pro ratione respondet libertas».[195] *Creatio ex nihilo* signifies therefore an act without a why, or that creation is dependent on nothing, on no other than on the original freedom of God. For the Cardinal creating means that God creates amongst all things from no other than from himself, that God creates all *ex se*, *ex se ipso* and to create all by himself means no other than from nothing, from nothing other than from his freedom or original will.[196] The *nihil* from the *ex nihilo* is no other than the nothing of the divine freedom which presupposes nothing else.

Cusanus does not go deeply into the question of divine freedom considering it only in relation to the created but indicates a still more original and unfathomable aspect of it, namely the freedom of God with regard to himself. Expressed in Cusanus' words God does not only create all things, but also himself.[197] According to some authoritative exponents of 20th-century philosophical thought in their history of Western thought the question of divine freedom has been thematized and so analysed thoroughly, but mainly, if not exclusively, by con-

193 Cf. *De ap. theor.*, h XII, n. 21, p. 132: «Sicut posse mentis Aristotelis se in libris eius manifestat, non quod ostendant posse mentis perfecte, licet unius liber perfectius quam aliud, et libri non sunt ad alium finem editi, nisi ut mens se ostendat, nec mens ad edendum libros fuit necesitata, quia libera mens est nobilis se voluit manifestare, ita posse ipsum in omnibus rebus».

194 Cf. *Comp.* 7, h XI/3, n. 21, pp. 16-17: «Et sicut mens nolens se amplius ostendere, a verbi vocalis prolatione cessat et, nisi indesinenter proferat, existere nequit, sic se habet creatura ad creatorem».

195 *Sermo* CCXVI, h XIX, n. 25, p. 94.

196 Cf. *De non aliud*, h XIII, c. 24, p. 57: «Creat, inquam, quoniam rerum similitudines notionales ex alio aliquo non facit, sicut nec spiritus, qui Deus, rerum quidditates facit ex alio, sed ex se aut "non alio"»; *De theol. compl.*: h X/2a, n. 5, p. 29: «Creator igitur, dum omnia creat, ad se ipsum conversus omnia creat»; *De poss.*, h XI/2, n. 73, p. 86: «Ideo de nullo alio creat, sed ex se, cum sit omne quod esse potest».

197 *De theol. compl.*, h X/2a, n. 14, p. 82: «Creatio enim in deo est visio. Creare, videre, intelligere, velle, mensurare, facere, operari et quaeque talia, quae deo attribuimus, capienda sunt ut nomina infiniti circuli. Unde non est magis absurdum dicere deum creare se et omnia quam deum videre se et omnia».

sidering God's relationship with the world, or understanding God as creator and saviour and examining his free and gratuitous choice in the creative and salvific process.[198] Within the widespread "oblivion" of the question of the freedom of God in relationship with himself or of God as freedom, the voice of Cusanus re-echoes with assurance as if detached from the chorus. The Cardinal does not ask himself only about the why and how from the One the many and from God the world, but – as Plotinus had already done in his day – also poses the more profound and original question of the whence and of the why is that which is the One or God himself.

Since the work of 1453, *De visione Dei* and *De theologicis complementis*, God has been conceived as vision and absolute sight[199] and inasmuch as such is endowed with an ontological foundation force characterized by wishing, doing, creating, constituting, causing, essentialising, measuring, comprehending and defining not only all things, but above all himself.[200] In order to comprehend and investigate such a daring conception we must refer above all to one of the highest works of the Cardinal, namely the *De possest*. Central to the work is the attempt to think of God as coincidence of *posse* and *esse*. Against Aristotle, but using fundamental concepts of Aristotelian metaphysics according to pathways quite other than peripatetic, in the *De possest* Cusanus once more takes up the distinction between power and act. The distinction according to the Cardinal is valid for finite things that are not at the origin of themselves, that are not all which can be, which can be other than what they are, but is not valid for the *being* which is origin of itself, which is power of being that what it is.[201] God in fact, not only in the Aristotelian sense is, is not simply *actus sine potentia*, that is to say without a power which precedes him,[202] but is he who can be, who has the capacity and the power to be. According to the Cardinal every creature being able to be that which is in act requires a cause in act in order to pass from the power to the act. In

198 Cf. P. Coda, *Il logos e il nulla. Trinità religioni e mistica*, Roma 2003, pp. 316-331.

199 On this conception and its sources cf. W. Beierwaltes, *Visio absoluta oder absolute Reflexion (Cusanus)*, in *Identität und Differenz*, cit., pp. 144-175; W. Beierwaltes, *Eriugena und Cusanus*, in Id., *Eriugena. Gründzuge seines Denkens*, cit., pp. 266-312.

200 On the wide range of meanings of the divine vision cf. *De vis.*, h VI, c. 8, n. 27-31, pp. 28-31; *De theol. compl.*, h X/2a, n. 14, pp. 80-83; *De non aliud*, h XIII, c. 23, pp. 54-56. On the theme cf. W. Beierwaltes, *Eriugena und Cusanus*, in Id., *Eriugena. Gründzuge seines Denkens*, cit., pp. 266-312.

201 Cf. *De poss.*, h XI/2, n. 7, p. 8: «Et dico nunc nobis constatare deum ante actualitatem, quae distinguitur a potentia, et ante possibilitatem, quae distinguitur ab actu, esse ipsum simplex mundi principium. Omnia autem quae post ipsum sunt cum distinctione potentiae et actus, ita ut solus deus id quod esse potest, nequaquam autem quaecumque creatura, cum potentia et actus non sint idem nisi in principio».

202 Aristoteles, *Metaph.*, 1071b17 ff.

order not to go ad infinitum in the series of the causes in order to pass to the act will therefore require *absoluta actualitas,* of the pure act.[203]But if the power cannot pass into act if not into virtue of the absolute topicality, of the pure act – and up to here Cusanus repeats Aristotle for whom the act precedes the power[204] – at the same time for Cusanus the act cannot exist without it being possible, without the *absoluta possibilitas.*[205] Such absolute power however, neither precedes nor follows absolute actuality, but in the Principle they coincide perfectly.[206] The distinction between act and power is valid for finite things which are not at the origin of themselves but not for the eternal and infinite Principle of all things, who is at the origin of himself.

God is his own power of being: he is in the Cardinal's expression: *possest,*[207] or trinitarially coincidence of *posse, esse* and of their unity. The declaration of *Gen* 17, 1 «Ego sum Deus omnipotens» means for the Cardinal a self-declaration of the autopoietic capacity of the Principle.[208] For Cusanus God has in himself the power of all things, of the world and *in primis* of himself. In order to comprehend this conception of the Principle as self-positioning and to examine his free trinitarian character, we must refer to other works of the Cardinal, and more especially to that precise, even elliptical, expression of the will of God which is the *non aliud*[209], where the thought of the One-God as freedom or will finds its highest expression.[210]

203 Cf. *De poss.*, h XI/2, n. 6, p. 7: «Nec potest ipsa iam dicta possibilitas prior esse actualitate quemadmodum dicimus aliquam potentiam precedere actum. Nam quomodo prodisset in actum nisi per actualitatem?».

204 Cf. Aristoteles, *Metaph.*, 1049b5.

205 Cf. *De poss.*, h XI/2, n. 6, p. 7: «Possibilitas ergo absoluta, de qua loquimur, per quam ea quae actu sunt actu esse possunt, non praecedit actualitatem neque etiam sequitur. Quomodo enim actualitas esse posset possibilitate non existente?»

206 Cf. *De poss.*, h XI/2, n. 6, pp. 7-8: «Coaeterna ergo sunt absoluta potentia et actus et utriusque nexus. Neque plura sunt aeterna, sed sic sunt aeterna quod ipsa aeternitas».

207 Cf. *De poss.*, h XI/2, n. 14, pp. 17-18: «Esto enim quod aliqua dictio significet simplicissimo significato quantum complexum "posse est", scilicet quod ipsum posse sit. Et quia quod est actu est, ideo posse esse est tantum quantum posse est actu. Puta vocetur possest».

208 Cf. *De poss.*, h XI/2, n. 14, p. 18: «Ideo dum deus sui vellet notitiam primo revelare, dicebat: "Ego" sum "deus omnipotens", id est sum actus omnis potentiae».

209 Cf. *De non aliud,* h XIII, c. 9, p. 20: «Voluntas Dei est "non aliud"».

210 For a full bibliography on the *non aliud* I take the liberty of referring to D. Monaco, Deus Trinitas, cit., pp. 337-341. For a full reconstruction of the state of the studies cf. *ibid.*, pp. 21-55. Amongst the more recent works on the *De non aliud*, cf. S. Grotz, *Negationen des Absoluten. Meister Eckhart. Cusanus. Hegel*, cit., pp. 204-225; P. Casarella, *Cusanus on Dionysius*, in *Re-thinking Dionysius the Areopagite*, eds. S. Coakley – C.M. Stang, Blackwell, Chichester 2009 pp. 141-146; F. Vengeon, *Nicolas de Cues, le monde humain. métaphysique de l'infini et anthropologie*, Jérôme Millon, Grenoble 2011, pp. 84-88; C. M. Cubillos, *Los múltiples nombres del Dios innombrable: una aproximación a la metafísica de Nicolás de Cusa desde la perspectiva de sus*

For generating to be authentic generating, that is to say for it to be freedom to present and choose something distinct, it must be generating of other than itself, that is to say the generated must be distinct from the generator, otherwise it would be simply a mere reaffirmation of the same, of itself. Yet, at the same time, if the freedom of generating presupposed the other than itself, then the generated as other thing than the generator, would presuppose that inasmuch as other than him, it would invalidate his generative beginningness. For the generating to be authentically free, it thus requires a paradoxical unity of association and distinction, or in other words a more original non-otherness. In theological terms if one started out from the sameness between Father and Son on the Cross, God himself would die, whereas if one started out from the otherness, then the death on the Cross and the Son himself would be mere *dókesis*, appearance.[211]Expressed in Cusanus' terms the negation of the sameness understood as *idem* does not mean immediately and necessarily affirmation of otherness, and especially of substantial otherness of the *aliud*. Likewise the negation of the diversity of nature, of the *aliud*, does not present the effective reality of the sameness, of the *idem*: *non idem* does not mean *aliud*, and *non aliud* does not mean *idem*.[212] The Trinity, the

nombres divinos, Eunsa, Navarra 2013, pp. 203-246; S. Gottlöber, *Das Prinzip der Relationalität: Grundzüge cusanischen Denkens als Parameter für Toleranz und interreligiösen Diskurs*, cit., pp. 215-222; H. Schwaetzer, *"Non-autre" comme la Trinité*, in *La Trinité chez Eckhart et Nicolas de Cues*, cit., pp. 145-153; F. Resch, *Triunitas*, cit., pp. 41-52, pp. 282-294;J. G. Ríos, *Metafísica de la Palabra*, Biblos, Buenos Aires 2014, pp. 255-272; J. G. Ríos, *Possest, non aliud, posse ipsum. Los nombres enigmáticos como manuductiones en el pensamiento cusano de senectud*, in Manuductiones. *Festschrift zu Ehren von J. M. Machetta und C. D'Amico*, eds. C. Rusconi, Aschendorff, Münster 2014, pp. 169-190; M. Rohstock, *Der negative Selbstbezug des Absoluten: Untersuchungen zu Nicolaus Cusanus' Konzept des Nicht-Anderen*, cit.; H. Schwaetzer, *Nichts anderes als Spiegel*, in *Der Bildbegriff bei Meister Eckhart und Nikolaus von Kues*, cit., pp. 155-166; S. Grotz, Über den Zusammenhang von Name und Negation bei Nicolaus Cusanus, in *Der Bildbegriff bei Meister Eckhart und Nikolaus von Kues*, cit., pp. 201-213; C. Cubillos, *Für eine Systematisierung der cusanischen Gottesnamen*, in *Der Bildbegriff bei Meister Eckhart und Nikolaus von* Kues, cit., pp. 179-199; S. Mancini, *Congetture su Dio*, cit., pp. 103-166.

211 Cr. F. Tomatis, *Inizio e parola di Dio, in Vernunft und Glauben. Ein philosophischer Dialog der Moderne mit dem Christentum*, cit., p. 60.

212 Cf. *Crib. Alk.*,h VIII, II, 8, n. 107, p. 86: «Nunc patet, quod, qui non attingunt li non aliud non esse idem et li non idem non esse aliud, non possunt capere unitatem, aequalitatem et nexum esse idem in essentia et non inter se idem. Ideo trinitatem in deitate non capiunt nisi in tribus diis». On the difference between *idem* and*non aliud* cf. D. Monaco, Deus Trinitas, cit., pp. 270-283. References to the essential difference between the divine name of *idem* of the *De genesi* and the divine name of *non aliud* in S. Dangelmayr, *Gotteserkenntnis und Gottesbegriff in den philosophischen Schriften des Nikolaus von Kues*, Hain, Meisenheim am Glan, 230 ff.; H. Schwaetzer, *Aequalitas*, Georg Olms, Hildesheim 2000, 115ff. In an opposite direction, also with regard to Cusanus' letter, go the reflections on the theme of G. Schneider, *Gott – das Nichtandere*, Aschen-

intratrinitarian relationships to be thought of in their unfathomable depth require reference to an original non-otherness, to the *non aliud*.

In other words if God is freedom, choice, and decision, then an otherness must be presupposed, namely the *Lógos* with regard to which it may make an act of freedom and carry out its choice of love. At the same time if we wish to think of the absolute beginningness of God such otherness cannot precede God. There cannot be another sameness different from that of God, otherwise a presupposition would be necessary for its divinity which would be God. We cannot presuppose the Son before God as his own other, otherwise God would not be eternal beginning, original freedom ; even if at the same time we want to conceive God as free choice of love we must presuppose before him such otherness in favour of which he makes his own choice.[213]Only by making room for the *alius*, the other than self, which is *non aliud*, not-other than self, and who in his turn freely decides and accepts this condition and thus becomes, chooses himself as *alius*, other according to the person, but *non aliud*, not-other according to nature, or divinely free, does the Christian God reveal himself intimately as *Deus Trinitas*.

In the *De non aliud* the German cardinal closely examines and improves on Proclus' interpretation of Plato's *Parmenides* by re-elaborating it in the light of the Gospel and of Christian theology, especially the idea of *non aliud* representing a profound and radical coming true and an original and vertiginous reformulation of the conception of the negation contained in Proclus' work. In Book VI of his *Commentary to Parmenides* Proclus identifies numerous meanings of the negation amongst which the highest one excels for which it sets itself in opposition to the affirmation, but is mother of affirmations. The negations applied to the One-one cannot indicate either something which albeit being able to be accepted by the First Principle has not been accepted, or something which could not be accepted by it, as though it was not suitable to accept it, but rather – starting from the presupposition that the cause is not identified with its objects caused – are predicated by the One because in generating all things he is not identified with any of them and therefore they indicate his generative and source power regarding all which is negated of him.

Correspondingly, the "non" of the *non aliud* does not mean mere static absence of otherness, but rather antecedence with respect to the *aliud* and its constitutive, generative, and creative force. According to Cusanus in fact the *non aliud* is not opposed to the *aliud*[214] – as it should be according to Aristotle's *principium*

dorff, Münster 1970, 104 ff.; G. Santinello, *Introduzione a Niccolò Cusano*, Laterza, Roma-Bari, 1971, pp. 130-133.

[213] Cf. F. Tomatis, *Inizio e Parola di Dio*, cit., pp. 55-61.

[214] Cf. *De non aliud,* h XIII, c. 6, p. 14: «Deus autem, quia non aliud est ab alio, non est aliud, quamvis non aliud et aliud videantur opponi; sed non opponitur aiud ipsi, a quo habet quod est

firmissimum – but is cognitive and constitutive principle of it, in that the same *aliud* is «non aliud quam aliud».[215] *Aliud* here indicates the widest extent of being thinkable. It is a sort of transcendental in the medieval sense. Indeed according to the Cardinal it precedes the same transcendentals constituting them inasmuch as such.[216] For Cusanus every thing is *non aliud quam* that thing: every thing participates in the *non aliud* in order to be that what it is[217]. The *non aliud* is not a simple *negatio* which sets itself against the *affirmation*. It does not indicate *stéresis* or *exclusio* at all – which would imply a shortcoming in the One – neither does it refer superficially to an entity which has as property, even if perfectly and completely the

aliud».

215 Cf. *De non aliud,* h XIII, c. 2, p. 6: «aliud enim cum sit non aliud quam aliud, utique "non aliud" praesupponit, sine quo non foret aliud». Cf. *De non aliud,* h XIII, c. 1, p. 5: «Quid enim responderes, si quis te "quid est aliud?" interrogaret? Nonne diceres: "non aliud quam aliud"?». In criticising Aristotle and the principle of non-contradiction directly the same cardinal in *De non aliud,* h XIII, c. 19, p. 46 states: «Philosophus ille certissimum credidit negativae affirmativam contradicere, quodque simul de eodem utpote repugnantia dici non possent. Hoc autem dixit rationis via id ipsum sic verum concludentis. Quodsi quis ab eo quaesivisset, quid est aliud, utique vere respondere potuisset: "non aliud quam aliud est." Et consequenter si quaerens adiecisset: quare aliud est aliud? sane quidem, ut prius, dicere valuisset: "quia non aliud quam aliud est"; et ita "non aliud" et aliud neque sibi ut repugnantia vidisset contradicere. Atque illud, quod primum principium nominat, pro viae ostensione perspexisset non sufficere ad veritatem, quae supra rationem mente contemplatur».

216 Cf. *De non aliud,* h XIII, c. 4, p. 10: «Quamvis unum propinquum admodum ad "non aliud" videatur, quando quidem omne aut unum dicatur aut aliud, ita quod unum quasi "non aliud" appareat, nihilominus tamen unum, cum nihil aliud quam unum sit, aliud est ab ipso "non aliud". Igitur "non aliud" est simplicius uno, cum ab ipso "non aliud" habeat, quod sit unum; et non e converso. Enimvero quidam theologi unum pro "non aliud" accipientes ipsum unum ante contradictionem perspexerunt, quemadmodum in Platonis *Parmenide* legitur atque in Areopagita Dionysio. Tamen, cum unum sit aliud a non uno, nequaquam dirigit in primum omnium principium, quod sive ab alio sive a nihilo aliud esse non potest, quod item nulli est contrarium, ut inferius videbis. – Eodem modo de ente considera; nam etsi in ipso "non aliud" clare videatur elucere, cum eorum, quae sunt, aliud ab aliquo minime videatur: tamen ipsum "non aliud" praecedit. – Sic de vero, quod quidem similiter de nullo ente negatur, et bono, licet nihil boni expers reperiatur. Sumuntur quoque ob id omnia haec pro apertis Dei nominibus, tametsi praecisionem non attingant. Non tamen proprie dicuntur illa post "non aliud" esse; si enim forent post "non aliud", qomodo eorum quodlibet esset non aliud quam id, quod est? Sic igitur "non aliud" ante ista videtur et alia, quod post ipsum non sunt, sed per ipsum». Therefore even the Good and the One which according to the Neoplatonic tradition were the most adequate names for the Principle prove to be inferior for the *non aliud* in their capacity to indicate the First. On this aspect cf. also: *De non* aliud, h XIII, c. 23, pp. 55-56; *De ven. sap.*, h XII, c. 21, n. 59, p. 57.

217 Cf. *De non aliud,* h XIII, c. 3, pp. 7-8: «Nam cum omne, quod quidem est, sit non aliud quam id ipsum, hoc utique non habet aliunde; a "non alio" igitur habet. Non igitur aut est aut cognoscitur esse id, quod est, nisi per "non aliud", quae quidem est eius causa, adaequatissima ratio scilicet sive definitio».

absolute absence of otherness and is not even a mere *negatio negationis*, a negation of the negativity of the finite, of the otherness that constitutes it,[218] although since it is *principium essendi et cognoscendi* of all[219] in that it defines every thing, giving to it its being and its being knowable [220] is pure expression of the infinite and free causality of the Principle, of God as creator.[221] It indicates the divine creative will operating every thing, its causal power which founds, conserves and gives its own singularity to all and to each thing that is not-other than that what it is.[222]

Yet the *non aliud* does not only define all things, but above all itself [223]. Central to the *De non aliud* is the unfathomable self-definition «non aliud est non aliud quam non aliud». According to the double sense that the definition takes on in this work – for which it has not only a logico-gnosiological value, but also an ontological and constitutive one[224] – the triple self-defining repetition of the *non aliud* indicates that God creates, constitutes and generates himself trinitarially.[225] The First is such in that it self-defines itself exactly because it is definition of

218 Cf. *De non aliud*, h XIII, c. 4, p. 9.

219 Cf. *De non aliud*, h XIII, c. 3, p. 7: «Deus igitur per "non aliud" siginificatus essendi et cognoscendi omnibus principium est. Quem si quis subtrahit, nihil manet neque in re, neque in cognitione. Quemadmodum luce subtracta iris aut visibile nec est nec videtur, et sublato sono nec est audibile nec auditur, sic subtracto "non aliud" neque est nec cognoscitur quidquam».

220 Cf *De non aliud*, h XIII, c. 6: p. 14: «sine quo non esse, non discerni aliquid possibile est».

221 Cf. *De ven. sap.*,h XII, c. 23, n. 70, p. 67: «Nam aequalitas est verbum illud ipsius non aliud, scilicet dei creatoris se et omnia dicentis et diffinientis».On the concept of *aequalitas* cf. H. Schwaetzer, *Aequalitas*, cit.; D. Monaco, Deus Trinitas, cit., pp. 132-138.

222 Cf. *De non aliud*, h XIII, c. 9, p. 20: «Et sic illa vides voluntate omnia determinari, causari, ordinari, firmari, stabiliri et conservari, et in universo relucere».

223 Cf. *De non aliud*, h XIII, c. 1, p. 4: «Quodsi toto nisu mentis aciem ad li "non aliud" convertis, mecum ipsum definitionem se et omnia definientem videbis».

224 Cf. *De non aliud*, h XIII, c. 22, pp. 52-53: «Meministi, puto, Platonem negare quid rei definitionem attingere, quia quidditati circumponitur, uti etiam Proculus explanat. Unde non fit ita, cum ipsum ‚non aliud' se atque omnia definit. Non enim sic ipsum principium quidditativum definit, quasi qui lineis circumpositis triangularem determinat seu definit superficiem, sed quasi superficiem, quae trigonus dicitur, constituat. [...] Video certe hanc, quam asseris definitionem solum veram et quidditativam, non esse illam, quam Plato mancam et defectuosam dicit». On the double meaning that the definiton takes in the *De non aliud* cf. D. Monaco, *Deus Trinitas*, cit., pp. 213ss.; C. Rusconi, *La definicíon que se define a sí misma y a todo*, in Nicolás de Cusa, *Acerca de lo no-otro o de la definición que todo define*, cit., pp. 336-346.

225 Cf. *De ven. sap.*, h XII, c. 14, n. 40, p. 39: «Nam non aliud est non aliud quam non aliud. Miratur de hoc secreto intellectus, quando attente advertit trinitatem, sine qua deus se ipsum non diffinit, esse unitatem, quia diffinitio diffinitum. Deus igitur trinus et unus est diffinitio se et omnia diffiniens». Cf. *De non aliud*, h XIII, c. 5, p. 13: «Quando enim primum principium ipsum se definit per "non aliud" significatum, in eo definitivo motu de non alio non aliud oritur atque de non alio et non alio exorto in non alio concluditur definitio, quae contemplans clarius, quam dici possit, intuebitur».

itself, and shows itself one-in-three.[226] In the perfection of the self-definition of the *non aliud* the Trinity is shown to be no other than oneness, and the oneness is no other than Trinity. Oneness cannot be but trina, otherwise it would not define itself, and the Trinity cannot be but oneness, otherwise it would not be definition of the First.[227] Thanks to the triple self-defining repetition of the *non aliud* Cusanus attempts to make reference to the original freedom or will of the Principle of self-constituting, of creating himself trinitarially. The expression is therefore the attempt to give voice to the purest theogony, to God's self-creation, who, inasmuch as he self-constitutes himself, he reveals himself as Trinity. For the Cardinal the Trinity is not to be understood as a mere summation of three distinct units, albeit consubstantial, but rather as a self-unfolding of the One, as self-correlation in which the Unity constitutes itself as Trinity, as Tri-unity. The *non aliud triniter repetitum* indicates the autopoietic power of the Principle, his power to manifest, to create, to generate himself trinitarially, his revealing himself at the same time as First Principle defined by nothing else and as freedom to present himself. Through the *non aliud* God shows himself as the only one who has in himself the capacity of being what he is, as he who gives life to himself originating himself from no other than from himself, and who by unfolding himself reveals himself in essence as Trinity. Cusanus' speculation reaches his most profound thought, namely God as freedom or original will of self-manifestation, self-constituting himself, who in self-creating himself reveals himself one and triune, that is to say *Deus Trinitas*.

[226] Cf. *De non aliud,* h XIII, c. 5, p. 12: «In explicatam igitur eius definitionem intueamur, quod videlicet "non aliud" est non aliud quam non aliud; idem triniter repetitum si est primi definitio, ut vides, ipsum profecto est unitrinum et non alia ratione, quam quia se ipsum definit; non enim foret primum si se ipsum minime definiret; se autem quando definit, trinum ostendit». Cf. *De ven. sap.,* h XII, c. 14, n. 40, p. 39: «Vides nunc aeternum illud antiquissimum in eo campo dulcissima venatione quaeri posse. Nam cum sit sui ipsius et omnium aliorum diffinitio, non reperitur in alio aliquo clarius quam in li non aliud. Attingis enim in eo campo antiquissimum trinum et unum, qui et sui ipsius diffinitio». About the domain of the *non aliud* of the *De venatione sapientiae* cf. W. Beierwaltes, *Venatio sapientiae: Das Nicht-Andere und das Licht*, in «MFCG», 32 (2010), pp. 83-104.

[227] Cf. *De non aliud,* h XIII, c. 5, p. 12: «Ex perfectione igitur vides resultare trinitatem, quam tamen, quoniam ante aliud vides, nec numerare potes nec numerum esse affirmare, cum haec trinitas non sit aliud quam unitas, et unitas non sit aliud quam trinitas, quia tam trinitas quam unitas non sunt aliud quam simplex principium per "non aliud" significatum».

4. *Deus Trinitas*

Introduced in the *Cribratio Alkorani* of 1460-1461, but better exploited and analysed in greater depth in the tetralogy of the *De non aliud* of 1461-1462 and in several other substantial pages of his 1462-1463 work the *De venatione sapientiae*, the fortunate and opportune expression *non aliud* represents perhaps the German thinker's more mature attempt to give voice to the *Mysterium Trinitatis*. In these later philosophico-theological endeavours in fact Cusanus' conception of the Trinity reaches its apex by revealing the true depth of his speculation[228].

Among the many divine epithets elaborated by Cardinal Cusanus throughout the entire length of his thinking the *non aliud* is undoubtedly one of his most original and speculatively meaningful ones, yet at the same time one of his most enigmatic. However, if set in relationship to the Trinity context in which it was originally used and if its theological-trinitarian and Neoplatonic sources are reconstructed then it becomes decisively clear, proving to be rich in historical and hermeneutic significances and implications.

In the first eleven chapters of Book II explicitly devoted to the question of the Trinity in the *Cribratio Alkorani* – although references to it are present throughout all three books making up the work – while addressing the Muslims, Cusanus attempts to outline a real and proper *manuductio*, literally a leading by the hand, as an introduction and guide to the Trinity. On the basis of the peculiar ontological *imago-exemplar* relationship which the soul enters into with the divine Principle outlined in the third book *De mente* of the 1450 work *Idiota*[229], the German cardinal tries to ascend from Trinitariety, which belongs to the soul in its operating, to the Trinity. The intellect, inasmuch as being free, operates in fact in likeness (*in similitudine*) of its divinely free Principle. As God when creating produces real things, so the intellect which is his image (*imago*) when operating produces likenesses (*similitudines*) of real things, that is notional entities, creating gnosiologically, there where the First creates ontologically[230]. Here emerges one of the central features of Cusanus' complex and articulated conception of the *mens*, namely its

[228] For a periodization of Cusanus' thought and a reconstruction thereof I take the liberty of referring to my D. Monaco, *Deus Trinitas*, with a preface by W. Beierwaltes, Città Nuova, Roma 2010, pp. 67-159. On the Trinity in Cusanus cf. R. Haubst, *Das Bild des Einen und Dreinen Gottes in der Welt nach Nikolaus von Kues*, Paulinus, Trier 1952; T. Schumacher, *Trinität, Zur Interpretation eines Strukturelements Cusanischen Denkens*, Herbert Utz, München 1997; W. Knoch, *Die historische und systematische Bedeutung der cusanischen Trinitätsspekulation*, in «MFCG», 33 (2012), pp. 19-36; F. Resch, *Triunitas*, cit.

[229] Cf. *De mente*, h. V, III, c. 3-4, n. 72-79, pp. 108-120. On the theme cf. G. Santinello, *L'uomo «ad imaginem et similitudinem» nel Cusano*, in «Doctor Seraphicus», 37 (1990), pp. 85-97; D. Monaco, *Deus Trinitas*, cit., pp. 250-269.

[230] Cf. *Crib. Alk.*, h. VIII, II, c. 3, n. 94, p. 78.

creative capacity, which precisely in its capacity to create notional entities and concepts, the world of conjecture and of knowledge is revealed to be *viva imago* of the Trinity, or of the essential fecundity and divine freedom, of the creative and generative power of God.

From the operating of the soul, through a self-awareness process of self-analysis of one's own gnosiological structures of the mind – in accordance with a reasoning going back to Augustine to whom is owed the merit of using a psychological key for understanding the Trinity – the German thinker attempts to ascend to the *Deus Trinitas*. The *intellectus* – the highest and most noble part of the *anima* – while operating freely operates trinitarially: its free nature presupposes its Trinitariety composed of *mens* or *conceptus*, *scientia* or *ars* and *voluntas*. From the *mens* or *conceptus* of all which it operates is generated the *scientia* or *ars* and from both the *voluntas*. According to the cardinal the noble quality of the intellectual nature or its freedom demands that the mind is not the science generated by it – being itself generated in fact it cannot be the generating mind – just as it demands that the mind and generated science are not the will deriving from both – in that whatever is derived is not the same as that which it derives from[231].

On the basis of the trinitarianity of the human *intellectus*, in keeping with his theological objective Cusanus tries to express the Trinity of God by associating the *mens* with the *Pater*, the *ars*, the *sapientia* or the *scientia* with the *Filius*, and the *voluntas* with the *Spiritus Sanctus*: if God intends himself then he generates by himself the concept or the Word of himself [232]. Generating Word and generated Word are neither the same thing nor even a different thing. Father and Son – and the same may be said of *Amor* which derives from both – in Cusanus' language are neither *idem* nor *aliud*. In readopting the trinitarian terms already used, beginning from the *De docta ignorantia (On Learned Ignorance)* the German cardinal states that if *Deus caritas est* – according to the text of *1 John* 4, 8 and *1 John* 4, 16 – then *non est aliud unitas, aliud aequalitas aliud utriusque nexus*[233], that is to say for God to be thought of as love it is necessary to understand that the three persons of the Trinity are not *aliud* one from the other. Contrary to the Muslims who are guilty of not understanding that Trinity does not mean tritheism, and guilty of affirming an absolutistic monotheism, Cusanus believes that whoever does not understand that *non aliud* does not mean *idem* and the *non idem* is not equivalent to the *aliud* is not capable of understanding that Father, Son and Spirit, although they are not-other in essence, are not the same thing amongst themselves, just as, although they

231 Cf. *Crib. Alk.*,h VIII, II, c. 2, n. 90-93, pp. 75-77.

232 Cf. *Crib. Alk.*,h VIII, II, c. 6, n. 102, pp. 83-84.

233 Cf. *Crib. Alk.*,h VIII, II, c. 7, n. 105, pp. 85-86.

are not the same thing, they are not-other in essence[234]. The confusion between *idem* and *non aliud*, between sameness and not-otherness lies at the basis of the erroneous tritheistic interpretation of the Trinity by the Muslims.

On the contrary only in a truly trinitarian perspective is it possible to think radically of freedom itself and of divine fecundity, understanding it as love, *caritas*, and *agápe*. The Christian God is not the pure act, the non-moving mover, the inert substance of Aristotle, nor the divinity of an absolute monotheism, but is *caritas*, kenotic love, and self-sacrifice for the other. If *Deus caritas est* we must think of a distinction which is not difference, substantial otherness – otherwise we would lapse into tritheism – but at the same time we must also think of a unity which is not an all-consuming nihilistic monolithic sameness or a tediously boring mathematical equivalence since we would lose the *proprium* of Christian trinitarian monotheism, God's being original freedom and love. As he writes in the *De visione Dei* – in which the Cardinal utilizes the tryad of Augustinian *amor amabilis, amor amantis* and *utrius nexus* – without the distinction between loving love, namely the Son, and love needing to be loved, namely the Father, there would be no freedom to love, but only the necessity[235]. In other words if God is freedom, choice, decision, love *caritas*, then an otherness must be presupposed, namely the *Lógos*, with regard to which such an act of freedom may be exercised, and his choice of love be made. At the same time if we wish to think of the absolute beginningness of God such otherness cannot go before God, it cannot be different from that of God, otherwise there would be a necessary presupposition for his divinity which would be God. We cannot presuppose the Son before the Father (or before God) as his own other, otherwise he would not be eternal beginning, original freedom, love. At the same timeif if we wish to conceive God as free choice of love we must presuppose him this otherness in favour of which he makes his own choice, otherwise he would be mere reaffirmation of the same[236]. The *non aliud* refers to these Trinity paradoxes. Sameness and difference refer to a more original non-otherness, to an oversubstantial *koinonía*, to *homooúsia*. In Cusanus' terms in order to remain faithful to the statement that *Deus caritas est* we must try to think of a non-otherness (*non aliud*) which is not sameness (*idem*), and of a non-sameness (*non idem*) which is not otherness (*aliud*) but difference (*alius*).

In that it is not mere sameness, *idem*, but negation of the *aliud*, the *non aliud* does not violate but rather permits the difference, the personal otherness. In its turn without its difference, the personal otherness, not even a living communion

234 Cf. *Crib. Alk.*,h VIII, II, c. 8, n. 107, pp. 86-87.

235 *De vis.*, h VI, c. 28, n. 80, p. 63.

236 On these themes cf. F. Tomatis, *Inizio e parola di Dio*, cit., pp. 95-108.

is thinkable, but only a mere boringly flat sameness. The *homooúsia* is communion of love among different persons.

The tetralogy *De non aliud* opens with the question: what is it that makes us know? Cusanus' answer of an apparently Aristotelian flavour is the definition[237]. Every thing in fact according to the cardinal is known in that it is defined as no other than itself. The other is no other than other, the sky is no other than sky, and so on[238]. Cusanus' definition does not come about by identifying a very close type and a specific difference, but each thing is defined through being *non aliud* than itself, or through a sameness, and an itselfness, not a non-static and self-referential sameness, but a constitutively dynamic and omnicorrelative one which sets the object of the definition not only in relationship to every other thing on a horizontal plane, but also, and above all, on one vertical to the intranscendible transcendence of the Principle expressed by the *non aliud*. Every thing reveals itself in relation not only to every possible other, or in relation to the totality of every other possible being, but also to the infinite principle transcending every thing, including the *non aliud* itself. Cusanus moves from the gnosiological question to find himself confronted by the same rational or discursive knowledge with something which passes beyond such cognitive power, and at the same time determines and founds it.

Earlier in the *Layman* Cusanus had spoken of a *praegustatio naturalis sapientiae*[239] and of the *mens* as *viva imago Dei*[240] stressing that the mind is a *divinum semen*, a divine seed[241] and is endowed with an innate capacity for judgment[242]. Such an innate capacity for judgment attributed to the *mens* is clearly defined and closely investigated in the *De non aliud*: the *non aliud* is *condicio sine qua non* of every judgment and therefore of all knowing. It is the presupposition of seeing and of knowing which the mind does not notice until one concentrates explicitly on its presupposition, in that preceding every search the mind does not pay any attention to it while carrying out its research: only if its attention is turned to the condition of its investigation does it see the principle and the means by which all searching moves. Cusanus adopts the Platonic and Neoplatonic metaphor of light and compares the *non aliud* with an intelligible light which allows one to see, without himself being the direct and immediate object of vision[243].

237 Cf. *De non aliud*, h XIII, c. 1, p. 3.
238 Cf. *De non aliud*, h XIII, c. 1, pp. 4-5.
239 Cf. *De sap.*, h V, I, n. 11 ff., pp. 19 ff.
240 *De sap.*, h V, I, n. 18, pp. 37-38.
241 Cf. *De mente*, h V, c. 5, n. 81, p. 123.
242 Cf. *Demente*, h V, c. 4, n. 77, p. 118-119.
243 Cf. *De non aliud*, h XIII, c. 3, pp. 6-8.

No thought can be formed by man's mind without the *non aliud,* in that it is the thought of thoughts, the principle of every thought[244]. The *non aliud* is the form, the constituent structure of the thinking and, at the same time, that which is always present in every thought ever thought, as its inevitable *prius*. It is the highest object of the mind and *simul* the form with which it thinks. The *non aliud,* however, continues in its transcendence regarding the thought inside the thought itself, since although being no other than thought thinking itself – reference to the non-moving mover thought of thought reminiscent of Aristotle – it is not the same as the thought itself, which inasmuch as such is *non aliud* than thought[245]. The *non aliud* albeit being *non aliud* than the thought in that its principle is being no other than thought that thinks itself, remains free from it, further from it, in the thought itself, free from it and beyond it, trascendent not only with respect to the thought, but to within its relationship with it. The *non aliud* finds one of its essential meanings precisely in its being *apex mentis*: it is the highest object of the thought and at the same time the form with which the mind thinks, although it is ulterior, free, beyond the thought, even in its relationship to it[246].

Thinking of itself in the act of thinking the soul becomes aware of its own essence and its basis, arriving at the source and the principle of its own unity and its own being. The thought withdrawing into itself discovers itself to be closely associated with a pre-reflexive origin which will never be fully understood just as it is in itself and which goes beyond the thought. The *non aliud* refers back to a going further which goes beyond the thought and which is image or seed of God, principle beyond his being, principle which precedes the thought, but which through the original capacity of judgment of the *mens* is principle thereof.

It is not a rigid and fixed content of the thought or a mere representation, nor the result of an abstraction of a logical-formal type, but represents an intuition which gathers up all what is subtracted from discursive comprehension. The *non aliud* therefore represents a sort of pre-knowing of the One-God without which we could in no way return to it, not even negatively, or conceive its inconceivability and express its ineffability. It is a hidden impression, a trace, a revelation of God which, inasmuch as basis and origin of the thought is beyond it. The *non aliud* is the imprint, the mark of the divine freedom which shines in the *mens*. Just as God creates real entities, including the world, so the mind creates the notional entities in the world of knowledge (the definitions)[247].

Yet it does not only reveal the link of the soul with God, but also the way that it must ascend to him in that not only does the *mens* know every thing through the

[244] Cf. *De non aliud*, h XIII, prop. VIII, p. 62.

[245] *Ibidem*.

[246] For a more extensive discussion of the subject, cf. D. Monaco, Deus Trinitas, cit., pp. 250-269.

[247] Cf. *De non aliud*, h XIII, c. 24, pp. 56-58.

non aliud, but the same *non aliud* is the divine constituent principle of the being of everything. In criticising Plato of the *VII Letter* who rejects the definition as the access to the *quid*[248], the essence, Cusanus claims not only the gnosiological value, but also the ontological value of the definition: the definition not only permits us to know the reality of the thing defined, but also, and primarily, constitutes the thing from within giving it its essence, making it be that what it is, or, that is to say, *non aliud* than itself[249]. The ontologico-constituent value of the *non aliud* with respect to the essence of things itself becomes clear if one concentrates on the fact that it is to be understood not only and simply as *apex mentis*, but also and above all – as the very sub-title of the work shows us – as *Directio speculantis*, as guide for those who speculate on things divine. It is a divine appellation, a way to the Principle, although just as it is the pilgrim who does not identify the way which leads him to the city with the city itself, so one must not identify the *non aliud* with God or God with the *non aliud*[250]. The purpose of the *De non aliud*, as of every work of the Cardinal's, is not to identify God through a name or concept which, however refined and articulate, would do no other than enclose it within a form, even if the form were without form that gives origin to every form, but rather the aim of Cusanus' thought is to trace a way, an uphill ascent towards the divine[251]. According to the Cardinal however, the *non aliud* is a special way towards the divine compared with the others, endowed with a very special speculative valency, in that in it as in a more precious enigma there shines the most unutterable name of God[252]. However even in this case it is not a matter of a rational all-embracing complete knowledge, but of a route which within a rational form of proceeding succeeds in reaching a dimension which goes beyond the limits of the *ratio*, until it understands in stupified *docta ignorantia* the mystery to which the *non aliud per speculum et in aenigmate* – according to the Cardinal's interpretation of *1 Cor* 13, 12 – refers[253].

According to the Cardinal's theorising the world is *Dei apparitio*, theophany[254]. The created is manifestation of the creator who is revealed more clearly in the *mens*, as we have seen, on account of the specific ontological status of the latter. In this speculative context the *non aliud* indicates the name of God inasmuch as creator[255]. *Non aliud* indicates in fact the will of God who leads towards being and brings things into being as no other than what they are. The *non aliud* indicates

248 Plato, *Epist.*, VII, 342b-344d.

249 Cf. *De non aliud*, h XIII, c. 22, p. 52.

250 Cf. *De non aliud*, h XIII, c. 2, pp. 5-6.

251 For a more extensive discussion on the subject, cf. D. Monaco, Deus Trinitas, cit., pp. 236-249.

252 *Ibidem*.

253 Cf. *De non aliud*, h XIII, c. 17, p. 43; c. 20, p. 49.

254 Cf. *De non aliud*, h XIII, prop. XII, pp. 62-63.

255 Cf. *De ven. sap.*, h XII, c. 23, n. 70, p. 67.

the will of God[256]. For this purpose in order to illustrate this meaning of the enigma of the *non aliud* Cusanus has recourse to the image of Trajan's column[257]. As the Emperor Trajan wishing to make his glory known to posterity had his column built which is said to be his because through his will it is what it is, and this column is not different from his will, even though it is not his will, but whatever it is, it is through his will which constitutes and determines it. Thus through the *non aliud* God signified he has created the universe and every part of it, wishing to show his glory, although every thing of the universe is not his will, though being constituted and determined by it.

As Cusanus writes in the *De venatione sapientiae* that of the *non aliud* is the hunting ground for the divine in which the Triune God is revealed with a most pleasant pursuit in that the *non aliud* is the definition of himself and of all things[258]. In fact not only is the *aliud non aliud quam aliud*, but the same *non aliud* is *non aliud quam non aliud*[259]. The self-defining triple repetition of the *non aliud* speaks of the uni-trinitariety of God, his being at one and the same time one and triune.

Cusanus rejects such uni-trinitariety in a very particular way: taking up once again and examining the dynamic conception of Johannes Scotus Eriugena's – yet even earlier that of Marius Victorinus and of the Greek Fathers' – of the Trinity as life[260], he conceives the triple repetition of the *non aliud* as the self-constitutive process of God himself. The *non aliud* does not only show us the freedom and will of the Principle with regard to creation, and to created entities – expounding himself in his capacity to define all things – but rather also and above all, thanks to his triple self-defining repetition *non aliud est non aliud quam non aliud*, the even more original and unfathomable freedom or will of the Principle to constitute himself, and to create himself[261]. Not only does God know himself trinitarially, but constitutes himself trinitarially according to the double value of the definition, which as we have seen is both logico-gnosiological and ontological-constitutive. God not only defines all things, but above all himself, or in Cusanus' language is *diffinitio se diffiniens*[262]. A defining himself and all things, which is a seeing, a constituting himself and every thing[263]. In other words in that God Primus defines

256 Cf. *De non aliud*, h XIII, c. 9, pp. 18-21.

257 Cf. *De non aliud*, h XIII, c. 9, p. 20.

258 Cf. *De ven. sap.*, h XII, c. 14, n. 40, p. 39.

259 Cf. *De non aliud*, h XIII, c. 1, p. 4; c. 5, p. 12; prop. III, p. 61;*De ven. sap.*, h XII, c. 14, n. 40, p. 39.

260 On the theme cf. E. Vansteenberghe, *Le cardinal Nicolas de Cues (1401-1464). L'action – La pensée*, cit., p. 296; W. Beierwaltes, *Eriugena. Gründzuge seines Denken*, cit., pp. 204-261; Id., *Identität und Differenz*, cit., pp. 57-74.

261 *De non aliud*, h XIII, c. 5, p. 13.

262 Cf. *De ven. sap.*, h XII, c. 14, n. 40, p. 39.

263 *De non aliud*, h XIII, c. 23, p. 54.

himself, in defining himself he shows himself uni-trinitarially constituted.

It must not be forgotten that at the basis of Cusanus' discourse on the Trinity almost as its prologue is the ineffability and the unknowability of God, his Mystery. In the *Cribratio Alkorani* Cusanus in fact writes that God may be considered both as Principle and as non-Principle. In the latter case, or not in relationship to the things created, he is neither One nor Triune, neither Father nor Son nor Spirit, but incomprehesible and ineffable[264]. For this purpose Cusanus makes a fine distinction between *Deus* and *Deitas* identifying in the *Deitas* the divine essence which in itself is neither generating nor generated[265]. According to the Cardinal although God and *Deitas* are the same thing, yet if one considers the *Deitas* no generating will be seen, whereas if God is considered it will be seen inasmuch as, with God being identified with the Generating Father, he is such precisely insomuch that he generates the Son, or since he is love and fecundity[266].

But how then, are we to think such *prius* of the *Deus Trinitas* itself to which the same trinitarian God is associated without re-understanding him in the Trinity, and at the same time without making the *Deitas* a sort of presupposition different from God which would be a God Primus? One way of considering it may be what John has taught us in the *Prologue* of the IV Gospel, that is to say as *arché* or *Beginning*[267]. Divine *Arché* to be considered in Cusanus' way of thinking as *non aliud*. Cusanus himself in fact indicates a furthering of the *non aliud* regarding God himself when he claims also that «God is no other than God»[268]. The *non aliud* represents an attempt to give voice to the *profunda Dei* of which the Scriptures speak (*1 Cor* 2, 10), of the *hypertheiótes* of Dionysian memory [269].

The same Trinity-generating is associated with a deeper mystery which goes on transcending the revelation itself. As God is not immediately referrable to his will

264 Cf. *Crib. Alk.*, h VIII, II, c. 1, n. 88, pp. 73-74.

265 Cf. *Crib. Alk.*, h VIII, I, c. 14, n. 63-64, p. 55.

266 *Ibidem.*

267 On the *non aliud* as St. John's *arché* cf. F. Tomatis, *Inizio e parola di Dio*, cit., pp. 95-108; Id., *Ipseità, diversità e dia-ferenza*, in «Teoria», 26, 1 (2006), pp. 31-35. On the theme I take the liberty of referring also to my D. Monaco, *Deus Trinitas*, cit., pp. 318-328. The term "Beginning" is here understood in the sense outlined by Massimo Cacciari, cf. M. Cacciari, *Dell'Inizio*, Adelphi, Milano 1990, especially on the *arché* of John's prologue as Beginnning pp. 167-219. For Cacciari's reading of Cusanus' *non aliud* cf. M. Cacciari, *Filosofia e Teologia*, in *La filosofia*, vol. II, ed. P. Rossi, Utet, Torino 1995, pp. 365-421; Id., *Della cosa ultima*, Adelphi, Milano 2004, pp. 68-80.

268 N. Cusano, *De non aliud*, h XIII, c. 2, p. 6.

269 Cf. Ps.-Dionysius Areopagita, *De divinis nominibus*, XIII, 3, cit., pp. 228-230. To these references can be added in a modern projection the Übergottheit by Silesius (cf. A. Silesius, *Cherubinischer Wandersmann*, ed. L. Gnädiger, Reclam, Stuttgart 1984, I, 15, p. 29) and Schellingian's "Dio prima di Dio" by Luigi Pareyson (cf. L. Pareyson, *Ontologia della libertà*, Einaudi, Torino 1995, pp. 133ff).

or freedom with regard to the world and creation, so he is not identifiable definitively with the Trinity-generating of himself. In his freedom God is superessential, or beyond his very essence, his free will. God's re-vealing himself in the creation and in the Trinity is not complete manifestation, perfect manifestation and extrapolation from the divine depths, nor does he annul the transcendence of God : the *Deus Trinitas*, the God revealed does not cancel out the *Deus absconditus*, but God in himself in being infinite always remains unknowable, transcendent, ulterior, and superessential. The Cardinal states that God can be understood both as Principle and as non-Principle and that in this latter case he is neither One, nor Trine, nor Father, nor Son, nor Spirit, but incomprehensible and ineffable.[270] Also in the self-reflection and self-constitution of the Trinity God in himself, in his infinity remains ulterior, really and truly his own *Deus absconditus*.

[270] *Crib. Alk.*,h VIII, II, c. 1, n. 87-88, pp. 73-74.

Part II

Human Freedom and Dialogical Thought

1. Man as Image of God

In order to differentiate the human mind from the rest of the created Cusanus makes use of a simile. Let us imagine that God shines in a mirror, faultless, upright, infinite and perfect, constituted by the Word of God, and that all the creatures are like contracted and curved windows, set diversely in a circle around that unique mirror of truth. Among these mirrors arranged in a circle around that divine mirror there are some, the creatures of an intellectual nature, that are not only more transparent and upright than the others, but which are like living mirrors, that is to say intellectual and free, endowed with the capacity to bend, to straighten themselves and purify themselves all by themselves[271]. Now – the simile goes on – while in the central divine mirror all the mirrors appear perfectly, that is to say all things just as they are in their truth, the bent and contracted mirrors reflect in various ways all differently, all in a different way, every thing not as it is in itself, but according to its own limited capacity of reflection. Thus every creature is like a mirror in which all things are reflected, and in which all the universe is reflected in a unique and singular way. But while all creatures have a capacity to manifest things according to a limited and fixed disposition assigned by the Creator himself, the living intellectual windows, that is to say the creatures endowed with mind are free to increase by themselves, thanks to their own intellectual faculties, their own capacity to perceive and reflect both the divine truth and the truth of everything[272]. Albeit comparing every creature with a mirror in

[271] *De fil.*, h IV, 3, n. 65, p. 48: «Sit igitur altissima resplendentia principii nostri dei gloriosi, in qua appareat deus ipse, quae sit veritatis speculum sine macula rectissimum atque inter minum perfectissimumque, sint que omnes creaturae specula contractiora et differenter curva, intra quae intellectuales naturae sint viva, clariora atque rectiora specula, ac talia, cum sint viva et intellectualia atque libera, concipito, quod possint se ipsa incurvare, rectificare et mundare».

[272] Cf. *De fil.*, h IV,, 3, n. 65-66, pp. 48-49: «Dico igitur: claritas una specularis varie in istis universis resplendet specularibus reflexionibus et in prima rectissima speculari claritate omnia specula uti sunt resplendent, uti in materialibus speculis in circulo anteriori ad se versis videri potest. In omnibus autem aliis contractis et curvis omnia non uti ipsa sunt apparent, sed secundum recipientis speculi condicionem, scilicet cum diminutione ob recessum recipientis speculi a rectitudine. Quando igitur aliquod intellectuale vivum speculum translatum fuerit ad speculum primum

which the image of the entire universe shines, Cusanus differentiates the mirrors which simply reflect the world from those mirrors endowed with mind having an essential relationship with God, which are capable of making themselves similar to the Creator by partaking of his most divine spark and of his creative power, and by being able to show the universe in their own way by modyfying its image, thanks to their own faculties and freedom. These mirrors are not only images of the creatures' universe, but of the same divine author of the universe himself.

Since his *creatio* takes place last in the Biblical narrative account contained in *Genesis*, Man represents the perfecting of all what has been made before, the final achievement of divine creation[273]. He makes a clear distinction between the mind and the other things created: the *mens* differs from all other beings since it is not simply enfolding, but image of God.

> Philosophus: Videtur, quod sola mens sit Dei imago. Idiota: Proprie ita est, quoniamomnia, quae post mentem sunt, non sunt Dei imago nisi inquantum in ipsis mens ipsa relucet, sicut plus relucet in perfectis animalibus quam imperfectis et plus in sensibilibus quam vegetabilibus et plus in vegetabilibus quam mineralibus. Unde creaturae mente carentes sunt potius divinae simplicitatis explicationes quam imagines, licet secundum relucentiam mentalis imaginis in explicando de imagine varie participent[274].

According to Cusanus therefore, one thing is the unfolding, while another thing is the image[275]. But what distinguishes being image from being simple unfolding?

Ever since the *De docta ignorantia* God has been thought of not as being opposed to the world, but as "all that can be" and "all that which is possible"[276]. According to Cusanus' terminology the One is conceived as *complicatio (enfolding)*

veritatis rectum, in quo veraciter omnia uti sunt absque defectu resplendent, tunc speculum ipsum veritatis cum omni reception omnium speculorum se transfundit in intellectual vivum speculum, et ipsum tale intellectuale in se recipit specularem illum radium speculi veritatis in se habentis omnium speculorum veritatem. Recipit autem suo modo in eodem vero momento aeternitatis vivum illud speculum quasi oculus vivus, cum receptione luminis resplendentiae primi speculi in eodem veritatis speculo se uti est intuetur et in se omnia suo quidem modo».

273 Cf. *Sermo I*, h. XVI/1, n. 15, p. 13: «Creavit autem ultimo Deus hominem, tanquam in quo complementum et creaturarum perfecto». Although man occupies a privileged place within creation, in that he is capable of mediating between the world of the spirit and the world of matter, the cardinal appears to extend his discourse to all creatures endowed with mind strarting from ther angelic ones as far as the more imperfect terrestial ones. On the theme, cf. G. Santinello, *L'uomo «ad imaginem et similitudinem» nel Cusano*, in «Doctor Seraphicus», 37 (1990), p. 86.

274 Cf. *De mente*, h V, 4, n. 76, p. 116.

275 Cf. *De mente*, h V, 4, n. 74, p. 113: «Attende aliam esse imagine, aliam explicationem».

276 Cf. *De docta ign.*, h I, I, 4, n. 11, p. 10.

of all things possible, that is infinite unity of all possibles, including the contradictory ones. Together with the concept of *complicatio*, Cusanus employs that of *explicatio*, (*unfolding*)[277]. If enfolding means containing in himself all things within the unity of his own power, then explicare means unfolding in the multiplicity all what was enfolded in the One[278].

Although having presented the scheme of Neoplatonic origin of a procession of the One by degrees and by intermediary hypostases, according to which the creative action would be directed not towards the universe *tout court*, but rather mediated through a strict hierarchical subdivision, the German thinker rejects this conception in favour of the simultaneousness of every creature: every thing is immediate *explicatio Dei* in that everything is a *contractio*[279], a divine contraction, that is direct participation by the creature, according to its own possibilities, in the divine universal *complicatio* in its unfolding itself. No hierchically-ordered *descensio*, not even the Neoplatonic One, Intellect, Soul is no longer conceivable in Cusanus' system.

The unfolding of the Principle is thought of neither as an emanation, nor as a multiplication, nor as a division, but rather as a sort of concentration of the universal into the particular, of the infinite into the finite, of the absolute into the contracted[280]. At the same time the participation of the Many in the One is not thought of as a *partem capere*, a taking part as if the things took part of the One, in that it is absolutely indivisible[281]. For Cusanus every thing is a contraction of God, that is a concentration of the divine power into one of its possibilities. In its unfolding the unity of all the possibles is in act in a contracted way, or all in the *mode* of that particular possible unfolding which contracts it. For Cusanus: «quodlibet in quolibet»[282], that is to say every unfolding of the One encloses in itself all the other possible manifestations of the One, the enfolding of all the possibles, but in fact limitedly to its unique, unrepeatable and individual exceptional capacity to manifest it. Every being is the contracted all.

[277] Cf. *De docta ign.*, II, 3, n. 107, p. 70.

[278] Cf. *De docta ign.*, II, 3, n. 105, p. 69.

[279] For a close examination of the various spheres of use of the concept of contraction, of its sources and its developments within Cusanus' work, cf. J. Hopkins, *Nicholas of Cusa's Metaphysic of Contraction*, Arthur J. Banning, Minneapolis 1983; G. d'Onofrio, *Nel cuore della rivoluzione gnoseologica: Cusano e la dottrina della* contractio *fra Medioevo e Rinascimento*, in *Cusano*, cit., pp. 7-24; S. Mancini, *Congetture su Dio*, cit., pp. 29-102.

[280] Cf. *De doctaign.*, h I, II, 4, n. 116, pp. 74-75.

[281] Cf. *De doctaign.*, h I, II, 2, n. 102, p. 67.

[282] Cf. *De doctaign.*, h I, II, 5, n. 117, p. 76.

According to Cusanus only the individuals are in act[283]. The One therefore unfolds itself into a plurality of individuals, of centres, which are unique and singular images and mirrors – in that there can never exist two equal things in the universe[284] – of the *complicatio* (*enfolding*) of all possibles. It is not a question of different collatable parts since it is as if every being were everything, inasmuch as contracted in a unique and singular way. The being is concentrated in so many unitary centres which partake of the unity of all, and not as parts of an all in all, a mirror of the infinite[285], a viewpoint on infinite unity[286]. Cusanus constantly denies the plurality of forms in God, defining God as *forma formarum*, form of all forms, inasmuch as form-maker, or creator of forms[287]. The cardinal conceives the form of all forms not as a static model which an outside activity must copy, but as a forming activity which by itself creates and models the being, imprinting on it an image of itself, and at the same time expressing itself as forming form. The plurality of forms is in contrast, in act in the plurality of the individual beings. The individuals are the reality of the formed forms which, inasmuch as such are pure and simple possibilities realized in their identifications. As God is form of forms or creative power, active, forming, so the created things or the formed forms, which are images of the divine exemplar, are they themselves active centres of formation. Every thing, clearly each in accordance with various degrees manifests God in that it manifests itself. Manifesting one's own being means expressing it and forming it, and in this expression also the absolute being of God proves to be expressed and manifested. Cusanus' universe is revealed therefore as a collection of individual beings, dynamic contraction of the unity of all, or in other words as a collection of monads, each reflecting in a different and individual way the creative and formative divine power inasmuch as it itself is power-forming containing every thing in itself.

283 Cf. *De docta ign.*, h I, II, 6, n. 124, p. 80; II, 6, n. 125, p. 80; III, 1, n. 184, p. 120. The existence in act of the single or the individual involves the recognition of the individuality of the substantial forms or to express it in more modern language a conception of reality of monadological mould. Cf. G. Santinello, *Il pensiero di Nicolò Cusanonella sua prospettiva estetica*, Liviana, Padova 1958, pp. 111-118; S. Mancini, *Congetture su Dio*, cit., pp. 29-102.

284 Cf. *De docta ign.*, h I, III, 1, 188, p. 122; *De ven. sap.*, h XII, 37, n. 109, p. 102; F. Vengeon, *Nicolas de Cues, le monde humain. métaphysique de l'infini et anthropologie*, Jérôme Millon, Grenoble 2011, pp. 53-88.

285 Cf. *De dato,* h IV, 2, n. 99, p. 74.

286 Cf G. Santinello, *Il pensiero di Nicolò Cusano nella sua prospettiva estetica*, cit., pp. 111 ff.; N. Herold, *Menschliche Perspektive und Wahrheit. Zur Deutung der Subjektivität in den philosophischen Schriften des Nikolaus von Kues*, Aschendorff, Münster 1975, pp. 21ff.

287 Cf. *De dato*, h IV, 2, n. 73, p. 98. Among the first to emphasise the reference to this terminology to Eckhart was Edmond Vansteenberghe, cf. E. Vansteenberghe, *Le Cardinal Nicolas de Cues (1401-1464). L'action - la pensée*, cit., pp. 427-428. Cf. moreover*De ven. sap.*, h XII, 39, n. 118, p. 109.

In the universal *explicatio Dei* the human *mens* appears to acquire an exclusive and privileged role. The mind in fact is not mere unfolding, but *viva imago Dei*[288], that is to say it enjoys a special ontological status. The formative creative divine power in fact finds its maximum reflection in the cognitive faculty which gives form to the world of knowledge.

The *mens* is living image or likeness in that it is capable of being increasingly likened, as far as possible, to its exemplar, to the infinite creative art: it possesses an innate force through which it can make itself more in keeping with the *ars divina*. In some passages of Cusanus' work, the same divine affiliation, the deification, the approaching near to God, appears to coincide with the greatest perfectioning of our intellect or of our knowledge of all things as likeness of the divine creative art, which is the Word. Ever since his second great theoretical work, the *De Coniecturis* Cusanus elaborated, more than a Christology, but rather a philosophy of the mind founded christologically, in which the latter inasmuch as close likeness of God («alta Dei similitudo») is seen as the unifying link between the finite and the infinite level, between the worldly dimension and the divine one[289]. Thus the mind is one of the fundamental themes of Cusanus' speculation. It represents the axis round which all his reflection rotates in that it is the unifying link between two essential poles of his thought, the one and the many, God and creation, and the two essential spheres, the gnosiological and the theological one, which is the very basis of his theorising. Thus the mind acquires a special status within his creating: it is the first and closest sign to the Creator in that in it his creative power shines most brightly[290].

[288] Cf. *De mente*, h V, 4, n. 74, p. 113; 4, n. 76, p. 116. On the *mens* as *viva imago Dei* cf. G. Santinello, *L'uomo «ad imaginem et similitudinem» nel Cusano*, cit., pp. 85-97; G. F. von Bredow, *Der Geist als lebendiges Bild Gottes (Mens viva dei imago)*, in «MFCG», 13 (1978), pp. 58-67; P. Moffitt Watts, *Nicolaus Cusanus. A fifteenth-century vision of man*, Brill, Leiden 1982, pp. 87-116; G. Cuozzo, Mystice videre. *Esperienza religiosa e pensiero speculativo in Cusano*, Trauben, Torino 2002, pp. 176-182; W. Dupré, *Spirit, Mind and Freedom*, in *Conflict and Reconciliation. Perspectives on Nicholas of Cusa*, ed. I. Bocken, Brill, Leiden 2004, pp. 207-221; H. Schwaetzer, Viva imago dei: *Überlegungen zum Ursprung eines anthropologischen Grundprinzips bei Nicolaus Cusanus*, in *Spiegel und Porträt. Zur Bedeutung zweier zentraler Bilder im Denken des Nicolaus Cusanus*, eds. I. Bocken - H. Schwaetzer, Uitgeverij Shaker, Maastricht 2005, pp. 113-132; J. Kreuzer, *Der Geist als imago Dei — Augustinus und Cusanus*, in K. Reinhardt - H. Schwaetzer (eds.), *Nicolaus von Kues in der Geschichte des Platonismus*, Roderer, Regensburg 2006, pp. 65-86; D. Monaco, Deus Trinitas. *Dio come* non altro *nel pensiero di Nicolò Cusano*, cit., pp. 250-269; J. Kreuzer, *Der Geist als lebendiger Spiegel. Zur Theorie des Intellekts bei Meister Eckhart und Nikolaus von Kues*, in «Meister-Eckhart-Jahrbuch», 4 (2011), pp. 49-66; K. Yamaki, Imago Dei. *Über "anthropozentrische" Bezeichnungen in der cusanischen Imago-Dei-Lehre*, in *Manuductiones. Festschrift zu Ehren von J M. Machetta und C. D'Amico*, cit., pp. 124-136.

[289] Cf. *De coni.*, h III, I, 1, n. 5, p. 7; *De fil.*, h IV, 6, n. 86, p. 62.

[290] Cf. *Comp.*, h XI/3, 8, n. 23, p. 19.

But what makes the mind so special? In what is the mind image of God? Cusanus refers the origin of the term *mens* to the act of *mensurare*, of measuring, by identifying in it the activity belonging to the mind, the mind's own proper activity: the mind is defined on the basis of its capacity to give *mensura* and *terminus*, that is measure and limit to every thing[291]. If the soul is called such considered in its role of animating the body, but understood instead as organ of knowledge itself it is called *mens* and from its activity which consists in *mensurare*. The mind therefore, being image and not simply *explicatio* of the *mens* or infinite *ars* of God, that is of his Word, in which, from which, and in view of which, all things have been created, has a special relationship of likeness to it. As the divine simplicity enfolds all things, so the mind which is its *imago* is the unfolding of the notion and of the measure of all things. Just as the divine mind gives being to all things, so the human mind gives place to the notion and to the measure of all things. As the mind of God by conceiving creates, so our mind conceiving becomes like the beings; as all things are in the infinite mind in their precision and truth, so they are in the finite mind or in the image or in the likeness of their truth, that is to say in their notion or measure. As all things are in God as exemplars, in our mind they are as likenesses; as God is *complicite* of all beings, so the human mind is *complicatio* of all measures. In this way Cusanus' affirmations are understood – of hermetic origin – according to which man is a human God, second or caused, that is creator of likenesses of all things, and is also *microcosmos* or *parvus mundus*, notional enfolding of all[292].

We may recall that for Cusanus knowing means comparing, by proportioning one thing with another: «comparativa igitur est omnis inquisitio medio proportionis utens»[293]. Every rational search moves from the known to the unknown by

[291] Cf. *De mente*, h V, 1, n. 56, p. 90.

[292] Cf. *De beryl.*, h XI/1, n. 7, p. 9. In the *De coniecturis* one speaks of «humanus deus», cf. *De coni.*, II, 14, n. 143, p. 143. In the *De dato patris luminum* di «deus humanatus»; cf. *De dato,* h IV, 3, n. 102, pp. 76-77. On the resumption of this hermetic theme cf. W. Dupré, *Der Mensch als Mikrokosmos im Denken des Nikolaus von Kues*, «MFCG», 13 (1978), pp. 68-87; K. Bormann, *Nikolaus von Kues: «Der Mensch als zweiter Gott»*, Trier, Paulinus, 1999; P. Arfé, *The annotations of Nicolaus Cusanus and Giovanni Andrea Bussi on the Asclepius*, in «Journal of Warburg and Courtauld Institutes», 62 (1999), pp. 29-59; Id., *Alberto Magno e Nicola Cusano interpreti dell'Asclepius*, in *Nicolaus Cusanus zwischen Deutschland und Italien*, cit., pp. 129-151; Id. (ed.), *Apuleius. Hermes Trismegistus. Aus Codex Bruxellensis 10054-56*, Winter, Heidelberg 2004, pp. 41-42; Id., *Ermete Trismegisto e Nicola Cusano*, in *La tradizione ermetica dal mondo tardo-antico all'Umanesimo*, eds. P. Lucentini - I. Parri - V. Perrone Compagni, Turnhout, Brepols, 2002, pp. 223-244; M. Thurner, *Explication der Welt und mystische Verinnerlichung. Die hermetische Definition des Menschen als "secundus deus" bei Cusanus*, in *La tradizione ermetica dal mondo tardo-antico all'Umanesimo*, cit., pp. 245-261; F. Vengeon, *Nicolas de Cues, le monde humain. métaphysique de l'infini et anthropologie*, cit., pp. 89-158.

[293] *De docta ign.*, h I, I, 1, n. 3, p. 6.

comparing them by means of proportion, that is to say what is searched for is to be set in relation to a certain presupposition by proportioning it with it, either immediately or through other passages that are always intermediary proportional and comparative, thus arriving at its definition. Number occupies a privileged role in an always cognitive procedure of human reason, and without it no proportion, distinction, order, harmony, or plurality is possible[294]. Comparison, proportion and measurement are the categories and the methods of positive discursive knowledge due to dianoetic reason (*ratio*), from which Cusanus distingushes that vision which sees but does not understand, which instead, belongs to the intellect (*intellectus*)[295]. Positive rational knowledge employs number as its essential and fundamental element[296]. Without number in fact our mind cannot do anything: assimilation, distinction, conceptual knowledge, measuring, which are the activities belonging to the *mens*, would not take place without it[297]. The mind measures in that it counts with numbers.

The cardinal distinguishes between beings which are produced by man and which inasmuch as such can be known by him precisely, and the real or natural beings which, inasmuch as such, are works of God and remain unknown to us through his precision.

> Coniecturas a mente nostra, uti realis mundus a divina infinita ratione, prodire oportet. Dum enim humana mens, alta dei similitudo, fecunditatem creatricis naturae, ut potest, partecipat, ex se ipsa, ut imagine omnipotentis formae, in realium entium similitudine rationalia exserit. Coniecturalis itaque mundi humana mens forma exstitit uti realis divina[298].

Most especially it is to be emphasised that in the writing *De coniecturis*, in which the first formulation of this doctrine recurs, numbers play a privileged and fundamental role[299]. In fact they represent both the principle of the rational construction of the mind, and the element of which all that which descends from infinite unity is composed. Yet the exactness of our mathematics depends on its capacity to reflect divine mathematics symbolically.

294 Cf *De docta ign.*, h I, I, n. 5, 13, p. 12; *De coni.*, h III, I, 2, n. 7-8, pp. 11-14.

295 On the differentiation of the cognitive faculties in Cusanus and his Neoplatonic sources cf. G. d'Onofrio, Vera philosophia. *Studies in Late Antique, Early Medieval and Renaissance Christian Thought*, cit., pp. 297-308.

296 On the theme cf. W. Schulze, *Zahl, Proportion, Analogie*, Aschendorff, Münster 1978; F. Nagel, *Nicolaus Cusanus uns die Entstehung der exakten Wissenschaften*, Münster, Aschendorff, 1984, pp. 6-85.

297 Cf. *De mente*, h V, 6, n. 95, p. 141.

298 Cf. *De coni.*, h III, I, 1, n. 5, p. 7.

299 Cf. *De coni.*, h III, I, 2, n. 7, p. 11-14.

> Symbolice etenim de rationalibus numeris nostrae mentis ad reales ineffabiles divinae mentis coniecturantes, dicimus "in animo conditoris primum rerum exemplar" ipsum numerum, uti similitudinarii mundi numerus a nostra ratione exsurgere[300].

Cusanus makes a distinction between real divine ineffable numbers and human rational numbers, or those of our mathematics, which are symbols thereof. As the first exemplar of the divine mind is the divine number, so the first exemplar of our mind is human number. As God creates the real world on the basis of real divine ineffable numbers which are the first exemplar of the things in his mind, so the human mind creates, produces the world of conjectures and measurings through the rational number which is the first exemplar of our knowledge. Thus things have a basis and a mathematical structure, winessed by the very Scripture which says that all the things have been disposed by God *in misura, et numero et pondere* (Wisdom. 11, 20)[301].

Also in the *De mente* dialogue Cusanus repeats the differentiation between divine numbers and mathematical number, and the symbolical relationship and of image that the latter has with the former.

> Arbitror autem viros Pythagoricos, qui ut ais per numerum de omnibus philosophantur, graves et acutos. Non quod credam eos voluisse de numero loqui, prout est mathematicus et ex nostra mente procedit – nam illum non esse alicuius rei principium de se constat –, sed symbolice ac rationabiliter locuti sunt de numero, qui ex divina mente procedit, cuius mathematicus est imago[302].

The number which proceeds from our mind is only a useful rational entity produced by our *mens* and useful for human and conjectural knowledge of things, yet it is not the number through which the divine mind has produced all things, the divine number, principle and substance of real entities. The first exemplar of the things in the creator's soul is divine number, likewise the exemplar of the conceptions of our mind is mathematical number[303]. The number of our mind, being image of the divine number, which is the exemplar of things, is exemplar of the notions[304]. The symbolical parallelism between rational number formed by our mind and the divine ineffable number ensures the validity of our measurings.

Thus Cusanus always distinguishes between divine ontological number and human gnosiological number. Knowledge and human measuring is never a pure

300 *De coni.*, h III, I, 2, n. 9, p. 14.

301 D. Albertson, *Gott als Mathematiker? Das Schöpfungsverständnis des Nicolaus Cusanus*, in «MFCG», 33 (2012), pp. 99-122.

302 *De mente*, h V, 6, n. 88, p. 133.

303 Cf. *De mente*, h V, 6, n. 94-95, pp. 139-141.

304 Cf. *De mente*, h V, 6, n. 95, p. 141.

creating or a pure activity, but is also always marked by a passivity, by a receiving. Human thinking remains linked to sensitivity from which it begins. It is necessary for the mind to be excited and moved by the sight of the sensitive world for it to be able to unfold by itself notionally the totality of things[305]. The plurality of things exists independently of us, the multiplicity of the world exists even if we do not see it, in that it is work of the divine creative intellect[306].

The level of knowledge does not coincide with that of reality, but the latter maintains a transcendence of its own with regard to our knowing, which can only make reference to it. Yet man possesses a *visus mentalis*, a mental vision, thanks to which he sees prior to every possible piece of knowledge with absolute certainty both what level of being is and its difference and ulteriority regarding the level of our knowledge. From this mental vision there derives a critical awareness of the gap, of the difference between our knowledge and reality, which allows us also to understand the link, the relationship between the two levels. Although we do not know things directly, our mind with being has, if not an immediate and direct relationship, then a mediated and indirect relationship, insomuch as knowledge refers to, and indicates that level of being, albeit without ever succeeding in identifying itself with it, nor in determining itself exactly and equally with it[307].

Thus Cusanus makes a distinction between being and knowing, between the ontological level and the gnosiological level. God creates the reality of things, creates ontologically, while man analogously creates the notions of things, and creates gnosiologically. Yet in this parallelism, circularity, being precedes knowing, that is to say there is a priority of the ontological level, of reality, over that of thought and knowledge. At the same time, although such priority persists only thanks to the mind which is artificer of the gnosiological level, of human knowledge, the ontological level sees its value recognised.

Exactly inasmuch as rational mathematics is a product of our mind its precision and its exactness is accessible to us; being its constructors we are able to grasp the truth of mathematical number[308]. Just as the precision of real things is in the hands of God since the numerical disposition exemplar with which they are constituted is work of the divine mind, the precision of our knowledge of human mathematics depends in contrast on the fact that rational numbers are our work[309].

305 Cf *De mente*, h V, 8, n. 85, pp. 128-129.

306 Cf. *De mente*, h V, 6, n. 93, p. 138.

307 Cf. G. Santinello, *Riflessioni sul concetto di analogia nel pensiero moderno*, in *Metafore dell'invisibile. Ricerche sull'analogia*, ed. G. Santinello, Brescia, Morcelliana, 1984, pp. 44-46.

308 Cf. *De poss.*, h XI/2, n. 43, pp. 52-53.

309 Cf. *De coni.*, h III, I, 2, n. 9, p. 14. On the idea that mathematics is a construction of the human mind and on the basis of its precision, cf. also *De beryl.*, h XI/1 n. 55, p. 63.

In one of his last works, Cusanus compares God with a money coiner and man as a money evaluator[310]. Without man's intellectual capacity to discern and evaluate things the possibility of knowing value would also come short, and things would be without value. Although it is not knowledge that institutes value, but it is God that creates things, and thus gives beginning, reality and value to them, it is man who measures them, identifies them and decides on their value[311]. God is like a money-coiner who having the power to create any kind of money, even having created such money and its value according to his own will, has entrusted the task of counting it, distinguishing it and evaluating it to a money changer, namely man, but keeping for himself the art of making money.

In Cusanus' perspective there no longer exists a fixed centre of the universe not only because the cosmos is infinite, but *also* because it is man who is to be centre of the universe with his capacity for *mensurare*, for measuring things. The vision of the centrality of the *mens* in the created universe cannot be set in relationhip with the precarious cosmological theses of the German thinker of the relativity of each point of movement and of each centre of the world. According to the Cardinal we cannot be aware of movement except in relationship to something fixed, and we are forced to presuppose poles or centres when we try to arrive at the measures of motions[312]. We fail to note movement except in relationship to something fixed or stable[313]. It is we ourselves therefore, who hypothesize fixed celestial poles so that we may observe movement and calculate but only on the basis of a stationary point of reference. The identification of a centre is a need for our rational faculty and for our capacity to measure which proves to be completely imprecise with respect to the reality of things. Astronomical measurings, as our every measuring, are far from precise[314]. Mathematical calculations and astronomical systems are abstract and approximative because there is a gap between our rational construction and the universe, between the constructions of reason and the structure of reality. They are therefore always conjectures. The universe no longer has the earth as its centre since its ontological centre is God, creator of the world, and its gnosiological centre is man with his capacity to measure the world.

310 Cf. *De ludo*, h IX, II, n. 110-121, pp. 137-149.

311 *De ludo*, h IX, II, n. 114, p. 140; II, n. 114, p 140.

312 Cf. *De docta ign.*, h I, II, 11, n. 159, p. 102.

313 Cf. *De docta ign.*, h I, II, 12, 162, p. 103.

314 Cf. *De docta ign.*, h I, II, 1, 9, p. 61.

2. Interfaith Dialogue in Cusanus

On the 29th of May 1453, Constantinople – which was not only one of the leading cities of Christianity, but also one of the symbolic places of its history – was conquered by the Turkish army led by Sultan Mohamed II. The news of the fall of Constantinople and of the slaughterings and sackings that followed quickly spread throughout Europe. The tragic event upset the European and Christian conscience, spreading a sense of anguish and terror against the Islamic enemy which was now at the gate. Fine intellectuals of the time also made a call to weapons and war as the only way to salvation.[315]

In such a harsh atmosphere, Cardinal Cusanus had the merit of suggesting a different way from the torn Christian conscience of the time[316]. Despite being aware of the danger that was looming over Christianity, the Cardinal understood that resorting to weapons would only have rendered the centuries-old conflict even more violent. During the months which followed the event, Cusanus wrote a text which was beyond its times, yet quite daring from its very title: the *De pace fidei, The Peace of Faith.* Paraphrasing but following Cusanus' intent: *Peace which starts from faith.*

The work tells of a vision had by a narrator, identifiable with Cusanus himself. It is a vision of a celestial assembly composed of angels and saints chaired by the Omnipotent aimed at examining the question of the tragic events that had taken place on Earth because of the diverse religious rites. Before such a council of excellencies is a group of sages belonging to different populations who, as representatives of the different confessions, are called to converse first with the Word, then

[315] On this topic cf. *La cadutadi Costantinopoli*, ed. A. Pertusi, 2 voll., Mondadori, Milano 1976; E. Meuthen, *Der Fall von Konstantinopel und der Lateinische Westen*, in «MFCG», 16 (1984), 35-60; R. Crowley, *The Holy War for Constantinople and the Clash of the West,* Hachette Books, New York 2005. For an overwiew of the historical context of Cusanus's works on religious dialogue, cf. J. E. Biechler, *Interreligious dialogue*, in *Introducing Nicholas of Cusa: a guide to a renaissance man*, eds. C. M. Bellitto - T. M. Izbicki - G. Christianson, Paulist, New York 2004, pp. 270-296.

[316] Literature on Cusanus' relationship with Islam is quite extensive nowadays, especially among the more recent contributions,cf. T. Bakos, *On faith, rationality, and the other in the late Middle Ages: A study of Nicholas of Cusa's manuductive approach to Islam*, Eugene, Oregon 2010; *Cusanus und der Islam*, eds. W. A. Euler – T. Kerger, Paulinus, Trier 2010; M. Costigliolo, *Islam e cristianesimo: mondi di differenze nel Medioevo.Il dialogo con l'Islam nell'opera di Nicola da Cusa*, Genova University, Genova 2012; *Nicolas de Cues et l'Islam*, ed. H. Pasqua, Peeters, Leuven 2013; W. A. Euler, *Cusanus' Auseinandersetzung mit dem Islam*, in «Das Mittelalter», 1 (2014), pp. 72-85; *Nicholas of Cusa and Islam Polemic and Dialogue in the Middle Ages*, eds. I.C. Levy – R. George-Turtkovíc – D. F. Duclow, Brill, Leiden 2014.

with Saint Peter and Saint Paul. The aim of the dialogue – in which the highest theological and philosophical themes are debated, such as the Oneness of God, Logos, Trinity, Incarnation, Christ, Law, a critique to idolatry, bliss, sacraments, - is to find certain agreement wherewith it is possible to build peace on Earth and to put an end to those violent acts perpetrated in the name of God. The objective of the dialogue between the representatives of the different religions with the Divine Word, Saint Peter and Saint Paul, is that of reaching the awareness that religion is only one, despite the diversity of rites. The work concludes on reaching an agreement in the heavens, wishing for a council to be presently held on earth, to be held in the city of Jerusalem as city of peace, so that the indication of the celestial assembly might find its realisation on Earth.

De pace fidei is certainly one of cardinal Cusanus' most well-known and most read texts. It is subject to various interpretations and still today scholars do not agree unanimously on certain crucial aspects of Cusanus' opinion, nor on the evaluation of the role of Christianity in relation to the sharp synthetic expression «religio una in rituum varietate»[317], which effectively sums up Cusanus' proposal.

When first reading it, we may distinguish two possible lines of interpretation[318]. According to the first line, the concept of *una religio* identifies essentially with Christianity, while other religions are multiple rites that relate to this one true faith. According to the second line of interpretation, instead, all religions – including Christianity – are imprecise, hypothetical rites of that one *religio* which does not identify with any particular creed and which cannot coincide with any of them, but in which all creeds blend and take part. However, both these hermeneutic options, although both provide valid reasons, appear to be incomplete and give rise to several relevant reservations. This incompletion is further testified by the variations in interpreting the two hermeneutic lines[319].

According to the first interpretation, if the *una religio* concept were identified with Christianity then the fundamental bases of Cusanus' speculation would be refuted – that is to say the definition of *docta ignorantia* and of the speculative character of human knowledge, the unobjectability of truth and Divinity – together with their ulteriority from our every expression of them. All the other religions would be rites that have a meaning only with respects to the one Christian truth as its partial revelations and its unfolding. The task of dialogue, then, is to

317 *De pace*, h VII, c. 1, n. 6, p. 7.

318 Cf. P. Gaia, *Introduzione*, in N. Cusano, *Opere religiose*, Utet, Torino 1993, pp. 57-64; A. Moritz, *Die Andersheit des Anderen – noch einmal zum Problem der Toleranz in Nicolaus von Kues' Dialog De pace fidei*, in «Litterae Cusanae», 1 (2006), pp. 1-17.

319 Cf. D. Monaco, *Dialogo interreligioso, intrareligioso e identità cristiana nel De pace fidei di Nicolò Cusano. Una prospettiva ermeneutica*, in «Filosofia e Teologia», 2 (2007), pp. 323-335; D. Monaco, *Cusano e la pace della fede*, preface by F. Tomatis, Città Nuova, Roma 2013, pp. 120-126.

lead them all to the one and only manifested truth by overcoming their singularity and depriving them of their partiality. However, it is clear that the *una religio* concept does not immediately identify with Christianity *tout court* and that the dialogue does not seek to convert all the non-Christians to Christianity.

If the second interpretation serves to equate all religious creeds as bearers of the same revelational value, and so if Christianity is considered only as a contracted realisation of the unreachable truth, then it is hard to understand why the dialogue would place the Word first, and then Peter and Paul at the centre of the Celestial Council. In the work all the representatives of the different religions do not debate with one another, but only do so with the *Logos* first and then with the two Apostles, who do not take part in the circle of the other religious representatives. They are in fact the centre of it and answer the wise men's questions because it is God's explicit will that they do so[320]. There seems to be an irremediable contradiction between the assignment of value to all the different religions and the privileged part taken on by the leading representatives of one of them. It appears contradictory that Christianity does not identify with the concept of *una religio,* whilst most of Cusanus' work concentrates on questions such as the Holy Trinity and the Incarnation – fundamental dogmas of the Christian religion. The second line of interpretation thus does not succeed in explaining the centrality of Christianity.

According to the writer of this piece, the only way to understand the contradiction intrinsic in the *De pace fidei* is to read the work and try to reconstruct its contents by setting them in the wider context of the Cardinal's philosophical speculation: Cusanus' position towards interfaith dialogue can only be fully grasped if it is thought of in the wider context of his philosophy[321]. However, although it is undeniable that any interpretation of the *De pace fidei* encounters many intrinsic complexities, according to the investigation carried out in this work it is not possible to understand the dialogue's contents without making its philosophical foundation explicit. The dialectic between the One and the many and that between the uniqueness of truth and the variety of its expressions are the speculative bases of the work[322].

320 K. Reinhardt, *Die cusanische Idee vom Frieden im Glauben nach der Interpretation von Raymond Klibansky (1905-2005)*, in «Litterae Cusanae», 1 (2006), p. 24.

321 For a more extensive analysis of the *De pace fidei* and a more detailed exposition of our interpretation, cf. D. Monaco, *Cusano e la pace della fede*, cit.

322 Cf. *De pace*, h VII, c. 1, n. 6, p. 7: «una religio in rituum varietate; *ibid.*, c. 4, n. 11, p. 11: «Ante enim omnem pluralitatem est unitas»; *ibid.*, c. 5, n. 15, p. 14: «Non est autem possibile plures esse aeternitates, quia ante omnem pluralitatem est unitas»; *ibid.*, c. 5, n. 17, p. 16: «Et qui dicit plures deos, dicit unum antecedenter omnium principium»; *ibid.*, c. 5, n. 17, p. 16: «Et non est possibile plura esse aeterna, quia ante omnem pluralitatem unitas»; *ibid.*, c. 7, n. 21, p. 20:

The dialectic between oneness and multiplicity – which had already appeared in other texts prior to the *De pace fidei* and was completed in his last work – is a necessary premise for understanding the theoretical proposal outlined in the work from 1453, a proposal dedicated to interfaith dialogue and to Cusanus' entire philosophy[323]. The view of the relationship between God and the world – between the One and the many – is shown through a close examination of the two most representative terms of the German philosopher's speculation – *complicatio* and *explicatio*. Thanks to the asymmetry between enfolding and unfolding – according to which an unfolded thing cannot be directly derived from an enfolded thing, while an enfolded thing necessarily derives from an unfolded thing – Cusanus manages to defend both God's freedom and omnipotence and the significance of the world, and it being theophany, trace and manifestation of its creator[324]. Using another Cusanus term, the world achieves meaning and value because it is a contraction of God (*contractio Dei*), that is the ability of God's infinite power to concentrate, individualise and actualise itself in each and every created thing. The creature and the finite being thus have a positive value in their singularity in that they are a manifestation of God's transcendence and infinity in their unique individuality[325].

Cusanus employs his view of the relationship between oneness and multiplicity also in a field of gnosiology, and develops a perspectivistic view of human

«Omnis autem multitudinis unitas est principium: quare principium multitudinis est aeterna unitas»; *ibid.*, c. 8, n. 22, p. 22: «In tantum enim res est in quantum una est».

323 For an interpretation different from ours, that is to say, one contrary to relating the proposal contained in the *De pace fidei* to Cusanus' entire body of metaphysics, cf. T.McTighe, *'Nicholas* of Cusas' *Unity-Metaphysics and the Formula religio una in rituum varietate'*, in *Nicholas of Cusa in search of God and Wisdom,* a c. di G. Christianson - T. Izbicki, Brill, Leiden 1991, pp. 161-172; K. Flasch, *Nikolaus von Kues. Geschichte einer Entwicklung*, Klostermann, Frankfurt am Main 1998, pp. 384-385; P. Valkenberg, Una religio in Rituum Varietate: *Religious Pluralism, the Qur'an, and Nichols of Cusa*, in *Nicholas of Cusa and Islam Polemic and Dialogue in the Middle Ages*, eds. I.C. Levy – R. George-Turtkovíc – D. F. Duclow, Brill, Leiden 2014, pp. 30-48.

324 *De docta ign.*, h I, I, c. 22, n. 69, p. 45: «Nam posita complicatione non ponitur res complicata, sed posita explicatione ponitur complicatio».

325 Cf. Cf. *De docta*, h I, III, c. 1, n. 188, p. 122: «Ut nihil sit in universo, quod non gaudeat quadam singularitate, quae in nullo alio reperibilis est, ita quod nullum omnia in omnibus vincat aut diversa aequaliter, sicut cum nullo ullo umquam tempore aequale in quocumque esse potest; etiam si uno tempore minus eo fuerit et alio maius, hunc transitum facit in quadam singularitate, ut numquam aequalitatem praecisam attingat»; *De ven sap.*, h XII, c. 22, n. 66, p. 64: «Sed una est omnium singularium causa, quae omnia singularizat, quae neque est totum neque pars neque species neque individuum neque hoc neque illud neque omne nominabile, sed est singulorum singularissima causa. Singulare cum sit ab aeterna causa singularizatum, numquam in non-singulare resolvi potest. A quo enim resolveretur ab aeterna causa singularizatum? Hinc singulare bonum numquam desinit, cum omne singulare sit bonum».

knowledge. The German philosopher combines an idea of truth as infinite with a speculative view of knowledge. Truth, in its unobjectability, unlimitedness and transcendence can be accessed and expressed by man only within certain singular and particular points of view which, rooted in finiteness, can convey the infinity of truth[326]. In this scheme, the mind (*mens*) has a central and essential role within the variety of creation, from an ontological point of view and because it is God's and the One's first self-manifestation. The *mens* and the One are the two fundamental principles in the German philosopher's speculation as a whole[327]. It is not by chance that they represent the axis around which his later philosophy rotates – the complete expression of his thought over the years. Only the *mens* can know the One or the *posse*, for it is a living image of God (*viva imago Dei*), unlike the rest of the created things, which are merely an unfolding of God (*explicatio Dei*)[328].

Thus the cognitive power of the mind is the image of the infinite divine *posse* it bears. In this way, Cusanus represents a historical turning-point: the centre of the

326 Cf. *De docta ign.*, h I, I, c. 3, n. 10, p. 9: «Non potest igitur finitus intellectus rerum veritatem per similitudinem praecise attingere. Veritas enim non est nec plus nec minus, in quodam indivisibili consistens, quam omne non ipsum verum existens praecise mensurare non potest, sicut nec circulum, cuius esse in quodam indivisibili consistit, non-circulus. Intellectus igitur qui non est veritas numquam veritatem adeo praecise comprehendit, quin per infinitum praecisius comprehendi possit»;*De theol. compl.*, h X/2a, n. 3, p. 15: «Est igitur veritas infinitas. Solum enim infinitas non potest esse maior nec minor»; *De coni.*, h III, I, prologus, n. 2, p. 4: «Quoniam autem in prioribus Doctae ignorantiae libellis multo quidem altius limpidiusque quam ego ipse nisu meo praecisionem veritatis inattingibilem intuitus es, consequens est omnem humanam veri positivam assertionem esse coniecturam»; *De coni.*, h III, I, prologus, n. 2, p. 4: «Cognoscitur igitur inattingibilis veritatis unitas alteritate coniecturali atque ipsa alteritatis coniectura in simplicissima veritatis unitate»; *De coni.*, h III, I, c. 11, n. 57, p. 58: «Coniectura igitur est positiva assertio, in alteritate veritatem, uti est, participans».

327 Cf. T. Leinkauf, *Nicolaus Cusanus. Eine Einführung*, cit., pp. 29-118.

328 Cf. *De mente*, h V, c. 4, n. 74, p. 113: «Attende aliam esse imaginem, aliam explicationem». Cf. *De mente*, h V, c. 4, n. 76, p. 116: «Philosophus: Videtur quod sola mens sit Dei imago. Idiota: Proprie ita est, quoniam omnia, quae post mentem sunt, non sunt Dei imago nisi inquantum in ipsis mens ipsa relucet, sicut plus relucet in perfectis animalibus quam imperfectis et plus in sensibilibus quam vegetabilibus, et plus in vegetabilibus quam mineralibus. Unde creaturae mente carentes sunt potius divinae simplicitatis explicationes quam imagines, licet secundum relucentiam mentalis imaginis in explicando de imagine varie participent»;*Comp.*, h XI/3, c. 8, n. 23, p. 19: «Et hinc in se reperit primum et propinquius signum conditoris, in quo vis creativa plus quam in aliquo alio noto animali relucet»; Cf. *De fil.*, h IV, c. 6, n. 86, p. 62: «Intellectus autem cum sit intellectualis viva dei similitudo, omnia in se uno cognoscit, dum se cognoscit»; *De mente*, h V, c. 7, n. 106, pp. 158-159: «Utitur autem hoc altissimo modo mens se ipsa, ut ipsa est dei imago; et deus, qui est omnia, in ea relucet, scilicet quando ut viva imago Dei ad exemplar suum se omni conatu assimilando convertit». Cf. also *De coni.*, h III, I, c. 1, n. 5, p. 7; *De fil.*, h IV, c. 6, n. 86, p. 62.

universe is no longer the earth, but the mind as God's living image in its creative power with regard to the world of knowledge. According to a *Leitmotiv* in the cardinal's thought, in the same way as God creates the world of being and the real entities, so man produces the world of knowledge and the entities that are part of it, in the image of the divine creation and the created being[329].

It is only in the view of these fundamental moments of Cusanus' philosophy that it is possible to re-examine the *De pace fidei* to understand its contribution to a philosophy of interfaith and intercultural dialogue. Cusanus identifies the origin of idolatry and the dangerous outcomes it may lead to with a reasoning that is narrowed down within the limits of the law of non-contradiction and the finite that absolutises itself by denying the transcendence of God and truth. The contradiction underlined at the beginning of this piece – that between the universality of the solution proposed and the particularity of the point of view used, between Christianity as one among the other religious creeds and the central position taken on by its representatives – reveals the contradictory nature intrinsic in Cusanus' thought, a contradiction Cusanus himself does not seek to solve because it is contradictory only at the level of finite discursive reasoning, but not at the higher level, that of intellect.

The cardinal goes beyond the Aristotelian-Scholastic model, which seeks to avoid contradiction at all costs and tries to confine the law of non-contradiction within the limits of the cognitive power it serves, the *ratio*, showing the ulteriority of the *intellectus* and its *visio*. What limits the two interpretations mentioned above is that they tone down the contradiction intrinsic in *De pace fide* instead of thematising it. It is definitely not to embellish the tale that the story opens with the intellectual abduction of the narrator who is caught up to an intellectual

[329] Cf. *De coni.*, h III, I, c. 1, n. 5, p. 7: «Coniecturas a mente nostra, uti realis mundus a divina infinita ratione, prodire oportet. Dum enim humana mens, alta dei similitudo, fecunditatem creatricis naturae, ut potest, participat, ex se ipsa, ut imagine omnipotentis formae, in realium entium similitudine rationalia exserit. Coniecturalis itaque mundi humana mens forma exstitit uti realis divina»; *De mente*, h V, c. 3, n. 72, p. 109: «Conceptio divinae mentis est rerum productio; conceptio nostrae mentis est rerum notio»; Cf. *De mente*, h V, c. 5, n. 85, p. 127: «Philosophus: Unde habet mens iudicium illud, quoniam de omnibus iudicium facere videtur? Idiota: Habet ex eo, quia est imago exemplaris omnium: Deus enim est omnium exemplar»; *De mente*, h V, c. 5, n. 81, p. 123: «Unde, quia mens est quoddam divinum semen sua vi complicans omnium rerum exemplaria notionaliter, tunc a Deo, a quo hanc vim habet, eo ipso, quod esse recepit, est simul et in convenienti terra locatum, ubi fructum facere possit, et ex se rerum universitatem notionaliter explicare»; *De beryl.*, h XI, n. 7, p. 9: «Nam sicut Deus est creator entium realium et naturalium formarum, ita homo rationalium entium et formarum artificialium, quae non sunt nisi sui intellectus similitudines sicut creaturae dei divini intellectus similitudines»; *De ludo*,h IX, II, n. 80, p. 98: «Deus vis est creativa, secundum quam virtutem facit omnia veraciter esse id quod sunt, quoniam ipse est entitas entium. Mens nostra vis est notionalis, secundum quam virtutem facit omnia notionaliter esse».

height where a *vision* opens up in front of him, a vision whose contents have been reported as far as *memory* may allow him, in order for them to be *communicated* to others. The elements mentioned – the vision, the memory and communication – recall two different cognitive fields, namely the *intellectus* and the *ratio*. Nicholas of Cusa presents the text as a vision he has transcribed based on his memory and within its limits which he wanted to render in a discursive and communicative way[330]. According to one of the philosopher's *leitmotifs*, it is only in the world of *ratio*, in discursive reason – which uses the law of non-contradiction as fundamental criterion of truth – that something that appears contradictory, whilst in the world of *intellectus* it is not so.

The *De pace fidei*'s very genre, dialogue, is essential for understanding Cusanus' speculative proposal. Not only does it report the philosophical contents of the work, but *is* also part of them. Significantly, the German thinker does not elaborate a theory of dialogue, he does not write a theoretical essay but presents a real dialogue. Therefore it is not a question of transcending one's historical situation, religious and cultural background, but of living it in terms of one's own perspective on reality, constantly deepening one's knowledge, until it is an unlimited openness towards dialogue. Dialogue can only be achieved when it originates from a concrete and resolute position. If every statement is a hypothesis, if every view always holds a certain position, if we are only one of the various single mirrors which reflect the one and only truth, then Cusanus' conclusion cannot be absolute and impersonal. He does not elaborate an objective and universal theory of interfaith dialogue but, by imagining a dialogue with the other creed, he searches for an answer from his own personal religious perspective, thus seeking the answer from Christianity, his own faith. Cusanus' perspective, therefore, is the Christian answer to interfaith dialogue. The addressees of his work are Christians whom he addresses in order to identify another different solution rather than that of the Crusade invoked by his contemporaries to stop the dramatic clash with the Islamic world.

The centrality of Christianity, the centrality of its highest representatives, is justified by the conjecturality, the contraction, the historicity, the particularity and the singularity of every attempt to give an answer. Every attempt to solve the problem of religious pluralism and the dialogue between different cultures and

330 Cf. *De pace*, h VII, c. 1, n. 1, pp. 3-4: «Accidit ut post dies aliquot, forte ex diuturna continuata meditatione, visio quaedam eidem zeloso manifestaretur, ex qua elicuit quod paucorum sapientum omnium talium diversitatum quae in religionibus per orbem observantur peritia pollentium unam posse facilem quandam concordantiam reperiri, ac per eam in religione perpetuam pacem convenienti ac veraci medio constitui. Unde, ut haec visio ad notitiam eorum qui hiis maximis praesunt aliquando deveniret, eam quantum memoria praesentabat, plane subter conscripsit».

religions is an attempt set within a particular conjectural perspective, a finite one. However, it is exactly in its contraction, historicity, particularity that Cusanus' proposal reveals its universal meaning, showing the universality of every answer's particular condition. Cusanus' search, since it is a deep analysis of a potential Christian way to dialogue, reveals how interfaith and intrafaith dialogue penetrate each other in a circularity, opening up to an ulteriority of sense. The encounter with the other stimulates us to deepen our individual and personal views as well as our religious, cultural and personal perspective, which can provide reasons for the dialogue to take place.

In order to illustrate this passage it is useful to recall the experiment of the all-seeing portrait, the image of the divine face, illustrated by Cusanus in his *De visione Dei.* In this speculative masterpiece – rarely and delicately beautiful, and with a mystical afflatus – which was written shortly after the *De pace fidei*, Cusanus proposes an experiment to the addressees of the text – the Tegernsee monks. Along with the manuscript of his work the Cardinal sends them a painting which represents an all-seeing man, who seems to be staring at all his observers at the same time. This man is used as a metaphor for God's image. First, the monks should hang the portrait on the wall towards the North, then all sit around it and look at it from different angles. While gazing at the portrait, they would experience the fact that the face stares at them so intensely that it does not seem possible that it might be looking in other directions at the same time. Even when one of the monks moved and changed his position, the portrait would keep following his moving without abandoning the other ones' staring, and still the person moving would feel as if he were the only one being looked at[331]. The only way that each one of the monks would know that the portrait is gazing at him and at others at the same time may only be achieved by means of dialogue, while asking each other and trusting each other[332].

Understanding that the divine gaze never abandons anyone, but follows everybody at the same time and in every direction they are moving, observing exclusively and contemporarily each and everyone, thus experiencing the infinity of truth can only be achieved through dialogue, by turning to the others and opening up to them. It is only in openness while in contact with each other with attention, faith and dialogue will it be possible to grasp the truth in its infinite-

331 *De vis.*, h VI, *praef.*, n. 4, p. 6: «Et dum attenderit quomodo visus ille nullum deserit, videt, quod ita diligenter curam agit cuiuslibet quasi de solo eo, qui experitur se videri, et nullo alio curet, adeo quod etiam concipi nequeat per unum, quem respicit, quod curam alterius agat».

332 Cf. *De vis.*, praef., n. 3, p. 6:«Et dum hoc experiri volens fecerit confratrem intuendo eiconam, transire de oriente ad occasum, quando ipse de occasu pergit ad orientem, et interrogaverit obviantem si continue secum visus eiconae volvatur, et audierit similiter opposito modo moveri, credet ei, et nisi crederet, non caperet hoc possibile».

ness and inexhaustibility, its otherness with respect to every finite and contracted perspective and to every historically and personally determined position or point of view. Considering oneself the only depositary of truth and of God's revelation is an ever-impending danger intrinsic in every finite position, thus always risking refuting one's finiteness by making it absolute. The encounter with the other increases our awareness of the singularity of every concern and expression of truth and – through dialogue, collaboration and attention towards the other – it helps us grasp the transcendence and infinity of truth, the possibility of many relationships with the divine truth, in which this truth in its ulteriority that needs to be constantly found is present simultaneously in each and every one with infinite love. We are driven from interpersonal and interfaith dialogue to intrapersonal and intrafaith dialogue, and then, in a roundabout manner back from intrafaith and intrapersonal dialogue to interfaith and interpersonal dialogue. It is a non-necessary but free dialectic,which requires our concern and our trust towards each other in a close analysis of the ulteriority of truth, always transcending but always exceeding such circularity too.

> Quisque enim intellectualis spiritus videt in te deo meo aliquid, quod nisi aliis revelaretur, non attingerent te deum suum meliori quo fieri posset modo. Revelant sibi mutuo secreta sua amoris pleni spiritus et augetur ex hoc cognitio amati et desiderium ad ipsum et gaudii dulcedo inardescit[333].

Interfaith and interpersonal dialogue is not a secondary and extrinsic element with regard to the possession of the truth of faith, aiming simply at avoiding conflict and favouring peaceful coexistence. Rather it is an essential moment of faith itself and of the search for divine truth. A fundamental step towards the investigation of one's faith as well as a personal and religious perspective. According to Cusanus' speculative proposal, dialogue between religions is not a necessity based only on practical reasons – as urgent and serious as they might be including bringing peace to earth – but its necessity, to which only man can respond, is rooted in the transcendence of truth, the infiniteness and freedom of God, and in the mystery and the ulteriority of his revelation.

The infinity and freedom of God and truth require a never-ending search which coincides with dialogue. For it is the continuous investigation of the singular personal and religious perspectives regarding infinite divine transcendence and an investigation of one's understanding of the infinite truth and its particular expression that an improvement is possible only through the dialogical encounter with other's, both singular and finite, personal and religious perspectives on the

[333] *De vis.*, h VI, c. 25, n. 117, p. 88.

inexhaustible truth. From Cusanus' viewpoint truth-bearing, cognitive and religious perspectivism has dialogue as its direct outcome. It is its very truth-bearing aspect that establishes the positive possibility and necessity of dialogue between different perspectives, for it is an exploration of one's own position and of the ever-ulterior truth.

Cusanus' proposal of dialogue is based on the double register that denotes his thought. On the one hand the negative register, according to which God's transcendence and unobjectability lay the foundations for dialogue among different positions as a common search for the divine that is always ulterior, since none of these positions is his precise expression, and on the other hand the positive register, according to which the variety of expressions of God who, as infinite and inextinguishable, is expressed and revealed in individual ways by each particular position and therefore is an encouragement towards dialogue as the way of understanding its singularly and uniquely revealed truth. In order to establish interfaith and intercultural dialogue, Cusanus wisely combines both the negative dimension of the hidden God, and the positive dimension of the plurality and variety of religious creeds. Both aspects – the ulteriority of God and the plurality of his expressions – combine to create peace based on faith. Dialogue is not accidental in the search for peaceful coexistence between different religions, but rather it is an essential moment in the search and investigation of the divine truth and in one's personal and common faith and religious perspective.

According to the *De pace fidei* peace will only be achieved through the evidence of the existence of a single faith, although it is expressed in a variety of confessions and religious creeds. It is not a question of persuading people to accept a faith that is different from the one they have always believed in. Rather it is a question of finding the one and only faith required everywhere. His proposal of a form of peace arising from faith is based on the idea that beyond every human attempt – both positive and historically finite – to think of, worship or give name to a divinity there is a negative dimension made of mystery and ultimate transcendence appertaining to God for he is infinite—the faith in the hidden God (*Deus absconditus*), which every religion safeguards against its turning into idolatry.

> Tu ergo, qui es dator vitae et esse, es ille qui in diversis ritibus differenter quaeri videris et in diversis nominibus nominaris, quoniam uti es manes omnibus incognitus et ineffabilis. Non enim qui infinita virtus es, aliquod eorum es quae creasti, nec potest creatura infinitatis tuae conceptum comprehendere, cum finiti ad infinitum nulla sit proportio[334].

[334] *De pace*, h VII, c. 1, n. 5, pp. 6-7.

Cusanus does not seek to deny the various historical and finite forms by which the divinity is expressed, conceived or worshipped in order to favour a non-temporal, indifferentiated faith in the hidden God. Instead he seeks to reconstruct the original dimension of mystery, ineffability and obscurity that is always preserved in every positive form of ritual. It is not about removing or overcoming single beliefs and religious traditions by branding them as wrong or inappropriate, but remembering their historical and human formation and understanding that it is starting from this finiteness and historicity that they might become the revelation of divine transcendence. It is about renewing that dimension of transcendence that lives inseparably yet unmistakably in each single and authentic positive expression of God and in each religious ritual. The aim is to reacquire awareness of the ulteriority – which is not outward appearance – of God, the consciousness that he is beyond every possible experience or manifestation, although he is in each and every one of them at the same time, in relation with each authentic expression of veneration or acceptance of the divinity. As already argued, that very plurality and historicity of religious rituals is the outcome of the divine will, as it is God who freely sends prophets and guides to humanity at different times in history.

> Deus, ut creator, est trinus et unus; ut infinitus, nec trinus nec unus nec quicquam eorum quae dici possunt. Nam nomina quae Deo attribuuntur, sumuntur a creaturis, cum ipse sit in se ineffabilis et super omne quod nominari aut dici posset[335].

It is not even possible to argue that God is triune, because he even goes beyond the concept of Trinity itself as well as that of One and that of infinity—they are all just names, therefore finite and imprecise. God is beyond every possible determination, beyond every expression words try to state and manifest. The very concept of truth is nothing but one of the options God may choose in order to manifest himself and communicate himself to men. According to the mystical and teleologic-negative tradition re-elaborated by the German thinker, the hidden God is beyond every possible positive determination which the various religious traditions ascribe to the divine, even beyond the Trinity – one of the fundamental dogmas of Christianity.

Clearly this does not imply that the Cardinal denies his belief in the Holy Trinity, as well as in the other positive expressions of his and the other religious creeds. Rather it means that he wants to restore the original mysterious dimension of cults, the one related to the divine transcendence that resides in each single authentic confession or religious creed. It regards a mystical dimension which – starting from the positive, historical expressions of Christianity – the Cardinal

[335] *De pace*, h VII, c. 7, n. 21, p. 20.

wants to show as approachable not only within Christianity but also within every religious expression which must preserve the difference between the human and the divine, as well as the transcendence of the latter. It is not a question of removing differences and diversities but of finding the intimate and essential faith in divine transcendence and God's mystery which every religion presupposes.

Cusanus' position regarding the dialogue between the various religions represents a different declination of the same idea which relates to the relationship between the One and many, the truth and its expressions – applied, in this case, to the relationship between God and the other religious confessions. The plurality or large number of cults positive expressions of the divine meaning is possible on the basis of their intimate and constitutive relation with faith in that mystical dimension of mystery which, on the one hand, makes them possible and, on the other hand, allows the hidden God to reveal himself as the unintelligible, obscure, infinite and ulterior face of the divine, present in every positive affirmation of him. It is a truth that is inseparable from its expressions, but at the same time it cannot be confused with them.

> Nam quod dicendum est, convenienter exprimi nequit. Hinc multiplicatio sermonum perutilis est[336].

Such synthetic affirmation is significant in Cusanus' method since it is not possible to convey God or the truth through any way of expressing them, for they are always finite and contracted. It is useful to multiply them in order to better prove their infinity. The variety of religious cults is not a limit and does not come with a negative value, but with a positive one, since it represents a manifestation of God's intelligibility and transcendence, as well as the best way man has to understand and prove his infinity. The negative moment, the transcendence, the ulteriority of God with respect to every negative determination, his infinity, provides a chance to move towards the positive moment, to the pluralisation of the forms of expression of truth and the divine. Although God transcends every affirmation, he never denies himself from enunciation, but he himself claims it and creates it, at the same time showing its limit, because it is in this relationship that his ulteriority is revealed. Therefore the plurality of positive expressions and of religious cults finds its foundation in God's transcendence. Although he is always revealed as ulterior, infinite and to be found, God inspires an inextinguishable search for new ways of expressing his mystery.

Again, it is all about a declination of the particular dialectic between the One and the many, the truth and the various perspectives elaborated by the Cardi-

[336] *De mente*, h V, c. 4, n. 74, p. 113.

nal. Like the plurality of the many and the contractions of the One and of the creatures, also the variety of rituals and religious cults and the multiplicity of the divine names express God's infinity, inexhaustibility and unobjectability.

> Sed immultiplicabilis infinitas in varia receptione melius explicatur, magna enim diversitas immultiplicabilitatem melius exprimit[337].

Not only does multiplicity not contrast with unity, but it is the best expression of infinity in the world of the finite.

> Sed quia unus est pater et fons luminum, tunc omnia sunt apparitiones unius dei, qui, etsi sit unus, non potesttamen nisi in varietate apparere. Quomodo enim infinita virtus aliter quam in varietate apparere posset?[338].

The variety of single individuals does not contrast with the oneness of the One in any way, but represents its best image and expression. In the same way the singularity of all things represents the most suitable image of God's absolute singularity, so the plurality or multiplicity of his explanations represents the best way to express his infinity, unobjectability and inexhaustibility. The plurality and variety of the world originate from the One's overabundance and opulence, and are sign and revelation of his infinity. According to an analogy – again imprecise – operated in *De visione Dei*, just as a painter uses different colours to portray himself and to have an image of himself, so God, being one, non-multipliable and indivisible, produces many portraits, because the best way his infinite power can reveal itself is in multiplicity[339]. Indeed, since the One is single and unitary and cannot be either multiplied or divided, so his manifestation best reveals his non-multipliability and absoluteness.

Just as the ability to know something is more likely to be achieved through the use of all the five senses rather than through two of them, in the same way - for no creature can be God's perfect and precise expression, because it only manifests itself in a contracted way - multiplying or plurifying the signs makes a better knowledge of God possible. The very aim of such manifestation through a variety of theophanies is the revelation of God: visible things only exist in order for man to see God in them, and to exhort man to approach Him. Thus man is enlightened by the variety of creatures and this *varietas* exhorts him to turn to the transcendent and infinite light that constitutes the essence of creatures.

337 *De sap.*, I, c. 25, n. 52, pp. 10-11.

338 *De dato*, h IV, c. 4, n. 108, pp. 79-80.

339 *De vis.*, h VI, c. 25, n. 116-117, p. 88: «Cum ipse unus sit immultiplicabilis saltem, modo quo fieri potest, in propinquissima similitudine multiplicetur. Multas autem figuras facit, quia virtutis suae infinitae similitudo non potest nisi in multis perfectiori modo explicari».

As in the sphere of knowledge the plurality of conjectures does not deny the uniqueness of truth and in the metaphysical and ontological spheres the plurality of the many does not deny the uniqueness of the One, so in the same way, from a theological-religious point of view the variety of rituals and of confessions does not deny or contradict the one God, but reveals his incommensurability and his inextinguishable power. Not only is the multiplicity of religious cults legitimated, but it also acquires an essential positive value for it is manifestation and evidence of the revelation of God's infinity as well as his transcendence. This is why the variety of rituals can increase devotion.

> Augebitur etiam fortassis devotio ex quadam diversitate, quando quaelibet natio conabitur ritum suum studio et diligentia splendidiorem efficere, ut aliam in hoc vincat et sic meritum maius assequatur apud deum et laudem in mundo[340].

The positive evaluation of variety and plurality allows the Cardinal to elaborate a proposal to solve the religious conflicts which does not aim to eliminate the differences among the various religious confessions, but seeks to investigate those differences with what might be addressed as a "competition" – a definitely pacific one – among the different religions in order for them to foster their specific and particular rites so that they can achieve God's approval in the eyes of the world.

The solution to religious conflict lies in the comprehension of the positive value of religious pluralism for not only can it increase devotion, but it can also represent a source of wealth through dialogue for deepening one's understanding of the divine and of truth.

> Et sunt omnes intellectuales spiritus cuilibet spiritui opportuni. Nam nisi forent innumerabiles, non posses tu, deus infinitus, meliori modo cognosci. Quisque enim intellectualis spiritus videt in te deo meo aliquid, quod nisi aliis revelaretur, non attingerent te deum suum meliori quo fieri posset modo. Revelant sibi mutuo secreta sua amoris pleni spiritus et augeturex hoc cognitio amati et desiderium ad ipsum et gaudii dulcedo inardescit[341].

It is not possible to read these passages from the *De visione Dei* and forget that it was written only few months after the *De pace fidei*, or that there is a relationship between the Cardinal's words and the multiplicity of religions. Cusanus strongly affirms the positive value of the plurality of knowers thought of not only as single subjects but also as plural subjects, hence as people and religious communities.

340 *De pace*, h VII, c. 19, n. 67, p. 62.
341 *De vis.*, h VI, c. 25, n. 117, p. 88.

The positivity of pluralism of knowing subjects and of religions is founded in the infinity of truth or God. It is because God and truth are infinite that such plurality acquires a positive value as a more adequate expression of them or the best way by which they can be known. If God, in his inexhaustibility and freedom reveals himself in the ever-plural singularity of the diverse religious perspectives, that very finite freedom to embrace his revelation is the object to which to turn. For only by having a dialogue with it will it be possible to understand the divine truth in its specific and unique free self-revelation to that finite freedom. At the basis of a possible positive evaluation of the plurality of religious rituals there lies Cusanus' view of the relation between the One and the many, according to which not only does the One reveal himself in the many as infinite and the many are always conjectural expressions of the One, but the theophanic element is the singularity of each finite being that acquires a value of its own because it is finite and singular, unrepeatable and the One's only expression. Therefore, not only is the plurality of confessions and cults legitimated by the very transcendence and divine infinity and is not a negative limit of faith and peace, but the variety of rituals becomes a potential source of wealth from a cognitive and religious point of view, an intranscendible moment of the investigation of one's own religious perspective.

The *De pace fidei* does not seek to provide a speculative basis for Christianity's claim to possess the one and only truth and divine revelation; rather it seeks to identify a Christian way towards interfaith dialogue which can drive a vision of Christianity forward as a space of legitimisation and encounter among the various religious confessions as signs that lead to the same truth of faith in one God. A potential universalistic meaning of Christianity also emerges as a message that gives space to the plurality of the religions and confessions in that they are one of the multiple manifestations of the same human experience of God, of the only search, relation and prayer for him. A vision of Christianity as an identification of the value of the various finite human expressions of the ever-transcending God, which can serve to legitimate every experience and single interpretation of the inexhaustibility of the only *veritas semper indaganda*, and potential space for dialogue between different expressions of the transcendental experience and the infinity of truth and God.

The formulation that probably best expresses Cusanus' position with regards to interpersonal, as well as interfaith and intercultural dialogue is the one he chose as a title for his work, namely *De pace fidei*, *On the Peace of Faith*. Indeed, in the various manuscripts of the work there are different variations of its title – a sign that the work was received in various ways even by the copyists themselves – among the titles, *De unitate fidei et sanctarum [sic] diversitate in unum reducenda*, *De concordia religionum*, *De pace et concordia unice fidei*, *De pace seu concordia fidei*[342]. However, in a letter to John of Segovia in which he presents his work to the theologian, Cusanus himself calls it *De pace fidei*, thus leaving no room for doubt[343].

The expression "peace of faith" provides an explanation for Cusanus' position, emphasizing that there is a constitutive duality in his proposal. First of all, peace originates from faith, or faith makes peace possible because it is only through faith towards the Other – who is so 'other' that he becomes 'not-other' – towards the infinite and inextinguishable God that a dialogue between different religious, cultural and personal perspectives can be achieved. Without any faith that can transcend the single finite positions no kind of dialogue would be possible, for truth should lie either in one of them – meaning the others can only be brought back to it even in violent ways – or there would be no truth at all, and free will would then reign, together with it violence. At the same time having faith in other people lets the law of non-contradiction be surpassed and prevents us from getting embedded in the *principium firmissimum*, both of which are obstacles to understanding the truth in the Other and also in the others. It is only by having faith and believing in what the other presents to us as the truth, by relying on the other, by abandoning habitual and rational certainties and risking betrayal that we are able to understand even what it might not be possible to know just through the perspective of our reason. However Cusanus is not inviting us to abandon reason supported by the law of non-contradiction, but he incites us to recognize it as one of the possible cognitive sources. Moreover, he is not suggesting that we deny the path of knowledge, but that we enrich and investigate it thoroughly and open up to a form of knowledge that may let us hear and comprehend the voice of the Other and to discuss with the others. All this should be achieved by accepting one's rationality, which is not negated in its validity to draw reality, but confined within its own limits and led back to its own finiteness by avoiding the risk and the danger of any absolutisation.

342 Cf. *De pace*, h VII, p. 3, note 1.

343 *Epistula ad Ioannem de Segobia*, II, in *De pace*, h VII, p. 97

3. Cusanus and Religious Tolerance

Among the works of Cusanus the *De pace fidei* met with considerable fortune.[344] The reasons for such fortune certainly include the theme, namely peaceful coexistence among different religions, which is currently being imposed at the heart of cultural debate in modern Europe. Its uniqueness stems from its being an almost isolated example of works on this theme coming down from that age. Unlike the apologetic and anti-Islamic ones both previous and coeval, this work was not prompted by a desire to denigrate or demonize the prophet Mohammed.[345]If the previous works dedicated to the dialogue between religions were mostly characterized by the emphasis on rhetoric, moral and intellectual inferiority, and by the humiliating debasement of the interlocutors who were stigmatised as infidels, Cusanus was amongst the first – an extraordinarily rare and precious exception perhaps only together with Raimondo Llull, Marsilio Ficino and Pico della Mirandola – not only to recognize the value of other religions but also to identify a source of richness in religious pluralism.

In the fifteenth century, a summary of the *De pace fidei* could be found under the title *theologia variorum sectarum consona* in the *Centheologicon* by the Dominican theologian and Dean of the University of Leuven, Heymeric de Campo.[346] The work was also known to the Spanish John of Segovia – sent to him by the Cardinal himself. The Iberian theologian had a rich epistolary exchange with Cusanus concerning the Turkish question and the attempt to find the speculative bases towards a possible dialogue with Muslim and the other religions.[347] However, if they were both consonant with the fact that the conflict with the Muslims which had flared

[344] On the history of the reception of the work cf. R. Klibansky - H. Bascour, *Praefatio editorum*, in *De pace*, h VII, pp. XL-XLV; R. Klibansky, *Die Wirkungsgeschichte des Dialogs* De pace fidei, in «MFCG», 16 (1984), pp. 113-125.

[345] Cf. Ó. De la Cruz Palma, *Alcuni argomenti nella polmeica antiislamica di Raimondo Lullo e Niccoló Cusano*, in *Ramon Llull und Nikolaus von Kues: Eine Begegnung im Zeichen der Toleranz – Raimondo Lullo e Niccolò Cusano: un incontro nel segno della tolleranza*, eds. E. Bidese - A. Fidora - P. Renner, Brepols, Turnhout 2005, pp. 25-40.

[346] Cf. R. Imbach, *Einheit des Glaubens. Spuren des Cusanischen Dialogs De pace fidei bei Heymericus de Campo*, in «Freiburger Zeitschrift für Philosophie und Theologie», 27 (1980), pp. 5-23

[347] Cf. R. Klibansky, *Die Wirkungsgeschichte des Dialogs 'De pace fidei'*, cit., pp. 113-114; See the important epistle from Cusanus to Segovia; cf. *Epistula ad Ioannem de Segobia*, in *De pace*, h VII, pp. 93-101. On the theme, cf. R. Haubst, *Johannes von Segovia im Gespräch mit Nikolaus von Kues und Jean Germain über die göttliche Dreieinigkeit und ihre Verkündigung vor den Mohammedanern*, in «Münchener Theologische Zeitschrift», 2 (1951), pp. 115-129; A. Alvarez-Gómez, *Über die Bedingungen des Friedens im Glauben bei Johannes von Segovia und Nikolaus von Kues*, Trier 2003; W. A. Euler – F.-B. Stammkötter, *Johannes von Segovia und Nikolaus von Kues im Gespräch mit dem Islam*, in *Cusanus und der Islam*, cit., pp. 49-64; W. A. Euler, *L'image de l'Islam*

up again after the siege of Constantinople had to be resolved not through armed warfare but by word, their interpretation of the Muslim religion proved a totally different matter. For the German thinker, despite essentially agreeing with Islam, it was a misunderstanding and heresy against the Gospel, whereas for the Spanish thinker it was an "Epicurean" religion and hence the naturalistic negation of Christianity.[348] Another Spanish thinker to be numbered among the connoisseurs of Cusanus' works, Juan de Torquemada, uses the *De pace fidei* incorporating it verbatim, though without ever mentioning its title, in at least two chapters of his *Defensiorum fidei contra Iudaeos, haereticos et Sarracenos.* Cusanus' text thence doubtlessly had an influence on Pius II, who was a close friend of his and who held Cusanus in high esteem, especially in his famous *Epistola ad Mahumetum II*,[349]in which he asked the sultan to convert to Christianity.

One of the key points in the studies of the fortune of the dialogue has always been the discussion on its possible influence on Italian humanism. The debate regarding the fortune of the work and more generally on Cusanus' thinking in this cultural context is still open, and we are far from reaching definitive conclusions. Ernst Cassirer was the first to defend the thesis of a decisive influence of Cusanus' thinking and of the *De pace fidei* on Italian humanists.[350] Basing himself on the studies by Pierre Duhem on the relationship between Cusanus and Leonardo da Vinci[351], the German philosopher reached conclusions that, examined on the basis of historical and philological documents, these conclusions appear excessively enthusiastic and optimistic. From the outset Eugenio Garin took a stand against Cassirer's

à la fin du Moyen âge: La correspondance entre Jean de Ségovie et Nicolas de Cues, in *Nicolas de Cues et l'Islam*, cit., pp. 9-20.

348 Cf. L. D'Ascia, *Il Corano e la Tiara. L'epistola a Maometto II di Enea Silvio Piccolomini (papa Pio II)*, Pendragon, Bologna 2001, pp. 28-19.

349 Cf. L. D'Ascia, *Il Corano e la Tiara. L'epistola a Maometto II di Enea Silvio Piccolomini (papa Pio II)*, cit., pp. 104-128. For the letter cf. Pius II, Papa (Aeneas Sylvius Piccolomineus), *Epistola ad Mahumetem*, eds. R. Glei – M. Köhler, WVT, Trier 2001.Cf. On the theme R. Glei, *Pius Aeneas und der Islam. Der Brief des Papstes an den Eroberer Konstantinopels*, in *Religiöse Kommunikation - Formen und Praxis vor der Neuzeit*, eds. G. Binder - K. Ehlich, WVT, Trier 1997, pp. 301-325; J. Helmrath, *Wege des Humanismus*, Mohr, Tübingen 2013, pp. 279-342.

350 Cf. E. Cassirer, *Individuum und Kosmos in der Philosophie der Renaissance*,eds. F. Plaga - C. Rosenkranz, in Id., *Gesammelte Werke. Hamburger Ausgabe*, XIV, Meiner, Hamburg 2002, pp. 54-84. On Cassirer's reading cf. K. Zeyer, *Cusanus in Marburg*, Aschendorff, Münster 2015, pp. 237-344. Cf. moreover G. Saitta, *Niccolò Cusano e l'umanesimo italiano*, Tamari, Bologna 1957. Giuseppe Saitta's studies too are based on positions which are perhaps 'too optimistic regarding the possibility of identifying a determinig influence by Cusanus' on Humanism.

351 Cf. P. Duhem, *Nicolas de Cues et Léonard de Vinci*, in Id., Études sur Léonard de Vinci, II, Hermann, Paris 1909, pp. 97-279. On the theme cf. also F. Fiorentino, *Il Risorgimento filosofico nel Quattrocento*, Tip. della Regia università, Napoli 1885 (rist. Forni, Bologna 1982), pp. 83-176.

position.[352] The famous Italian historian of philosophy in fact expressed himself negatively, rejecting support for a possible influence of Cusanus on the Italian thinkers of the Italian fifteenth century. As further confirmation, Garin indicated the lack of historical evidence to support Cassirer's thesis on the one hand, and the complete non-involvement of Cusanus in the problems and the spirit of Italian Platonic and Humanistic Renaissance on the other. Today, thanks to new philological data and in view of new and more detailed studies, there is a tendency to prefer more balanced and moderate positions, tracing some of the elements that might suggest a circulation of Cusanus' ideas in the Italian context, but without necessarily defining precise influences or dependencies.[353]And this, pending new studies to verify or disprove the debated hermeneutic options. Cesare Vasoli has distinguished himself by recalling scholars' attention to the fact that the verification of the relationships between Cusanus and the Italian humanistic world remains an open problem still awaiting a solution. He emphasises how important it is to examine this point in order to retrace the history of the rebirth of Platonism and other philosophical and religious aspects of the late fifteenth century, which remain hitherto almost unexplored. Such studies, according to the Italian scholar, more than establishing dependencies or successions, should aim towards demonstrating assured connections and relationships that are well enough verified to recreate the thick network of connections and links, exchanges of interest and intellectual solicitations that might have spread Cusanus' thinking among the personalities and societies of that age.[354]

352 E. Garin, *Cusano e i Platonici italiani del Quattrocento*, in *Nicolò da Cusa in Nicolò da Cusa. Relazioni tenute al Convegno Interuniversitario di Bressanone nel 1960*, cit., pp. 75-100. Also has minimized Cusanus' influence on humanism M. Seidlmayer, *Nicolaus von Cues und der Humanism*, in *Humanismus, Mystik und Kunst in der Welt des Mittelalters*, by J. Koch, Brill, Leiden 1959, pp. 1-38.

353 Cf. K. Flasch, *Nikolaus von Kues und Pico della Mirandola*, in «MFCG», 14 (1980), pp. 113-120; Id., *Cusano e gli intellettuali italiani del Quattrocento*, in *Filosofie del Rinascimento*, ed. C. Vasoli, Bruno Mondadori, Milano 2002, pp. 175-192. An interesting reconstruction of philological and historical data, which would indicate some positive data on the reception of Cusanus on the peninsula has been given ed. P. O. Kristeller, *A Latin Translation of Gemisto Plethon's De Fato by Johannes Sophianos dedicated to Nicholas of Cusa*, in *Niccolò Cusano agli inizi del mondo moderno*, cit., pp. 175-193. On the influence of Cusanus' thought on Humanistic-Renaissance and Protomodern thinking cf. also S. Meier-Oeser, *Die Präsenz des Vergessenen. Zur Rezeption der Philosophie des Nicolaus Cusanus vom 15. bis zum 18. Jahrhundert*, Aschendorff, Münster 1989;G. Gawlick, *Zur Nachwirkung cusanischer Ideen im siebzehnten und achtzehnten Jahrhundert*, in *Nicolò Cusano agli inizi del mondo moderno*, cit., pp. 225-239;H. Schnarr, *Frühe Beziehungen des Nikolaus von Kues zu italienischen Humanisten*, in *Nicolaus Cusanus zwischen Deutschland und Italien*, cit., pp. 187-213; P. R. Blum, *Nikolaus von Kues und die italienische Renaissance*, Paulinus, Trier 2015.

354 Cf. C. Vasoli, *Cusano e la cultura umanistica fiorentina*, in *Nicolaus Cusanus zwischen Deutschland und Italien*, cit., pp.75-90.

With regard to the *De Pace Fidei*, Cusanus' theoretical proposal contained in his work cannot by any means be assimilated to that of other thinkers of his time, but yet there are common elements of interest within the various perspectives. Marsilio Ficino's position, according to whom there is a unique and original revelation which is expressed in many different languages extending diachronically through an endless chain of wisdom, and which moves from the ancient oriental theologians to the Greek philosophers and Christian religion, reaching contemporaries, is certainly not akin to that of Cusanus'.[355] Likewise completely different is Pico della Mirandola's plurality of synchronically possible paths which in parallel lead man to the divine.[356] Nevertheless, viewpoints like those of Ficino or Pico della Mirandola's might show some influence from Cusanus in revealing that same tension towards *pax fidei* and in acknowledging the value of the different religious experiences as God-given. [357] Ficino, Pico and Cusanus are all inspired by the quest for common grounds and elements of proximity among the different religious confessions, particularly in the case of Islam and Christianity.[358] From a historical point of view to assess the possibility that Ficino and Pico had some knowledge of Cusanus' texts or thought, we should reconsider the role that Pierleone da Spoleto – physician to Lorenzo dei Medici – held. A close friend of both Marsilio's and Pico,'s he possessed two of the three manuscripts of the *De pace fidei* existing in Italy.[359]

As has been observed, there is a tradition of imaginary and visionary ecumenical dialogues which started with Cusanus' *De pace fidei* arriving indirectly, despite the relative differences, at the *Colloquium Heptaplomeres* by Jean Bodin (1593-

355 Su Ficino cf. T. Leinkauf, *Cusanus, Ficino, Patrizi. Formen platonischen Denkens in der Renaissance*, Trafo, Berlin 2014, pp. 123-308.

356 It is now certain that Pico possessed a summary of Cusanus'*De coniecturis*, cf. A. Tura, *Un incunabolo Grimani e due codici pichensi nella Bibliothèque Nationale di Parigi*, in «La Bibliofilia», 99 (1997), pp. 181-189.

357 On the theme cf. R. Klibansky, *Praefatio*, cit., pp. XLII-XLIII; G. Santinello, *Nicolò Cusano e l'utopia dell'unità culturale e religiosa nel Quattrocento*, in «Archivio di filosofia», 53 (1985), p. 387; H. De Lubac, *Pico della Mirandola. L'alba incompiuta del Rinascimento*, Milano 1975, pp. 311-331, 372-377; R. Celada Ballanti, *Pensiero religioso liberale. Lineamenti, figure, prospettive*, Morcelliana, Brescia 2009, pp. 125 e ff.

358 Cf. On Ficino cf. L. D'Ascia, *Il Corano e la Tiara*, cit., pp. 33-36. For both Ficino and Cusanus, rather than being members of other religions, Muslims and Christian heretics. On Pico cf. K. Flasch, *Nikolaus von Kues und Pico della Mirandola*, cit., pp. 113-120; Id., *Cusano e gli intellettuali italiani del Quattrocento*, cit., pp. 175-192.

359 Cf. C. Vasoli, *Niccolò Cusano e la cultura umanistica fiorentina*, cit., pp. 85ss. On Pierleone da Spoleto, his relationship with Ficino and Pico, Cusanus' codes and his notations cf. M. Rotzoll, *Pierleone da Spoleto. Vita e opere di un medico del Rinascimento*, Olschki, Firenze 2000; F. Bacchelli, *Giovanni Pico e Pierleone da Spoleto. Tra filosofia dell'amore e tradizione cabalistica*, Olschki, Firenze 2001.

1596) – who knows and cites Cusanus' text[360] – extended, in addition, to the dispute on his *Conclusiones Nongentae* (1486), drawn up in Rome for the epiphany of 1487 by Pico della Mirandola, but also to the *De Christiana religione* by Ficino and the *Sinodo sulla libertà di coscienza* (1582) by Dirck Coornhert.[361] On this matter we may also cite the celestial assembly of the gods convened by Jove in the *Spaccio della bestia trionfante* by Giordano Bruno, which is an almost ideal counterbalance of the Christian one by Cusanus[362]. If a certain fortune of the *De pace fidei* can be assessed in the English-speaking and French cultural environments,[363] regarding an Irenicist and Concordist vision of the relationships among different religions, another author who certainly cannot be overlooked who was thoroughly acquainted with Cusanus' work, namely Guillaume Postel, doubtlessly drew inspiration from it in drafting his *De Concordia orbis*.[364] Although from a historical and philological viewpoint we are far from a precise reconstruction of influences, one cannot get away from the fact that, from Cusanus onwards, regarding peace among religions, there is a genuine chain of dialogical and ecumenical proposals which develops, almost as a sort of philosophical genre having spread far and wide throughout those centuries.

The fourth edition of the works by the Cardinal, that of Basle of 1565, opened with a dedication of the printer-editor Henric Petri to the dean and senate of the university, in which it was said that many had pleaded with him to reprint the

360 Cf. S. Meier-Oeser, *Die Präsenz des Vergessenen. Zur Rezeption der Philosophie des Nicolaus Cusanus vom 15. bis zum 18. Jahrhundert*, cit., pp. 18, 170, 175.

361 Cf. C. Vasoli, *De Nicolas de Kues et Jean Pic de la Mirandole à Jean Bodin: trois «colloques»*, in *Jean Bodin. Actes du Colloque Interdisciplinaire d'Angers (Angers, 24-27 Mai 1984)*, 2 voll., Universitè d'Angers, Angers 1985, I, pp. 253-275; R. Celada Ballanti, *Pensiero religioso liberale*, cit., pp. 107-242. Rudolph Stadelmann links together under the banner of interreligious dialogue the *De pace fide* the *Colloquium* of Bodin, Lessing's *Nathan the Wise* and the work of Sebastian Frank; cf. R. Stadelmann, *Vom Geist des Ausgehenden Mittelalters*, Niemeyer, Tübingen 1929, pp. 89-159; 226-227. Eugenio Garin identifies in the research into religious-philosophical peace a main theme in common with the thought of Cusanus, Ficino, Pico and Erasmus; cf. E. Garin, *Erasmo*, Cultura della Pace, S. Domenico di Fiesole, 1988, pp. 7-16. Further on these themes cf. W. A. Euler, *'Pia philosophia' et 'docta religio'. Theologie und Religion bei Marsilio Ficino und Giovanni Pico della Mirandola*, Fink, München 1998; Id., *Die Religionverständnis von Cusanus und Ficino*, in *Nicolaus Cusanus zwischen Deutscheland und Italien*, cit., pp. 511-526. In addition to these names the influence of the ideas contained in the *De pace fidei* is to be closely examined in thinkers such as Thomas More, Sébastien Castellion and John Donne.

362 Cf. R. Celada Ballanti, *Pensiero religioso liberale*, cit., p. 111.

363 Cf. R. Klibansky, *Die Wirkungsgeschichte des Dialogs 'De pace fidei'*, cit., pp. 114-119; ID., *Praefatio*, cit., pp. XLII-XLIII.

364 Cf. R. Klibansky, *Die Wirkungsgeschichte des Dialogs 'De pace fidei'*, cit., p. 119; S. Meier-Oeser, *Die Präsenz des Vergessenen. Zur Rezeption der Philosophie des Nicolaus Cusanus vom 15. bis zum 18. Jahrhundert*, cit., pp. 346-347.

work of the thinker Cusanus who was committed to making the Church more peaceful and harmonious. If we connect this indication with the geographical collocation and the historical moment of this edition, namely that same Basle which was the capital of the debate on religious tolerance in the Sixteenth Century, it becomes evident under which light the Cusanus' texts were read in the Swiss city.[365] An interest in the *De pace fidei* was doubtlessly documented at that time in Germany where there had been a translation of several extracts in 1538-1539 by Johannes Kymeus, campaigner for the theses of Reform.[366] Despite being a great opponent of Cusanus, whom he saw as the supporter of the Papal cause against the Germans, Kymeus, saw in the *De pace fidei,* an anticipation of the Protestant and Lutheran doctrine of the justification by faith alone (*ex sola fide*).

However, only in 1643, during the Thirty Year's War, was there to be a complete translation of the *De pace fidei*.[367] A superficial summary of this work is present in a text of the eighteenth century by the Protestant theologian Johann Salomo Semler.[368]But for the *Wirkungsgeschichte* of this work, what is of particular interest is the fact that it aroused the attention of the important writer and philosopher of the German Enlightenment, namely Gothold Ephraim Lessing (1729-1781). During the last years of his life, Lessing made every effort to obtain a translation of it, which he commissioned Konrad Arnold Schmid to produce. As is shown in their correspondence, Schmid translated the text and sent it to Lessing asking him to correct and revise it. However, due to the death of the latter, it was never published and is now lost.[369]Another translation of this work, which in fact is an incorrect paraphrase of the text, was instead published in 1787 by Elias Kaspar Reichard with some additions by the aforementioned theologian, Semler.[370]

365 Cf. L. Perini, *Nicholas di Cusa in the mirror of his editions*, in *Nicolaus Cusanus zwischen Deutschland und Italien*, cit., pp. 289-301.

366 Cf.. J. Kymeus, *Des Babst Hercules wider die Deudschen*, ed. O. Menzel, Winter, Heidelberg 1941.

367 As we are told by Raymond Klibansky the only copy of the translation known was lost during the 1943 bombings. A photocopy is conserved in his Montreal archive. Cf. R. Klibansky, *Die Wirkungsgeschichte des Dialogs 'De pace fidei'*, cit., p. 120, note 125.

368 In the work J. S. Semler, *Versuch eines fruchtbaren Auszugs der Kirchengeschichte*, 3 voll., Hemmerde, Halle 1173-1778, II, p. 172. Cf. R. Klibansky, *Die Wirkungsgeschichte des Dialogs 'De pace fidei'*, cit., p. 122.

369 Cf. *ibid.*, pp. 122-125; Id., *Praefatio*, cit., pp. XLIV-XLV; On the theme, cf. W. A. Euler, *Il De pace fidei di Nicolò Cusano e la parabola dell'anello di Lessing*, in *Cusanus*, cit., pp. 59-74; Id., *Religionsfriede und Ringparabel. Die religionstheologischen Ideen von Cusanus und Lessing*, in «Cusanus Jahrbuch» 4 (2012), pp. 3-24.

370 Cf. R. Klibansky, *Die Wirkungsgeschichte des Dialogs 'De pace fidei'*, cit., p. 124, note 35; Id., *Praefatio*, cit. p. XLIV.

Nonetheless, it is relevant to emphasize that during the same years in which he worked on the translation of the *De pace fidei,* Lessing was also engaged in writing his *Nathan the Wise,* whose drama is actually set at the time of the Crusades in Jerusalem, city sacred to the three monotheist religions, namely Judaism, Christianity and Islam. Cusanus' text also concludes by proposing Jerusalem as common centre of religions and peace. In Lessing's work, Saladin the Sultan invites the Hebrew Nathan to indicate which of the three monotheist religions is in his opinion the truest. In reply, Nathan the wise recounts the parable of the ring.

This parable tells the story of a man who possessed a ring of great value that « has secret power in that it renders pleasing to both God and men the person who wears it and has trust in its magic charm».[371]The object was always bequeathed to the most beloved son, though, because the man had three sons and loved them equally, he was faced with the problem of having promised it to each one of them. He then had two other rings made, which were so indistinguishable that he himself could not recognize the original. Before dying, he handed each son his ring and each considered himself to be the legitimate prince of the house. The sons, who clearly represent the three great monotheist religions – in the same way the father is to be identified with God – then accuse one another of imposture and bring their case before a judge. According to the judge since the ring had the power of rendering a person loved by and agreeable to god and men, because of their behaviour, none of them possessed the real ring. The response deserves to be quoted:

> Nathan: Therefore accept things as they are. That is, if each one of you is certain that he received his ring from his father's hands, let him look on his ring as true and as authentic. It is likely that your father was no longer prepared to tolerate in his own house the tyranny of a single ring. It is certain that he loved all three of you equally. Indeed he did not wish to humiliate two of you in order to favour one. Come now! Try to imitate his incorruptible love and without prejudice! Let each one compete with the other to show in the light of day the virtue of the stone in

[371] Gotthold Ephraim Lessing, *Nathan der Weise*, in Id., *Sämtliche Werke. Unveränderter photomechanischer Abdruck der von Karl Lachmann und Franz Muncker 1886 bis 1924 herausgegebenen Ausgabe von Gotthold Ephraim Lessings sämtlichen Schriften*, vol. III, De Gruyter, Berlin 1979, p. 90. The parable of the ring does not date back to Lessing but has its sources in certain Medieval Islamic , Jewish and Christian authors, who reformulate on every occasion with different senses and meanings. It is also found in Boccaccio, especially in his famous work Dec*ameron* of 1348. However, Lessing's version differs from Boccaccio's. Cf. F. Niewöhner, *Veritas sive Varietas. Lessings Toleranzparabel und das Buch Von den drei Betrügern*, Schneider, Heidelberg 1988; K.-J. Kuschel, *"Jud, Christ und Muselmann vereinigt"? Lessings "Nathan der Weise"*, Patmos, Düsseldorf 2004; A. Aurnhammer – G. Cantaruffi – F. Vollhardt (eds.), *Die drei Ringe*, De Gruyter, Berlin 2015.

> his ring. And let him strive to aid its power with meekness, with a peaceful disposition, benevolence and heartfelt confidence in God! If then the magic of your rings appears to work in favour of your latest progeny, that is among the grand-children of their grandchildren then shall I after thousand times a thousand years not fail to summon them again before this tribunal. A wiser man than myself will sit here and speak. Go now! So spake that modest judge.[372]

The parable of the ring by Lessing, indicates a competition as solution to the question of religious differences, a completion of love and devotion, that is to say, as a challenge in the concrete religious practice. Although the differences between Cusanus and Lessing must be held constant, it is necessary to highlight the fact that the *De pace fidei* too does not aim at abolishing the differences among different religions, but aims at analysing those differences in what might be defined as a sort of peaceful competition among religions, in order to cultivate their rites carefully so as to obtain more praise from God and the world.[373]

The relationship between true religion and love, the latter identified with the only essential law truly wanted by God, is fundamental both in Cusanus and Lessing. The very same comment by Lessing that the ring had to be worn with faith for it to produce its effects means that its power of rendering loveable and pleasing to God and men is not linked to the object itself, but to the way it is worn, and the way one relates to it.

The distance of Cusanus' perspective from that of the Enlightenment has long been discussed, reaching an almost unanimous negative response.[374] As Bruno

[372] Gotthold Ephraim Lessing, *Nathan der Weise*, cit., pp. 94-95.

[373] *De pace*,h VII, c. 19, n. 67, p. 62. Cf. anche *De pace*, c. 1, n. 6, p. 7.

[374] On the differentiation between Cusanus' perspective and the modern idea of tolerance cf. B. Decker, *Die Toleranzidee bei Nikolaus von Kues und in der Neuzeit*, in *Nicolò da Cusa. Relazioni tenute al Convegno Interuniversitario di Bressanone nel 1960*, cit., pp. 197-213; K. Jaspers, *Nikolaus Cusanus*, Piper, München 1964, p. 220; M. Watanabe, *Nicholas of Cusa and the idea of tolerance*, in *Niccolò Cusano agli inizi del mondo moderno*, cit., pp. 409-418; G. Santinello, *Nicolò Cusano e l'utopia dell'unità culturale e religiosa nel Quattrocento*, in «Archivio di filosofia», 53 (1985), pp. 381-391; M. Cacciari, *Geofilosofia dell'Europa*, Adelphi, Milano 1994, pp. 149-159; M. L. Lanzillo, *Tolleranza*, Il Mulino, Bologna 2001, p. 28; A.A. Akasoy, *Zur Toleranz gegenüber dem Islam bei Lullus und Cusanus*, in *Ramon Llull und Nikolaus von Kues: Eine Begegnung im Zeichen der Toleranz – Raimondo Lullo e Niccolò Cusano: un incontro nel segno della tolleranza*, cit., pp. 105-124.For a different perspective on the theme, cf. A. Moritz, *Die Andersheit des Anderen – noch einmal zum Problem der Toleranz in Nicolaus von Kues' Dialog De pace fidei*, cit.; W. Hoye, *The Idea of Truth as the Basis for Religious Tolerance According to Nicholas of Cusa with Comparisons to Thomas Aquinas*, in *Conflict and Reconciliation. Perspectives on Nicholas of Cusa*, ed. I. Bocken, Brill, Leiden 2004, pp. 161-176; J. Decorte, *Tolerance and Trinity*, in *ibid.*, pp. 107-117; S. Gottlöber, *Das Prinzip der Relationalität: Grundzüge cusanischen Denkens als Parameter für Toleranz und interreligiösen Diskurs*, cit.; M. Watanabe, *Cusanus, Islam and Religious*

Decker has synthetically and efficaciously written, Cusanus would have been an adherent of Enlightenment before the Enlightenment.[375] However, according to the German scholar, there is an aspect in common between the idea of tolerance of the Enlightenment and Cusanus' perspective: both natural rational universal religion theorized by the Enlightened and Cusanus' *una religio* do not coincide with any of the historical religions. If Cusanus is definitely not a forerunner of the Enlightenment, the question regarding the fortune of his vision of peace among religions is far from being resolved and acceptance would first be required of the idea that a single viewpoint on religious tolerance does not exist, and that the notion has a complex backcloth and multiple formulations.[376]

If we wish to identify a train of modern thought on tolerance towards which Cusanus is perhaps more disposed than to any other– and that, after all, seemed to have among its sources Cusanus' thought as well - then it is to be found in Lessing and in his vision of religion and peace. Unlike many other authors of the Enlightenment, Lessing does not profess to pass over every historical religion in an abstract religion of reason.[377] Although, both for Cusanus as for Lessing there are common bases, religions are varied and multiple and are distinguished from one another in their different concrete historical expressions.[378] Cusanus' idea of a "religio in rituum varietate" could well be somewhat expressive of Lessing's attitude. Not by chance, according to some, would we find a conceptual schism in Cusanus' pages which would find its peak in several modern thinkers who, together with Kant and Schleiermacher, count Lessing himself among their ranks. The change in the conceptual paradigm would be made by the distinction between *religio* and *fides christiana* set out in Cusanus' pages. These two notions would no longer be identified, being ab-

Tolerance, in *Nicholas of Cusa and Islam Polemic and Dialogue in the Middle Ages*, eds. I.C. Levy – R. George-Turtkovíc – D. F. Duclow, Brill, Leiden 2014, pp. 14-16;

375 Cf. B. Decker, *Die Toleranzideebei Nikolaus von Kues und in der Neuzeit*, cit., pp. 202-203.

376 Cf. F. Lo Monaco, *Tolleranza*, Guida, Napoli 2005, p. 7. On the theme cf. C. J. Nederman – J. Ch. Laursen (eds.), *Different and Dissent: Theories of Toleration in Early Modern Europe*, Rowman, Lanham 1996.

377 Cf. Gotthold Ephraim Lessing, *Die Erziehung des Menschengeschlechts*, art. 77, in Id., *Sämtliche Werke. Unveränderter photomechanischer Abdruck der von Karl Lachmann und Franz Muncker 1886 bis 1924 herausgegebenen Ausgabe von Gotthold Ephraim Lessings sämtlichen Schriften*, vol. XIII, cit., p. 432,. On the theme cf. G. Nenne, *Lessings theologische Schriften im Zusammenhang seines Werkes*, in *Lessing in heutiger Sicht*, eds. E. P. Harris - R. E. Schade, Jacobi, Bremen 1977, p. 40;W. A. Euler, *Il De pace fidei di Nicolò Cusano e la parabola dell'anello di Lessing*, in *Cusanus*, cit., pp. 59-74.In *Education of the Human Race* the claims of truth of the contents of religions are however judged much more positively than in the parable of the three rings.Cf. B. Bothe, *Glauben und Erkennen. Studien zur Religionsphilosophie Lessings*, Hain, Meisenheim 1972.

378 Cf. Gotthold Ephraim Lessing, *Nathan der Weise*, cit., pp. 92-93; Engl. trans. cit., 93-94..

sorbed one by the other, but separate and different, initiating a process of categorisation of religion, which became something discernible from the individual faiths.[379]

Clearly there are certain important and irremovable differences between Cusanus' viewpoint and that of Lessing's. For the Cardinal, man is capable of recognizing in his learned ignorance the truth in its being unlimited and transcendent, and for this reason he is tolerant, while for the philosopher of German enlightenment, man is not capable of obtaining truth theoretically, but reaches the certainty of true faith only through morality. Cusanus and Lessing however, come together in the vision of different religions since all aimed at obtaining the love of God and love for one's neighbour, and in the affirmation that differences are not unsurmountable barriers. Indeed these differences can help one live one's own faith in a more authentic and fuller way when they become an occasion for meeting and not clashing, a moment for "competing" in devotion and love, elements in which is eventually to be found the expression of a true feeling of religion.

4. *Pia Interpretatio*

From the title and structure of the *De pace fide* it is possible to say that Cusanus is not a forerunner of modern tolerance since, despite what we have seen, certain features might make us think that he could have influenced the development of this category in the modern age. However, Cusanus is not an "enlightened" thinker prior to the Enlightenment, as we are faced with a theoretical construct which is an alternative to that of religious tolerance.

The modern idea of religious tolerance, at least in its Lockean-liberal classical vision, assumes an indifference towards positive religions and their contents.[380] It is based on the distinction between a public sphere and a private sphere. A distinction aimed at neutralizing differences by relegating them equally to the intimate dimension of the individual's conscience and towards neutralizing religious affiliation by transforming it into something personal and private. And all in the name of order and of peaceful co-existence. Tolerance means bearing whoever is not recognized as equal and choosing a practical solution that accepts the lesser evil, the existence of the tolerated, and avoiding the outbreak of a conflict.

It is not by chance that Voltaire, one of the fathers of modern tolerance, uses an image, that of the Stock Exchange, taken from economics. According to Voltaire,

379 Cf. R. Celada Ballanti, *Pensiero religioso liberale*, cit., pp.46 ff.

380 Cf. C. A. Viano, *Introduzione*, in J. Locke, *Lettera sulla tolleranza*, ed. C. A. Viano, Laterza, Roma Bari 1994, p. VII; M.L. Lanzillo, *Tolleranza*, cit., pp. 85ff.

at the stock market of London, a Hebrew, a Muslim, a Brahmin, a Chinaman, a Christian, and a Protestant trading pacifically are made equal only under the law of economic profit.[381] The image is not casual, because the liberal response to religious conflict deactivated the conflict of values bringing it back to a conflict of interests through the expulsion of religion from the political field. Tolerance is based, moreover, on the recognition of indifference to differences, not essential to the modus operandi of the market and the spread of the rising modern economy.

Furthermore, the idea of religious tolerance, at least in its modern-enlightened point of view, seems to imply a setting aside of the question of truth. Truth and tolerance would not be compatible, as the claiming of truth would render tolerance itself impossible. One tolerates what one does not assume to be true, so not by chance is one of the etymological meanings of the term *tollere* "to bear with patience".[382] Tolerance in its modern enlightened version – consider for example Bayle and Voltaire but also in the German sphere Lessing of *Nathan the Wise* – is based upon the fallibility of human knowledge and on the impossibility of reaching the truth.

A trait which is common to the conceptions of religious tolerance is that it always implies the idea of an exclusion. Even though those who are tolerated are many, those many never become all. Sometimes it is the Catholic who deals with the implications, because of his faith to the Roman pontiff, whereas at other times it is the atheist, as he undermines the basis of a civil co-existence with his unbelief (Locke, Milton, Voltaire).

The theories on tolerance share the exclusion of those who do not recognise the principle of tolerance as they presuppose the superiority of the viewpoint of tolerance itself. Even on the impossibility of reaching the truth there is no debate, as the impossibility of reaching the truth is truth itself.

Clearly a close analysis of the history of the notion of tolerance would bring about that which for reasons of time necessarily make even a brief reconstruction rather problematic.[383] However, the ones already explained are some of the fundamental elements of the classic liberal and enlightened viewpoints on religious tolerance.

381 Cf. Voltaire, *Lettres philosophiques*, ed. R. Pomeau, Garnier-Flammarion, Paris 1964, VI, p. 47; Id., *s. v. Tolérance*, in Id., *Dictionnaire philosophique*, 2 voll., ed. C. Mervaud, in *Les Oeuvres complètes de Voltaire*, XXXVI, Voltaire Foundation, Oxford 1994, p. 552. On Voltaire's complex conception of tolerance and on the various stages of the development of his thought cf. M. L. Lanzillo, *Voltaire. La politica della tolleranza*, Laterza, Roma-Bari 2000.

382 Cf. M. L. Lanzillo, *Tolleranza* cit., pp. 18, 82-85; M. Cacciari, *La maschera della tolleranza*, in *La maschera della tolleranza*, Bur, Milano 2006, pp. 134ff.

383 Cf. F. Lo Monaco, *Tolleranza*, Guida, Napoli 2005.

Moreover, not by chance do the modern theories on religion develop tolerance as an answer to a problem which originally came from within European society, following the clash among Christian confessions. The concept of tolerance took root in Europe in order to solve the clash among the several confessions in Europe. The theoretical-strategic mechanism of neutralizing the religious conflict that has come about is hence already culturally determined and made to respond to specific problems.

It is not by chance, therefore, that our globalised world, marked by the exchange of views among religions and cultures which are highly heterogeneous, poses, in terms of tolerance, relevant questions which do not appear to find an easy answer within such a theoretical paradigm. In other words, faced with the new requirements for recognition and visibility among one's own differences as well as with the reappearance of religions in the public sphere – after their disappearance had been prematurely declared – the liberal-enlightened vision responds inadequately by saying that the difference is of no importance and is to be restricted to the private sector. Today we are present at rising issues of recognition of religious and cultural differences – not only coming from outside the Western world, but inherent in the same area of Western culture and spirituality- which do not ask to be standardized, but to be recognised as they are in their own specificity and otherness. The last few decades have brought to the fore the question of tolerance, highlighting its status as a concept undergoing a crisis.

On many fronts we are witnessing an upsurge in the theoretical issue of proceeding towards a radical revision of the notion itself, if not of driving beyond tolerance. But clearly not to be understood as a putting aside of the concept that tolerance wishes to communicate, which is peaceful co-existence, but rather as a search for new ways for encounter.

The Cardinal's position is totally different from the liberal-enlightened one. Cusanus, unlike tolerance theorists engaged in comparing and confronting different Christian sects, aims at finding solutions to a different problem, which is that of Christianity's relationship with other religions. His proposal, in fact, is not that of peace regardless of faith (as modern theorists of tolerance seem to think) but that of a peace which is born of faith, in which it is precisely from faith that peace can spring. In Cusanus there is no indifferentist attitude towards the religious contents nor does he exclude the possibility of reaching truth. For Cusanus it is the ability of reaching truth itself which makes the encounter and the dialogue with the other possible.

The problems left open by the two dominant interpretations of the work mentioned earlier, might be summed up in the contradiction between the essentiality and the particularity of Christianity, between the Christian religion as a positive religion and as a religion in itself. The Christian religion is a peculiar and determinate religion if compared to others, and at the same time has a centrality and a universality in the dialogue which leads towards identifying it as *una religio*. In other words what appears to take shape in this work is a strong contradiction between the value given to the other religions and the privilege entitled to the Christian religion. Christianity is at one and the same time the model, the paradigm upon which one can approach closer to the other religions, and above all to a particular faith.

It is a contradiction Cusanus is aware of, but which he does not intend to resolve, probably also because it is not necessary, or even possible, to resolve. Cusanus is well aware that the contradiction is such in the sphere of reason but not in the superior sphere of the intellectual consideration of faith.

It is not for a mere literary or aesthetic fact that Cusanus presents the work in the first chapter as the narration of a vision he had after a meditation lasting several days on the tragic events of Constantinople. This long meditation brought about a rapture of such intellectual intensity that created the vision he tells about. The work is not presented simply as the outcome of rational argumentation, but refers to a different dimension. The very literary form of the *De pace fidei*, namely the dialogue, is not an element extrinsic to its content, as if it were a mere receptacle of its speculative proposal. The choice of the device is not indifferent to the message Cusanus tries to convey. On the contrary, and significantly so, Cusanus elaborates a theory of dialogue or a religious treatise on dialogue among religions, and also enacts real conversing. Clearly there was a medieval tradition of dialogical works among representatives of different religions, but there were also other traditions. So why does Cusanus choose the form of dialogue?

In addition, it has to be stressed yet again that Cusanus does not make the different representatives of the different religions talk amongst each other, but makes the word of God, Saint Paul and Saint Peter speak to representatives of individual religious traditions.

We must not forget, as has often been the case, *who* it was who wrote the *De pace fidei* and to *whom* the work is addressed. Cusanus is writing shortly after the fall of Constantinople and becomes involved in the debate taking place in Europe, as his letters to eminent people of that time also demonstrate, with regard to the question of Christians responding with arms. *Cusanus is speaking as a Christian to Christians* showing them a pacific way to resolve the religious conflict.

Only if we take these these two aspects into consideration is it possible to interpret the dialogue correctly and to understand Cusanus' proposal. Cusanus expresses himself from the viewpoint of the Christian faith, from within it, without abandoning it, in order to bring about an exchange of ideas with the other, but rather he finds this affiliation the reasons and paths towards dialogue. Secondly, he does not address the believers of different confessions with a view to their conversion but tries to show Christians a way leading towards encounter and dialogue.

From Cusanus' persective it is not a matter of renouncing one's own religion, or putting aside one's own identity: communicating is possible, in fact, only by starting from one's own personality and affiliation to one's own tradition and culture. From one's own faith. In fact, there is no panoramic overview covering all standpoints, no gazing down from any fixed height, but it is always starting from otherness (Cusanus' conjecture), from a situation, an identity, a point of view that one communicates and relates to the other. It not possible to communicate by putting oneself aside, one's own roots, one's existential and common entrenchment, one's tradition, but communicating is always possible by starting from one's own determinate perspective. For Cusanus in interfaith dialogue it is not a matter of relating with the other by putting aside Christ and his centrality – by proceeding as Saint Anselm does as direct and indirect imitations *remoto Christo or sola ratione,* or as Abelard does by putting aside his religious garments. On the contrary Cusanus tries to communicate with others by starting from his own faith and his own being Christian.

The idea then is of those theologians and philosophers of religion defined as pluralists or theocentricists for whom there is only one essence of religions. In order to reach it, it is necessary to relativize one's own faith in Jesus Christ by considering him as one of the many figures or models or ways towards salvation, so that rather than promote dialogue, from Cusanus' perspective, they actually make dialogue impossible. Indeed, as hermeneutics teach us, there cannot be any communication if one of the interlocutors drops out from the very beginning rather than honestly risk his own identity, his position, his personality, and his perspective. The danger inherent in the pluralist position – according to which there is a unique noumenal essence belonging to the religions of which the single experiences and traditions are phenomenic realities- and that while one believes one is promoting plurality, a unitary and equalizing model is in fact constructed imposing itself from above over all the different forms of religious experience, while underestimating their own specific characteristics[384].

The core idea, despite perhaps our being unaware thereof, is that there exists an overall view of religions which permits an objective confrontation. But in order for this to happen religions have to be transformed into something different and their specificity would fall short. Religions are neither objects nor do they have to do only with reason, but rather they are characterised for involving what least objectivistic there is, namely rational sense and to imply that what goes beyond reason, namely, faith.

384 Cfr. M. Pagano, *Ermeneutica e interculturalità,* in «Annuario filosofico», 26 (2010), pp. 135-148.

The concept that it is not possible to transcend one's own affiliation and identity leads in contrast to respecting religious traditions and their individuality and otherness. Cusanus' every effort to find features among Christian dogmas and truths in common with those of other religions, both in the *De pace fidei* and in the work of some years later that the *Cribratio Alkorani,* is an attempt to use a kind of analogical method.

And it is precisely in the very possibility of being able to read the *de pace fidei* and the *Cribratio Alkorani* in continuity that gives one of the most convincing proofs of being able to interpret Cusanus' thinking. It must be borne in mind that the work *Cribratio Alkorani* was written in 1460, some seven years after the *De pace fidei*, and is a text explicitly dedicated to a confrontation wth Islam. In this text Cusanus tries to rediscover exactly what in the Koran and in Mohamed's teachings is in agreement with the Gospel, and on the basis of such agreements tries to trace in it large fragments and rays of truth. Only too often have commentators seen a sharp discontinuity between the two works, reading in the *de pace* an irenicist Cusanus, while in the *Cribratio* a Cusanus who has realised that communication is impossible, and who embarks on the road of polemical confrontation with Islam. Indeed the same method is used in both works, that can be defined, by using an expression used by the cardinal himself to indicate the methodology of the *Cribratio,* which we may define as *Pia Interpretatio.*[385]

Pia Iinterpretatio is an attempt to find analogies, that is to say, moments of continuity and similarity between one's own experience of faith and truth and the religious experience of the other recognised as other. Cusanus aims at defining, recognising and interpreting the similarities in diversity. *It is therefore a method useful for the Christians – whom we repeat Cusanus addresses –* to try to exchange views with other religions and representatives of other confessions. From the view-

[385] Cf. *Crib. Alk.*, h VIII, II, 1, n. 86, p. 72; II, 12, n. 119, p. 72; II, 13, n. 124, p. 99; II, 19, n. 154, p. 125. On the theme cf. L. Hagemann, *Der Ḳur'ān in Verständnis und Kritik bei Nikolaus von Kues*, Knecht, Frankfurt am Main 1976; J. E. Biechler, *Nicholas of Cusa and Muhammad,* in «The Downside Review», 101 (1983), pp. 55-56; J. Hopkins, *The Role of Pia Interpretatio in Nicholas of Cusa's Hermeneutical Approach to the Koran*, in *Concordia discors. Studi su Niccolò Cusano e l'umanesimo europeo offerti a Giovanni Santinello*, cit., pp. 251-273; T. Kerger, *Pia interpretatio. Vier christliche Theologen im Gespräch mit dem Islam*, Paulinus, Trier 2010, pp. 164-225; P. Valkenberg, *Sifting the Qur' an: Two Forms of Interreligious Hermeneutics in Nicholas of Cusa*, in *Interreligious Hermeneutics in Pluralistic Europe*, eds. D. Cheetham – U. Winkler – O. Leirvik – J. Gruber, Rodopi, Amsterdam 2011, pp. 27-48; G. Gobillot, *La singulière clairvoyance de Nicolas de Cues à l'égard du Coran*, in *Nicolas de Cues et l'Islam*, ed. H. Pasqua, Peeters, Leuven 2013, pp. 35-86; H. Pasqua, *Nicolas de Cues et l'Islam*, in *Nicolas de Cues et l'Islam*, cit., pp. 1-7; T. Kerger, *La* Cribratio Alkorani*: un project de dialogue avec l'Islam*, in *Nicolas de Cues et l'Islam*, cit., pp. 21-34; M. Watanabe, *Cusanus, Islam and Religious Tolerance*, in *Nicholas of Cusa and Islam Polemic and Dialogue in the Middle Ages*, cit., pp. 14-16.

point of the Christian religious experience – which we recall is always an experience of truth – this is perhaps a possible way towards the other which permits reaching a dialogue with the desire for knowledge and for getting to know one another without sacrificing essential elements including truth, identity and faith. Moreover, rather than taking away the richness of plurality of religious experiences this perhaps allows one to respect the different traditions by taking them into consideration individually, in their otherness without standardizing them.

This is probably a reinterpretation and application in a modern key of an old doctrine established by the Church Fathers, and in particular already present in the works of Saint Justin, namely that of the *semina verbi* or of the *logos spermatikos*[386]. The universal revelation of the Word or Logos, which illuminates every man, means that in the different religions, rites and customs of peoples it is possible to find seeds or rays of Divine Truth and to recognize its elements of grace and redemption. Probably from the point of view of religious conscience which experienced truth in Revelation - namely from the Christian standpoint Cusanus adopts – finding analogies in the other, moments of continuity with the truth that one had experienced is far from being a debasement, but rather a highly respectful and defferential way of addressing the other.

As Cusanus himself says, one knows what is unknown by starting from what is known. We understand others always in reference to ourselves, through analogies with ourselves. Such knowledge of the other is also reflected in the knowledge of ourselves, leading us to deepen our own identity and perspective in a fertile and virtuous circle.

As in the experiment of the *de visione dei* already mentioned, communicating with the other is only possible by starting out from faith, from the trust we put in the other. Without this initial action there is no possibility of encounter or dialogue. The believer, according to Cusanus, in the case of the experiment of the monk who keeps his gaze focused on God and receives the divine gaze by having faith in him, finds in the experience of trust in God a model of trust and faith in the other as well. For Cusanus, in the experience of relying on the Other which appertains to the believer, the man of faith, it is possible to trace the path to be followed also in the relationship with others. Faith therefore, rather than being an obstacle as the modern-enlightened mindset would appear to think, can be the driving power for opening up dialogue, and the force for the strength of peace among religions and cultures.

[386] Cf. Iustinus, *Apol.* I, 3746, 2-4; II, 7, 3; II, 10, 1-8; II, 13, 3; in Id., *Apologie pour les Chrétiens*, ed. C. Munier, Cerf, Paris 2006, pp. 251-253, 340-342, 348-350, 362.

Part III

Readings

1. *Thinking the One with Cusanus. Werner Beierwaltes' Reading*

> Unum est, quod omnes theologizantes aut philophantes in varietate modorum exprimere conantur[387].

With these words taken from Nicholas Cusanus' *De filiatione dei* the basic guiding idea might be summed up of Werner Beierwaltes' research (Klingeberg am Main 1931), directed – according to the programme title of one of his main texts which reveals a truly metaphysical interest by Beierwaltes – in *Denken des Einen*[388]. The expression, which might be translated also as "Thinking the One" has been rendered on explicit indication by Beierwaltes himself by "Think the One" that is also implying an imperative nuance –"one must think the One"[389] – which again implies some sort of necessity.

The very subtitle of this work, *Studien zum Neuplatonismus und ihrer Wirkungsgeschichte*, i.e. *Studies on Neoplatonic philosophy and on the History of its influences* is also equally representative of the progression in thought of the German scholar and philosopher who - spurred on by the intranscendible necessity of the thought to think the One – has concentrated his attention specifically on ancient Neoplatonism (Plotinus and Proclus, in particular) by following their traces and reconstructing the *Wirkungsgeschichte* in early Christian theology, in the Middle Ages, in the Renaissance, in German Idealism and in contemporary philosophy, with his capacity for close examination which makes him one of the

387 *De fil.*, h IV, c. 5, n. 83, p. 59.

388 W. Beierwaltes, *Denken des Einen. Studien zum Neuplatonismus und dessen Wirkungsgeschichte*, Klostermann, Frankfurt am Main 1985.

389 Cf. G. Reale, *Significato e portata del* Pensare l'Uno *di Werner Beierwaltes*, in W. Beierwaltes, *Pensare l'Uno. Studi sulla filosofia neoplatonica e sulla storia dei suoi influssi*, Vita e Pensiero, Milano 1992, p. 20. On Beierwaltes thought cf.moreover S. Mancini, *Beierwaltes e la trascendalità del pensiero*, in «Giornale di Metafisica», 1 (2007), pp. 191-210; Id., *Beierwaltes nella corrente dell'eriugenismo: la duplex theoria e lo statuto trascendentale della manifestazione*, «Annuario Filosofico», 22 (2006), pp. 117-134; Id., *Congetture su Dio*, cit., pp. 167-200; Id., N. Scotti, *Aspetti di attualità teoretica del pensiero procliano negli studi di Werner Beierwaltes*, «Giornale di Metafisica», 1 (2007), pp. 120-145.

leading international authorities on the Neoplatonic tradition and on the history of its influences[390].

Beierwaltes dedicated an impressive number of essays to Cusanus within a time span of almost fifty years of study, first trying to reconstruct the relationship of his thought with Greek and Medieval philosophy, and then to examine the characteristics which make him a thinker of the Renaissance, as well as being open to modernism[391]. Such interests have led him to reflect on Cusanus' acceptance of

390 Amongst the main volumes published by Beierwaltes cf.: W. Beierwaltes, *Proklos. Grundzüge seiner Metaphysik*, Klostermann, Frankfurt am Main 1965; Id., *Platonismus und Idealismus*, Klostermann, Frankfurt am Main 1972 [II. ed. 2004]; Id., *Identität und Differenz*, Klostermann, Frankfurt am Main 1980; Id., *Denken des Einen. Studien zum Neuplatonismus und dessen Wirkungsgeschichte*, cit.; Id., *Eriugena. Grundzüge seines Denkens*, Klostermann, Frankfurt am Main 1994; W. Beierwaltes, *Platonismus in Christentum*, Klostermann, Frankfurt am Main 1998; Id., *Das wahre Selbst. Studien zu Plotins Begriff des Geistes und des Einen*, Klostermann, Frankfurt am Main 2001; Id., *Procliana. Spätantikes Denken und seine Spuren*, Klostermann, Frankfurt am Main 2007.

391 Cf.: W. Beierwaltes, *Deus oppositio oppositorum. Nicolaus Cusanus, De visione Dei XIII*, cit., pp. 175-185; Id., *Cusanusund Proclus. Zum neuplatonischen Ursprung des non aliud*, cit., pp. 138-140; W. Beierwaltes, Visio absoluta. *Reflexion als Grundzug des göttlichen Prinzips bei Nicolaus Cusanus*, in Id., *Identität und Differenz*, cit., pp. 144-175; Id., *Subjektivität, Schöpfertum, Freiheit. Die philosophie der Renaissance zwischen Tradition und neuzeitlichem Bewusstsein*, in *Der Übergang zur Neuzeit und die Wirkung von Traditionen*, Vandenhoeck & Ruprecht, Göttingen 1978, pp. 15-31; W. Beierwaltes, *Identität und Differenz als Prinzip des cusanischen Denkens*, in Id., *Identität und Differenz*, cit., pp. 105-143; W. Beierwaltes, *Über die Cusanus-Ausgabe*, in *Ceterum censeo... Bemerkungen zur Aufgabe und Tätigkeit eines philosophischen Verlegers*, Meiner, Hamburg 1983, pp. 26-30; W. Beierwaltes, *Einheit und Gleichheit. Eine Fragestellung im Platonismus von Chartres und ihre Rezeption durch Nicolaus Cusanus*, in Id., *Denken des Einen*, cit., pp. 368-384; Id., *Das Seiende Eine. Zur neuplatonisches Interpretation der zweiten Hypothesis des platonischen Parmenides: das Beispeiel Cusanus*, in Id., *Procliana. Spätantikes Denken und seine Spuren*, cit., pp. 215-222; W. Beierwaltes, Visio facialis. *Sehen ins Angesich. Zur Coincidenz des endlichen und unendlichen. Blicks bei Cusanus*, cit.; Id., *Die Cusanus-Ausgabe. Nicolai de Cusa Opera Omnia iussu et auctoritate Academiae Litterarum Heidelbergensis ad codicum fidem edita*, in «Jahrbuch der Heidelberger Akademie der Wissenschaften», 1987, pp. 101-106; Id., *Eriugena und Cusanus*, in Id., *Eriugena*, cit., pp. 295-329;Id., *Der verborgene Gott*, in Id., *Platonismus im Christentum*, cit., pp. 130-171; Id., "Centrum tocius vite".*Zur Bedeutung von Proclos' "Theologia Platonis" im Denken des Cusanus*, in *Procliana. Spätantikes Denken und seine Spuren*, cit., pp. 191-214;Id., *Mystische Elemente im Denken des Cusanus*, in *Deutsche Mystik*, cit., pp. 425-448; Id., *Das Verhältnis von Philosophie und Theologie bei Nicolaus Cusanus*, in «Philotheos», 1 (2001), pp. 150-176; W. Beierwaltes, *Hans Gerhard Senger. Ein Leben mit Cusanus*, in «Litterae Cusanae», 2 (2002), pp. 50-65; Id., *Nicolaus Cusanus: Innovation durch Einsicht aus der Überlieferung – paradigmatisch gezeigt an seinem Denken des Einen*, in *Procliana. Spätantikes Denken und seine Spuren*, cit., pp. 165-190; Id., *Dank und Gedanken*, in *Nicolai de Cusa Opera Omnia. Symposium zum Abschluß der Heidelberger Akademie-Ausgabe. Heidelberg, 11. und 12. Februar 2005*, eds. W. Beierwaltes- H. G. Senger, Winter, Heidelberg 2006, pp. 9-19; Id., *Visio dei. Die mystiche Theologhie des Nicolaus Cusanus im Kontext benediktinischer Spiritualität*, in «Studien

Neoplatonism (especially of Proclus', Dionysius' and Iohannes Scotus Eruigena's) and on his reformulation of certain *Leitmotifs* of Neoplatonic thought. Exposure to the historical relationship has however, always been inextricably bound to his systematic interest in the main concepts which make Cusanus' thought a complete oneness in course of development in itself.

For Beierwaltes at the basis of Cusanus' thought of the One lies the interpretation of the first two hypotheses of Plato's *Parmenides* not as relating to two different objects, but as regarding the same Principle. In the wake of Dionysius' thought and the exigencies dictated by faith in Christian revelation, the "One-above-being", which is before and beyond being, completely unrelated and transcendent, and the "One-that-is", being in a full sense, intellect which thinks itself and which coordinates the multiplicity, as being strictly distinct from Plotinus and Proclus, are identified by Cusanus[392]. The One is no longer conceived as completely unrelated, but rather, in the light of the Trinity, as trinitarially self-relational and self-constituting oneness which, despite its reflexive self-unfolding must be conceived as non-multiple and non-different before all multiplicity and difference. Thus moreover, a paradoxical dialectic of transcendence and immanence of the divine Principle begins to takes shape, which is, at the same time, *omnia in omnibus*, "all in all" and *omnium nihil*, "nothing of all"[393]. This dialectic for Beierwaltes is already a motive for supporting Neoplatonic thought, in Cusanus takes on a new

und Mittleitungen des Benediktinerordens und seiner Zweige», 117 (2006), pp. 81-96; Id., *Theophanie. Nicolaus Cusanus und Johannes Scottus Eriugena. Eine Retractatio*, cit., pp. 153-175; W. Beierwaltes, *Venatio sapientiae. Das Nicht-Andere und das Licht*, cit., pp. 83-104; Id., Preface by D. Monaco, Deus Trinitas, cit., pp. 9-14. Some of the main essays by Beierwaltes on Cusanus are now collected in a Spanish translation in the volume: W. Beierwaltes, *Reflexion metafisica y espiritualidad*,Span. trans by A. Ciria, EUNSA, Pamplona 2005.

392 On the Neoplatonic and Cusanian interpretation of *Plato's Parmenides* cf. W. Beierwaltes, *Das Seiende Eine. Zur neuplatonisches Interpretation der zweiten Hypothesis des platonischen Parmenides: das Beispeiel Cusanus*, cit., pp. 215-222; W. Beierwaltes, *Denken des Einen. Studien zum Neuplatonismus und dessen Wirkungsgeschichte*, cit., pp. 193-225.

393 Cf.: W. Beierwaltes, *Deus oppositio oppositorum. Nicolaus Cusanus, De visione Dei XIII*, cit., pp. 175-185; Id., *Identität und Differenz als Prinzip des cusanischen Denkens*, in Id., *Identität und Differenz*, cit., pp. pp. 105-143; Id., *Eriugena und Cusanus*, cit.; Id., *Der verborgene Gott. Cusanus und Dionysius*, in Id., *Platonismus im Christentum*, cit., pp. 130-171; W. Beierwaltes, "Centrum tocius vite". *Zur Bedeutung von Proclos' "Theologia Platonis" im Denken des Cusanus*, in Id., *Procliana*, cit., pp. 191-214 On the theme moreover cfr.: J. Stallmach, *Das Nichtandere als Begriff des Absoluten*, in *Universitas. Dienst an Wahrheit und Leben. Festschrift für Bischof Dr. Albert Stohr*, cit., pp. 329-335; M. Alvarez-Gómez, *Die verborgene Gegenwart des Unendlichen bei Nikolaus von Kues*, cit., pp. 179-199; K. Kremer, *Gott – in allem alles, in nichts nichts. Bedeutung und Herkunft dieser Lehrer des Nikolaus von Kues*, cit., pp. 188-219; J. Stallmach, *Immanenz und Transzendenz im Denken des Cusanus*, in *Transzendenz. Zu einem Grundwort der klassischen Metaphysik*, cit., pp. 183-192.

shape in the light of the Christian concepts of creation and incarnation and of Dionysian-Eriugenian reflection. The immanence of the Principle in its being is considered more productively, thanks to the different evaluation of the created: the world becomes essentially theophany, revelation, image, mirror, participation, unfolding of God, without its nullifying or consuming divine transcendence.

For Beierwaltes this conception which constitutes the Neoplatonic-Christian system at the basis of the cardinal's thought is the foundation or the main theme of the original elaboration of those enigmatic names or divine conceptual images – *coincidentia oppositorum*, *idem*, *visio absoluta*, *possest* and *non aliud* – which represent one of the most original elements of Cusanus' speculation[394]. These names of the divine Principle which are not exhaustive since, inasmuch as words they are always fruit of the finite human *ratio*, are rather enigmatic images which referring to what in its own proper sense remains unnameable are used in order to approach ever more closely, even if always indefinitively, towards the *praecisio absoluta* of God's being in himself.

The free but not necessary dialectic between the *Deus absconditus* and the *Deus incarnatus* of concealing and manifesting proper to the Christian God revealed does not refute nor impede the thought, but rather demands it and excites it, showing at the same time its limit. On the one side therefore on account of their determining structure language and thought are not able to express God, who is not something determinate, while on the other there is the constant necessity on the part of language and thought of having to turn their attention to the basic foundation which makes speaking and thinking possible[395]. This is why despite all the methodical reserves regarding the possibility of giving name to the *Deus absconditus*, to the never abandoned assertion of *docta ignorantia*, Cusanus has always tried to name God, through creating new pathways, concepts, names or conceptual images, none of which may be considered as a definitive step.

The concept of *infinitas absoluta* is the primary perspective of all Cusanus' decisions attempting to express God's being as an absolute. Such *infinitas*, inasmuch as negation of the finite, *negatio negationis*, is to be understood as coincidence of every opposition in the sense of equality which excludes every individual differentiation, being unitary and equalising *complicatio* (enfolding) which embraces all the possible in itself. God's infinity is therefore primarily made clear by Cusanus through the idea of *coincidentia oppositorum* which shows the difference of divine origin from the level of the finite. The finite, in fact, is always something determinate through its sameness and therefore other or different from the other which it lacks, otherness which may progress as far as the contrary or contradictory op-

394 Cf. W. Beierwaltes, *Der verborgene Gott*, in Id., *Platonismus im Christentum*, cit., pp. 130-171.
395 Cf. W. Beierwaltes, *Der verborgene Gott*, in Id., *Platonismus im Christentum*, cit., pp. 130-171.

position; it is therefore a togetherness with an ever diverse intensity of oneness and otherness, sameness and difference. Divine origin is rather like *coincidentia oppositorum,* the absolute maximum of oneness and self-likeness. It is in itself the negation of all finite, *infinitum*. That which in the sphere of the finite is determinate in its being through otherness and opposition, in the infinite is surpassed in its otherness or opposition in that in it the maximum, which is at the same time the undifferentiated minimum, and is all that which can be. To think of the absolute Oneness as *coincidentia oppositorum* enables one to understand, according to a well known Cusanian adage, that between the finite and the infinite there is no proportion[396].

Beierwaltes succeeds in grasping, however, that the doctrine of the *coincidentia oppositorum* even earlier in the *De docta ignorantia* has two moments. According to the first, in fact, God enfolds the opposites into oneness, but for the other, as in the Neoplatonic tradition, God *supra omnem oppositionem est*[397]. Consequently and paradoxically according to the *De docta ignorantia* God is beyond the opposites and, at the same time, is their *coincidentia.* In the ensuing *De visione Dei* (1453)[398] Cusanus purposefully does not identify the thought of the *coincidentia oppositorum* with absolute infinity, but refers it back to a previous level or condition with respect to the vision of the infinite: the *coincidentia oppositorum* again becomes a conceptual form of intellectual thought which in order to reach the infinite must be surpassed in a visioning which is neither comprehensive nor considered as objective. Cusanus therefore uses the metaphor of the "wall of Paradise" in order to indicate the *coincidentia oppositorum* beyond which God is supposed to dwell[399]. This modification is due, according to Beierwaltes, to the risk that the concept of *coincidentia* might bring about a false understanding of the oneness of God as a co-existence of opposites or as their intransigence. Nevertheless this variation does not mean that the idea of the *coincidentia* is surpassed, but rather that it is thought of at the basis of the "wall of Paradise" metaphor, and is indication of an experience of the limit of the concept. For Beierwaltes therefore, the metaphor of the wall of opposites does not indicate any basic change in Cusanus' thought, but rather an affirmation and clarification of the implications of what was already

396 Cf. *De Docta ign.*, h I, I, c. 1, n. 3, pp. 6-8: «propter quod infinitum ut infinitum cum omnem proportionem aufugiat, ignotum est».

397 Cf. *De docta ign.*, h I, I, c. 4, n. 11-12, pp. 10-11.

398 On the *De visione Dei*cf.: W. Beierwaltes, *Visio absoluta oder absolute Reflexion (Cusanus)*, in Id. Identität und Differenz, cit., pp. 144-175; W. Beierwaltes, Visio facialis. *Sehen ins Angesich. Zur Coincidenz des endlichen und unendlichen. Blicks bei Cusanus*, cit.; W. Beierwaltes, *Visio dei. Die mystiche Theologhie des Nicolaus Cusanus im Kontext benediktinischer Spiritualität*, cit., pp. 81-96.

399 Cf. *De Vis.*, h VI, c. 9, n. 37, p. 35; c. 11-12, n. 43-50, pp. 40-43.

contained in it[400]. For progress towards the *visio Dei* Cusanus is therefore aware that the *coincidentia oppositorum* cannot be valid as an immediate expression and at the same time a final expression of the infinite, as its original way of being, but as a level necessary for passing to the *infinitas absoluta*[401]. Despite this, the infinite cannot be seen without a passing through of the thought of the coincidence of opposites or contradictory statements because it is the enfolding being beyond opposition and contradiction.

For the German scholar *coincidentia oppositorum* beyond every opposition may therefore be thought of in accordance with another expression of Cusanus' as *oppositio oppositorum sine oppositione*[402]. This wording which Cusanus relates to Dionisyius, but which does not find any textual confirmation in him – even though it might be reconstructed from various elements of his thought – finds a reliable source, according to Beierwaltes in the work of Iohannes Scotus Eriugena[403]. In fact in Book I of the *Periphyseon* is found the expression *oppositorum oppositio*, which in the copy which Cusanus possessed has been evidenced with a marginal note[404].

For Beierwaltes the formula *oppositio oppositorum sine oppositione* has two meanings. According to the first the opposition of the opposites is to be understood as opposition to all opposites, that is as otherness or absolute difference without opposition from the opposition. This first meaning speaks of the immeasurable otherness of the Principle. *Sine oppositione* within itself and outside itself means that the being of absolute origin is absolute simplicity and oneness. The concept of *oppositio oppositorum sine oppositione* is thus shown as an interpretation

400 Cf.W. Beierwaltes, *Mystische Elemente im Denken des* Cusanus, cit., in *Deutsche Mystik*, cit., pp. 425-448.

401 Cf. *De Visione Dei*, h VI, c. 10, n. 38-41, pp. 35-38. The idea of God as *ultra* or *super coincidentiam oppositorum* is already contained in a marginal annotation to Dionysius, cf. L. Baur, *Nicolaus Cusanus und Pseudo Dionysius im Lichte der Zitate und Randbemerkungen des Cusanus*, cit., marg. 589, and in *Apol.*h II, n. 21, p. 15.

402 Cf. *De Vis.*, h VI, c. 13, n. 54, p. 46; *Apol.*, h II, n. 21, p. 15; Id., *De theol. Compl.*,h V/2a, n. 13, p. 78; *De non aliud*, h XIII, c. 19, p. 47.

403 The idea of God as *oppositio oppositorum sine oppositione* comes from Cusanus attributed to Dionysius without it being possible to find any direct confirmation in Dionysius' text. Cf. *Apol.*, h II, n. 21, p. 15; *De non aliud*, h XIII, c. 19, p. 47. Cf. on the theme: L. Baur, *Nicolaus Cusanus und Pseudo Dionysius im Lichte der Zitate und Randbemerkungen des Cusanus*, cit., p. 51. The doctrine of the *oppositio oppositorum sine oppositione* became a topos of Beierwaltes' interpretation of Cusanus, on the theme of which cf.: W. Beierwaltes, *Deus oppositio oppositorum. Nicolaus Cusanus, De visione Dei XIII*, cit., pp. 175-185; Id., *Eriugena und Cusanus*, in Id., *Eriugena*, cit., pp. 266-312; Id., *Mystische Elemente im Denken des Cusanus*, in *Deutsche Mystik*, cit., pp. 425-448.

404 Cf. J. Koch, *Kritisches Verzeichnis der Londoner Handschriften aus dem Besitz des Nikolaus von Kues*, in «MFCG», 3 (1963), p. 98.

of the *coincidentia* since it indicates the beyond-categorical difference from all of the divine Principle through the otherness and the opposition to the determinate derivatives, inasmuch as oneness beyond opposites.

The second meaning in which the concept of *oppositio oppositorum* closely examines the fundamental thought of the coincidence of the opposites lies instead in its indicating at the same time the origin of the opposition of opposites. Absolute opposition is therefore, the foundation which operates in all opposites, bringing it about that, inasmuch as reciprocally opposites, they are what they are. In this way it is the foundation of their distinction and their self-identity or self-equality. The enfolding principle is absolute coincidence, infinite equality and so, at the same time, foundation and origin of the dividing and unfolding of the opposites as constitutive elements of the world. It is all in all, every thing is contraction of it, although it remains incontractable. In it all is identical to it. The *oppositio oppositorum* is origin of the opposition of the opposites in that it is the enfolding of them.

God is therefore *oppositio oppositorum* in that he is the foundation of the respective opposition of opposites, and is the opposite who operates in all opposites, and who determines all opposites. However, since it is not possible to think nothing opposite with respect to the universal foundation of opposites, God paradoxically with respect to the first aspect, is active opposition with regard to every other thing. God therefore negates of himself all that which is opposite, for which precisely inasmuch as *oppositio oppositorum* is not affected or determined by him.

This interpretation responds to a central element of Neoplatonic thought closely examined by Cusanus, namely that God *in spite of* or *because of* his being in every being is separate from and raised above every being, and therefore is all and nothing together. In this way the idea of *coincidentia oppositorum* would not be surpassed in the sense of being left behind, but rather, according to the meaning of Hegel's *aufheben* or of the Latin *tollere* would be surpassed by being brought to a higher level of truth, studied closely as *oppositio oppositorum sine oppositione,* and opening up the way to that divine name which represents one of the key features in Cusanus' thinking, namely the *non aliud.*

According to Beierwaltes the *non aliud* represents a fusion and a radicalisation not only of the *coincidentia oppositorum* and of the *oppositio oppositorum sine oppositione*, but also of the enigmatic names of *idem* and *possest*[405]. In Cusanus' first essay *Deus oppositio oppositorum* (1964)[406] the German scholar interprets the *non aliud* as expression of the oneness of the Principle with himself because of his otherness or absolute difference from all other, reassociating it with the sense of

[405] Cf. W. Beierwaltes, *Der verborgene Gott. Cusanus und Dionysius*, cit., in Id., *Platonismus im Christentum*, cit., pp. 130-171.

[406] Cf. W. Beierwaltes, *Deus oppositio oppositorum. Nicolaus Cusanus, De visione Dei XIII*, cit., pp. 175-185.

transcendence implicit in the expression *oppositio oppositorum sine oppositione,* and identifying it as negative wording of the immanence of the Principle expressed positively by the enigmatic name of *idem.* More generally, according to the German scholar there is a relationship of oneness between the *idem* and the *non aliud*: the not-other would be the negative wording of the *idem*, the negative expression of that which sameness expresses in the affirmative[407]. Again in *Identität und Differenz als Prinzip des cusanischen Denkens* (1978), in dispute with the Norwegian Wyller, Beierwaltes affirmed that the *idem* is the linguistically positive wording of the *non aliud*[408]. The *non aliud* would therefore represent, according to Cusanus' principle for which negations are more adequate than affirmations, a radicalisation of the *idem* in a negative sense.

Nevertheless for Beierwaltes, apart from the idea of *idem*, the *non aliud* represents a going thoroughly into the idea of *possest.*[409] *Possest* and *non aliud* are both a clarification and an articulation of the thought of infinite Oneness understood through the conceptual pair of *complicatio (enfolding)* and *explicatio (unfolding).* Like the *possest*, the *non aliud* is union of poles which negate themselves or are opposites within the same dimension, a oneness which fully precedes the dimension of opposition, and through which the latter, just as that of the difference, is made possible. The *possest* precedes possibility and reality absolutely, and is the foundation which permits their relationship, just as the *non aliud* precedes sameness and difference, which makes their relationship possible. The *non aliud* is without otherness, does not lack anything which could limit it in itself and in its creative work externally. It is a force or a power united trinitarially to which Cusanus rightly attributes the predicate of *virtus actu infinita*[410]. The *non aliud* is *possest*, creative force which has all the possible in itself.

The same conception of God as *visio absoluta*, studied closely by Beierwaltes in several conclusive contributions on the theme[411], contains some important theoretical elements of Cusanus' thought developing from the *non aliud.* Above all conceiving God as *visio absoluta* means for Beierwaltes conceiving him as vision or thought of himself who, in view of the coincidence of seeing, thinking and creating in God, indicates a reflexively self-constituting himself or, according to the *De non aliud*, his being *conceptus absolutus*[412], a self-constitution of himself inasmuch

[407] Cf. *Ibidem.*

[408] Cf. W. Beierwaltes, *Identität und Differenz als Prinzip des cusanischen Denkens*, in Id., *Identität und Differenz*, cit., 105-143,

[409] Cf. *Ibidem.*

[410] Cf. *De non aliud*, h XIII, c. 7, p. 16.

[411] Cf. W. Beierwaltes, Id., *Eriugena und Cusanus*, in Id., *Eriugena*, cit., pp. 266-312; Id., *Visio absoluta oder absolute Reflexion (Cusanus)*, cit., pp. 144-175.

[412] Cf. *De non aliud*, h XIII, c. 20, p. 49.

as absolute self-reflection. Such oneness does not constitute itself, therefore, in such a way that it, as in the Proclian context, excludes relationality. Rather it is, and is alive precisely because of this. Seeing in the absolute is, precisely through the exclusion of the difference, pure self-conceiving, expressing oneself and seeing onself. Absolute seeing however, is not enclosed in itself, but opens up to the constitution of otherness which is nonetheless connected to its own origin. Absolute seeing like the *non aliud*, penetrates, comprehends and renders every being alive as its essence and together transcends it. The small amount of absolute seeing that can be taken from a being, the same amount the latter could surrender to its own sameness. The world through absolute seeing which constitutes being then becomes theophany, manifestation, unfolding, image of the absolute, according to the method of contraction. The finiteness of man becomes the site of manifesting and operating of the absolute in that it is the infinite seeing that sees and is manifested in finite seeing. The *visio absoluta* is therefore, according to Beierwalte's interpretation of Cusanus' One-God, at the same time transcendent, inasmuch as absolute with respect to finite seeing, and immanent inasmuch as foundation of finite seeing. As seeing-oneself is a self-constituting of God and in this way foundation for the creation *ad extra*, so absolute self-definition of the *non aliud* implies a definition of every other thing. In this single trinitarian act the subject of the vision, the visible and the act of the subject are reciprocally distinct, but despite this, must be thought of as a unitary relationality in itself, or as dynamic unity in itself in virtue of the concept which sees and creates itself. The elimination in the *De non aliud* of the difference through a triple *non aliud* indicates precisely the contemporary oneness of the *visio* or of the self-definition of the absolute concept.

For Beierwaltes, beginning from the years of the *De Beryllo* (1458) and the *De Principio* (1459) Cusanus notes the need for revising the theory of the absolute Principle on the basis of the philosophical conception of Proclus' oneness, and it is precisely thanks to the *non aliud* that the concept of One is conceptually and terminologically defined. None of the "names" coined by Cusanus, in Beierwaltes' opinion, succeeds in summing up in a single word the oneness of transcendence and immanence in or as God, nor in clarifying it better than the *non aliud*[413]. The n*on aliud* indicates that God is absolute difference with respect to all that is other, and at the same time that he is not different from the other, but operates in him as his essence, as identifying, singularising and distinguishing foundation. At the same time in that *non aliud est non aliud quam non aliud*, he defines himself, and in defining himself, since the definition is not to be understood in a logico-formal sense, but in an ontological sense (he is not the simple verification of that which

413 Cf. W. Beierwaltes, *Der verborgene Gott. Cusanus und Dionysius*, in Id., *Platonismus im Christentum*, cit., pp. 130-171.

already is), creates himself, and self-constitutes himself trinitarially. The no*n aliud* refers to the trinitarian self-unfolding of God, whose fulfilment is the Trinity as *non aliud triniter repetitum*. The same self-definition as self-creation then makes its presupposition of the definition of the other, the non-otherness of the absolute who manifests himself in the singular reality, in that every thing is no other than what it is, is the constitutive foundation of the existence of every single being, of its identity and individuality. The *non aliud*, apart from being definition which defines every thing, is however at the same time also that which is defined in every other, so that in every other, one may fully see theophanically only the not-other in what is defined. In every single reality is manifested therefore the not-other as not-other than it, at the same time however its manifestation refers back to its transcendence.

One of the many merits of Beierwaltes' studies was that of showing that Cusanus understood the enigma of the *non aliud* as an explanation and as a continuation of Proclus' theory of the One. The *non aliud* in fact, as shown by Cusanus' important *marginalia* to Proclus, in particular to the *Teologia Platonica* and to the *Commentary on Parmenides*, represents a radicalisation or a re-interpretation of Proclus' absolute One[414]. Both are as follows, namely origin which in itself is beyond all opposites; before affirmation and negation; from nothing other; before the other; before sameness and otherness; nothing of all and at the same time cause of all. If the affinities are close, nevertheless the divergencies are no less so. While Proclus' Absolute One is in itself without relation, beyond all oppositions and relative beings, only in itself, Cusanus' *non aliud*, albeit being beyond all opposites, is in itself trinitarian. Moreover, for its unrelatedness Proclus' One does not think, in that even if it thought only of itself it would already be related to itself, whereas Cusanus' *non aliud* is an absolute concept, thinking and defining itself and all things. Against Proclus' exclusion of thought, and therefore also of self-reflection by the One – and Cusanus, Beierwaltes observes, was fully aware of this presupposition – is the trinitarian *non aliud* as *conceptus absolutus* which defines itself refexively[415]. For Cusanus the divine *triunitas* shows itself as self-foundation which defines itself and that in this self-definition – to be thought of ontologi-

[414] On Cusanus' marginal annotations to Proclus' texts cf.: W. Beierwaltes, *Philosophische Marginalien zu Proklos-Texten*, cit., pp. 49-90; Id., *Cusanusund Proclus. Zum neuplatonischen Ursprung des non-aliud*, in *Niccolò Cusano agli inizi del mondo moderno*, cit., pp. 138-140.

[415] Cusanus was fully aware of the differences: suffice it to consider marginal annotation 152 to the *Theologia platonica*. Cfr H. G. Senger, *Die Exzerpte und Randnoten des Nikolaus von Kues zu den lateinischen Übersetzungen der Proclus-Schriften. Theologia Platonis-Elementatio theologica*, cit., marg. 152. On the differences between Proclus' system and that of Cusanus'cf.:Id., *Cusanus und Proclus. Zum neuplatonischen Ursprung des non-aliud*, in *Niccolò Cusano agli inizi del mondo moderno*, cit., pp. 138-140; Id., *"Centrum tocius vite". Zur Bedeutung von Proklos' Theologia Platonis im Denken des Cusanus*, cit., in Id. *Procliana*, cit., pp. 191-214.

cally – moves out of itself with thought and love. Certainly the self-differentiation which is realised in this movement must not be understood as in the non-thinking One as an additional otherness which in fact separates itself and which upsets and destroys the oneness, but as the self-opening that does not permit scission at all, nor the opposite of the first not-other in the second not-other, being indistinct from it thanks to the mediation of the third not-other which fuses both into the absolute Trinity[416]. Despite the affinities, the basic differences between Cusanus' *non aliud* and Proclus' absolute One are given by the Christian context in which Cusanus thinks and operates, particularly by the need to reflect on the Trinity, the creation, the incarnation and the personality of God. Precisely on the basis of these presuppositions, writes Beierwaltes, in thinking of the *non aliud* as Trinitarian self-concept and its paradoxical coincidence of transcendence and immanence Cusanus has decidedly gone beyond Dionysius' and Proclus'. The *non aliud* systematizes and brings Cusanus' reflection on the One to a happy conclusion by representing the conceptual figure of his search for the name of God[417].

On the basis of Cusanus' conception of the One it is possible to understand one of the most productive theses for contemporary philosophy of the German scholar, the outcome of his intensive research into Cusanus and Neoplatonism. According to Beierwaltes, Cusanus' henological and Neoplatonic reflection questions the legitimacy of Heidegger's well known thesis whereby the history of Western metaphysics is characterized by the oblivion of the ontological difference between being and entity. In fact, if by "ontological difference" is meant the qualitative distinction between being and entity, for which being must be thought of co-originally with nothing, as «not of being»[418] or as the «totally other with respect to the entity»[419], then it may be rightly stated, together with Beierwaltes, that the intention starts from Cusanus' own conception of the One-God as *non aliud* (and of the Neoplatonic conception of the One in general) of thinking of the absolute difference of the Principle from every being and not only of representing him as a different being, which even if understood in a superlative sense remains included within the same dimension.

For Heidegger Western thought has always, yet exclusively, perceived being as "foundation", without the "not-thought of" of metaphysics, that is the prospective character of being, the *ereignet* of the *Ereignis*, its *Abgrund*, being without foundation. However this criticism does not accept the paradoxical oneness of a positive and negative approach to the First Principle elaborated by Neoplatonism

416 Cf. *De non aliud*, h XIII, c. 5, p. 13.

417 W. Beierwaltes, *Der verborgene Gott. Cusanus und Dionysius*, in *Der verborgene Gott. Cusanus und Dionysius*, in Id., *Platonismus im Christentum*, cit., pp. 130-171.

418 M. Heidegger, *Zur Seinsfrage*, Klostermann, Frankfurt am Main 1959, p. 38.

419 M. Heidegger, *Zur Seinsfrage*, cit., p. 40.

and by Cusanus, and by confining the affirmative side of it does not recognise the otherness and the transcendence of the One-God, which is indeed foundation of all, in that the being which is other with respect to the One-God can only be through It-He himself, but which at the same time is in essence beyond the being-foundation and the being-cause, namely It or He – as Plotinus perceptively knew – is cause not "in himself", but only "for us "[420]. When we call him cause in fact we rather express "we ourselves": the connection of the other with the same identical, but not this identical self. In Proclus the parodoxical oneness of a positive and negative approach was to find adequate expression in the conception of the One as foundation without foundation, or cause without cause[421]. For Cusanus, as we have seen, God is "principle of all" and, at the same time its negation, "nothing of all". Although the principle operates as cause or essence of all things, it is not in fact thought of at the level of entity, but rather it is in all the remaining nothing of all, it is in the world, but not in the way of the world.

Heidegger's interpretation of Western metaphysics as essential and preordained form of oblivion of being reduced to entity is possible therefore, paradoxically, on the basis of another form of oblivion, that of the authentic speculative and historical meaning of Platonic and Neoplatonic thought on the part of Heidegger himself. This criticism against Heidegger and his related re-assessment of Neoplatonic henology certainly represents one of the most precious outcomes which, thanks to his very close studies on Neoplatonism Beierwaltes confers on contemporary philosophical reflection.

2. Cornelio Fabro, Reader of Cusanus

In the studies on Cusanus' thought it is an almost unknown fact that numbered among the cardinal's readers is Cornelio Fabro (1911-1995), well known for having been one of the leading twentieth-century interpreters of the thought of Thomas Aquinas. In *La nozione metafisica di partecipazione secondo san Tommaso* of 1939 and in *Partecipazione e causalità secondo san Tommaso* of 1960 the Italian thinker provided an interpretation of Thomas' metaphysics as a conciliation and surpassing of Platonism and Aristotelism, in the sense of Hegel's *Aufhebung*, that is not of a mere leaving behind but of a surpassing in order to bring it to a higher

[420] Cf. Plotinus, *Enn.*, VI, 9, 3.

[421] Cf. *Proclus, Théologie platonicienne*, vol. II, cit., II, 9, p. 58.

level. Yet, although the studies on his thought have multiplied[422] in the last few years, no one has dwelt on his interpreting of Cusanus' thought.

In addition to several references to the contents of his work, Fabro analyzes Cusanus' thinking in his famous work of 1960 *Partecipazione e causalità* – now republished as vol. 19 of his complete works – in particular in a short but concentrated paragraph entitled *Il parmenidismo pitagorico di Cusano*[423]. The Pythagorean element which is also referred to in the title heading comes to correspond to the theological use of arithmetic and geometry. Fabro emphasizes the fact that this use gives shape to a methodical approach to mathematics which neither consumes nor represents the personal and final method of Cusanus' speculation. He realises that both mathematics and geometry, just as the notion of *coincidentia oppositorum*, have a purely symbolical-anagogical function, and that in the cognitive movement of ascending towards God activated by Cusanus they constitute only a first used methodology and not the final outcome of his theological development. Mathematics and *coincidentia* represent a first step in a journey which sets out to aspire towards a *visio Dei* which is *ultra coincidentiam contradictoriorum* and which ventures beyond the use of mathematics and geometry. Thus Pythagoreanism does not assume any particular relevance in Fabio's interpretation which dwells for the most part on other features.

By not concentrating his attention on the theme of *coincidentia* Fabro easily manages to set himself beyond the debate that developed within the *Cusanus-Forschung* among the Thomist interpreters. In fact only too often has *coincidentia* monopolized the attention of those readers, becoming project of a heated historiographic debate. In fact if a first group of scholars, authors of important studies to be set during the opening decades of last century criticised Cusanus' doctrine by interpreting it as being opposed to that of the Thomists (Albert Stöckl, Michael Glossner, Edmond Vansteenberg), the new generation, whose works are to be located in the second half of last century, has seen in the *coincidentia* a conception that teaches nothing new with respect to the scholastic one of the oneness of attributes in God, being only a precarious version of Aristotelian theory of the pure act as containing in itself every possible positive value and perfection (Paul Wilpert, Joseph Stallmach, Carlo Giacon). Although the new line of interpreta-

422 On Fabro and his thought: cf. M. Pangallo, *L'essere come atto nel tomismo essenziale di Cornelio Fabro*, Libreria Editrice Vaticana, Città del Vaticano 1987; Id., *Il principio di causalità nella metafisica di s. Tommaso. Saggio di ontologia tomista alla luce dell'interpretazione di Cornelio Fabro*, Libreria Editrice Vaticana, Città del Vaticano 1991; G. Mazzotta, *Ipotesi su Fabro*, in «Euntes Docete», 50 (1997), 213-231; E. C. Fontana, *Fabro all'Angelicum*, Edivi, Segni 2007; Id., *Fabro e l'esistenzialismo*, Edivi, Segni 2008; E. C. Fontana, *Metafisica della partecipazione. Genesi e significato della scoperta fabriana*, Edivi, Segni 2011.

423 Cf. C. Fabro, *Partecipazione e causalità secondo s. Tommaso*, Edivi, Segni 2010, pp. 553-567.

tion has the merit of stressing the continuity between Cusanus' thought and the scholastic one by not removing all possible connections and by showing how unjustified the accusation of pantheism made against Cusanus was, it nevertheless runs the risk of completely annulling their points of differentiation. Fabro's merit is that of clearly understanding the differences between the two positions, without however concentrating his attention obsessively on the theme of the coincidence of the opposites, and knowing how to interpret the latter in correct hermeneutic transposition.

Fabro's critical strategy consists in interpreting Cusanus as an exponent of Avicennian Neoplatonic Parmenideism, that is to say as being numbered among those thinkers who in following Parmenides deny the truth of being to the multifarious, and in uniting his thought with that of Meister Eckhart's. He represents neither a forerunner of modern thought, nor can his philosophy be set in the Thomasism trend, but rather his work is the expression of a very precise doctrinal movement, which proves most composite in that it includes Platonism, Neoplatonic metaphysics of the Oneness of Proclus' and Dionysius', Eckhart's Avicennism, Colonia's Albertism and the metaphysical formalism of Iohannes Scotus Eriugena, Avicenna and of the Platonists of the School of Chartres. Fabro mainly lodges two criticisms against the German philosopher, namely 1) having conceived creation neoplatonically as a necessary, and not as a free, act on the part of God; and 2) having thought of a participation without causality, that is not giving a positive foundation to the creation as something extrinsic, something «other» and «different» with respect to its cause, to the Creator.

According to Fabro, unlike Thomism – for whom biblicly indentified God with the *esse ipsum* is endowed with knowledge and love, and therefore creates freely – Neoplatonism conceives the derivation of the creatures as an emanation, that is as a procession necessary and free without causation which the One undergoes. The One of the Neoplatonists, who is beyond being, necessarily gives life to being. Cusanus, according to Fabro, shares the Neoplatonic vision of the origin of the multipicity and, furthermore, in following Meister Eckhart affirms the eminence of *intelligere* over *esse*. The essence of God consists in pure *intelligere*, in which its very causality is unfolded: in this way there is a perfect coincidence between God's knowledge and creation. The origin of being, thought of as creative knowledge, is eternal and necessary.

However, the idea of God as pure *intelligere* reveals Eckhart and Cusanus' dependence on another thinker who was first to conceive God as pure thought, namely Aristotle. The Philosopher conceives the Non-moving Mover as pure thought and more specifically as thought of thought[424]. If Fabro clearly has very

[424] Aristoteles, *Metaph.*, XII 7, 1072b18-24; XII 9, 1074b35.

good reasons for attributing to Neoplatonic thought – at least a part of it – a vision of the passage from the One to the many as outcome of a necessary process and not as outcome of free choice, the conception of God as pure *intelligere* and necessary and necessited cause would be made to date back even earlier to Aristotle.

The question within Cusanus' texts appears to be formulated differently from Fabro's interpretation. In fact he criticises Aristotle no less, and also Plato, for thinking that the Principle operates according to the necessity of nature[425]. On the contrary the First Principle acts freely, creating voluntarily[426]. God in fact, who is not necessitated by anything, was, and is, free to create as not to create.[427] Cusanus certainly thinks the One as beyond being, but unlike the ancient Neoplatonists he thinks so in a Christian fashion *at the same time* as the being itself endowed with intellect and free will, a free and personal Creator. The two aspects, otherness with regard to the being is sameness with the being itself, must not be separated. Also the sameness in God, well understood by Fabro, of creating and knowing, just as knowing and wishing, of reason and will, does not lead to conceiving the creation as necessary, but only to not keeping these aspects strictly separate in God.

Fabro says moreover, that the elimination of every intermediary and the rejection of every from of emanation constructed on hypostases and intermediary degrees leads towards attributing an even more intimate affiliation of the *processio rerum* to the divine eternity, to the intimate life of God. It is not possible to conceive a creation of different things by God since divine creating is identical with his being and has God himself as its end. Hence Cusanus' affirmation that God created himself. Two absolutely different moments would therefore seem to be confused, namely the Trinity progression or Trinity-generating, which is necessary and constitutes the intimate life of God and creation, which is free choice with regard to finite reality. In reality the affirmation that God does not only create all things, but also himself should be interpreted differently. In fact in the process of knowing himself God generates himself: hence the affirmation that God creates himself[428]. In knowing himself God generates himself trinitarially and in creating himself he knows himself. A speculative example is given by the divine name used by Cusanus in one of his last works, the *Directio speculantis seu de non aliud*. According to the German thinker «non aliud est non aliud quam non aliud», that is God defines himself trinitarially. However, seeing the definition having as its centre the *non aliud* not only has a gnosiological but also an ontological value, while

425 Cf. *De beryl.*, h XI/1, n. 38, p. 43. The same criticism against Plato and Aristotle is repeated in *ibid.*, n. 67-68, p. 78.

426 Cf. *Ibid.*,n. 37, pp. 42-43.

427 *Crib. Alk.*,h VIII, II, c. 2, n. 90, p. 75. Cf. moreover *De ven. sap.*,h XII, c. 27, n. 82, pp. 78-79.

428 Cf. *De theol. compl.*, h X/2a, n. 14, p. 82.

the triple repetition indicates that God in defining himself constitutes, generates, and creates himself trinitarially.

Yet between the creation of himself, that is Trinity-generating, the intimate life of God and the creation of the world and of the finite, there is no confusion, since Cusanus maintains their difference. While the first is a self-defining movement, of self-knowing and self-generating which does not imply any diversity or differentiation, but consists in a dynamic and relational reaffirmation of the same, the second, the creation of finite beings, represents a *contractio*, a contraction of God, a concentration of the single entities created, which are only images lacking truth. According to the terminology of the *De non aliud*, the three Trinity persons are *non aliud*, that is to say they are not diverse, are not other thing or other substance, but only *alius*, that is to say they are distinct one from the other. Although *alius* is the Father, *alius* the Son and *alius* the Spirit, they are not *aliud*. If the *alius* refers to the distinction of the persons, the negation of the *aliud* indicates the oneness of the substance : Father, Son and Spirit are other according to the person – *alius* – but not other – *non aliud* – according to nature. The creation of the world implies instead the creation of things which are constitutively *aliud*, that is to say different, the ones from the others.

Fabro distinguishes the Platonic and Neoplatonic vision, to which Cusanus also adheres, from the speculative proposal elaborated by Thomas: for the *doctor angelicus*, author of a grandiose synthesis and an original re-elaboration and *Aufhebung* of Platonism and of Aristotelianism, the entities are constituted by a real composition of essence and *esse* and really take part in the truth of being. Contrary to Platonism for which taking part eliminates causality and to Aristotelianism for which causality excludes participation, in Thomistic thinking the two aspects involve each other.

Moreover the Thomistic system is also distinguished from the Neoplatonic: the *esse ab alio*,which counterdistinguishes Neoplatonic multiplicity does not in fact indicate causality, but process. To say that the creature is entity by participation does not mean merely indicating that it is a being "dependent on…", but rather implies being different, being other, as other thing or reality. For there to be causality the effect not only cannot be without cause nor become identical to it, but in the sphere of being itself must necessarily be different from its cause. Thomas distinguishes the Creator, defined as *esse per essentiam*, that *is* the being itself, from the creature, defined as *esse per participationem*, which *has* being through participation. The *esse* for essence demands absolute perfection and simplicity, the *esse* through participation involves division and real composition, that is division into the multiplicity of the real essence of the fullness of perfection of the divine *esse* and the composition of every creature of its own essence or perfection with its proper act of being.

Fabro's interpretation sees the Dionysian-Avicennian-Eckhartian vision, supported also by Cusanus, as pantheistic in that it conceives the creature as *nichil* in itself, being that which is only in God. Although not reduced to a mere phenomenon, as it was later to be in Idealism, the creatures according to this vision are really only *imagines* and *vestigia*. For the Eckhartian-Avicennian approach the *esse* is God who does not compose himself with the essence as act and power. But if the *esse* is one and total the entities seem to constitute a simple dialectic moment, a *purum nihil*, a counterfigure of the *esse ipsum*. On the contrary for Thomas the *entia* have the *esse* perfectly participating in the essence as first fundamental act. Every creature possesses its own formal act (essence) and its real act (*esse* as *actus essendi*). The creature is really *ens* because in addition to the essence it has its act of *esse* distinct from its essence and from divine *esse*. Eckhart instead knows only one single act that is God. According to Fabro there exist therefore two different versions of participation, namely an Aristotelian-Thomist one according to which *esse* is a principle (*actus essendi*) constitutive of reality which constitutes the limit of the causality, and the other a Parmenidean-Avicennian one according to which the *esse* is a flux of causality.

In Thomist thought the likeness between Creator and creation is not, as in Avicennian-Eckhartian thought, only a relationship of exemplaristic derivation, just as unlikeness does not reside only in imperfection or in the finiteness of the creature, but the latter receives its *esse* in its finite essence as act of its own power, and therefore really distinct from the essence, while in God the *esse* is identified with the essence. For Thomas the entities *participate in the* Essere and this means that their essere does not identify with the Essere itself: the difference lies in the participation itself. The many are other than the One. In other words if for Thomas there is a difference between the Essere (Being: verbal noun) and the essente (being: adjective), for the metaphysics of Dionysian-Avicennian inspiration God himself is the being (essere) of the esistenti (existing). The *esse* and the *forma essendi* are one thing only and it is God himself who is act of all that which is in act according to an essential belonging. God is not only the *actus essendi* but also the *esse* as *essentia*, the essence of all things. The visible world is therefore simple indefinable reality of true being which is the *Essentia omnium* and the *forma essendi* of all. Participation is thought of as flux in act and the creature operates, intends and wishes as in *umbra Dei*. The creature does not have a being of its own in act, nor consists and operates in an order of its own. The essence of the creatures is distinguished from that of God as the image from its divine archetype, but its *esse* is the same divine *esse*, even if in accordance with the mode of its essence and not in accordance with the divine one. There remains missing the one which thomastically we may define as emerging act of *esse*.

According to Fabro, in keeping with the Dionysian-Eckhartian conception, Cusanus interprets participation as a form of likeness to God, who remains the only *esse* of all the real entities. Divine causality does not have an extrinsic limit in itself, but is a flux, a beam which illuminates the nothing of the creatures, for which God is the essere of all things existing. In support of his interpretation which sees God as the only *esse* of all the essences and real entities as mere reflections of God, Fabro cites a passage of the *Directio speculantis* in which the quiddity of things seems to refer totally to the *non aliud*.

> Quidditas igitur, quae "non aliud", quidditatis ipsius aliud quidditas est, quae quidem quidditatis est prioris relucentia[429].

The problem raised by Fabro does not regard so much the transcendence of the Creator regarding the creation, which would be safeguarded, but the lack of positivity of the creature which would not exist in itself, but would come to be only a manifestation of God without possessing a real and proper acting of its own being. It seems that the essence of the creature distinguishes itself from that of God only as image with respect to his exemplar; an *imago* which does not have an essere of its own, but whose essere is the same divine *esse*. The distinction would consist therefore only in the modes: in the creature the divine *esse* would be unfolded in a contracted way as in an image or special and concentrated manifestation, while in God it would be enfolded as absolute Unity.

Cusanus had already found himself facing such criticism and had attempted to formulate a response. The Aristotelian Johannes Wenck – Professor at Heidelberg and supporter of the Conciliarist movement, in which Cusanus himself had also taken part, but from which he later dissociated himself – had in 1442 written a polemical libel against the *De docta ignorantia* entitled *De ignota letteratura*. In this writing the name of Cusanus was compared in fact with that of Meister Eckhart, whose condemnation was referred to. The response was not immediate: only in 1449, after his nomination as cardinal became public in 1448, did Cusanus write an *Apologia doctae ignorantiae* in explicit opposition to Wenck's criticisms.

Against Wenck's text many criticisms and accusations were lodged, amongst which by far the most serious was that of making God coincide with the creature, that is to say by annulling the being of the creatures he made them coincide with God[430]. In more modern language, the accusation was that of having embraced pantheism. However, rather than cancelling their distinction Cusanus had kept God and world sharply distinct. In his system God was not merely form of things, as Wenck seemed to think, but *forma formarum*, that is God was neither this nor

429 *De non aliud*, h XIII, c. 8, p. 17.

430 Cf. *Le "De ignota letteratura" de Jean Wenck de Herrenberg contre Nicolas de Cuse*, ed.E. Vansteenberghe, Aschendorff, Münster 1910, p. 24.

that, neither sky nor earth, but form of all forms. God was the most simple and perfect Form and the being of all things, without being any of them[431].

The other accusation, being more subtle and with which instead Fabro sympathizes, regarded the identification of the *Esse* with God supported by Eckhart. According to Wenck this identification took all existence from the beings in their own genre[432]. On the question of creature participation Cusanus' response consisted in operating a distinction between form-forming and form formed. God is Form of forms who confers being, although it is then the form of the earth which confers being to the earth, and the form of fire which confers being to fire. But the form which confers being is God, who forms every form. Nevertheless if God is form-forming that does not mean that the beings do not possess a form formed of their own. The image or the creature has a form which it confers onto it that being of which it is image, and the form of the image is form formed, while what there is of truth in it receives it from that form which is truth and exemplar. In the same way it is in God that every creature is that being which it is. In God each creature, which is image of him, is in its own truth. But not for this is the existence of things annulled in their own form[433]. According to Cusanus if God sets himself as being, or that it is he who brings it about that the forms are this or that being, the existence of things is not annulled in their being, but is established[434].

Yet Fabro, who knows these texts, does not accept this response. From Fabro's point of view, which is Thomist, Cusanus relapses into an absolute metaphysical formalism, which refers all metaphysical reality back to transcendental formalities. But since these forms in the final analysis are identified in God, all being is once again referred back to God who absorbs all causality into himself. The German thinker does not recognise any real distinction in the creature between essence and being, between *forma* and *actus essendi*. Nevertheless Cusanus certainly does not identify the Creator with the creature, in that God does not resolve himself in

431 Cf. *De coni.*,h III, II, c. 6, n. 98, p. 95; *De docta ign.*, h I, I, c. 23, n. 70, p. 46;II, c. 7, n. 130, p. 84; II, c. 9, n. 148, p. 94; *Apol.,* h II,n. 37, p. 26.

432 Cf. *Le "De ignota letteratura"*, cit., p. 26.

433 Cf. *Apol.,* h II,n. 37, p. 26: «Moyses nominat eum formatorem: "Formavit igitur Deus hominem", et cetera. Si igitur ipse est formarum forma, ipse dat esse, licet forma terrae det terrae esse et forma ignis igni. Forma vero, quae dat esse, Deus est, qui format omnem formam. Unde, sicut imago habet formam, quae dat ei esse hoc, per quod est imago, et forma imaginis est forma formata et id, quod est veritas, non habet nisi ex forma, quae est veritas et exemplar: sic omnis creatura in Deo est id, quod est. Nam ibi est omnis creatura, quae est imago Dei, in sua veritate. Per hoc tamen non tolluntur subsistentiae rerum in suis propriis formis».

434 *Apol.*, h II, n. 38, p. 26: «Similiter etiam, quando allegat magistrum Eckhardum; nam Eckhardus circa principium Genesis, ubi praemittit de esse, postquam probavit Deum esse ipsum esse et qui dat esse et formas particulares hoc et hoc esse: subiungit per hoc non tolli subsistentias rerum in proprio esse, sed potius fundari».

any of the existing beings, but rather the latter, or better their form, is only image of God, that is to say the creature does not receive that foundation that Fabro, and before him Wenck, from a Thomist viewpoint ask from him, that is an act of proper being, but only a negative establishing[435]. In other words although God does not resolve himself in any creature, in that he transcends all and each infinitely, nevertheless the being of the creature resolves itself totally in its depending on being, in its *ab esse*[436].

3. Cusanus and Leibniz. Philological Introduction and Status Quaestionis

3.1. Testimonies

The present contribution sets out on an attempt to reconstruct the debate among scholars concerning one of the fortunate moments of Cusanus' thought in modern times, that is to say the reception of his thought by Gottfried Wilhelm Leibniz. Leibniz's case is of great interest in the field of studies related to the fortune of Cusanus's work because – unlike other philosophers, such as Hegel and Schelling, upon whom the *Cusanus-Forschung* has also focused – there are documents in which Leibniz explicitly refers to Cusanus[437]. However, although several creditable scholars have already investigated this moment of *Rezeptionsgeschichte* of Cusanus's thought, some recent data suggest that the topic should be readdressed from a new perspective and with new research.

[435] Criticism also shared by A. Bonetti, *La ricerca metafisica nel pensiero di Nicolò Cusano*, Paideia, Brescia 1973.

[436] Cf. *De docta ign.*,h I, II, c. 2, n. 102, p. 67: «Quis denique intelligere potest Deum esse essendi formam nec tamen immisceri creaturae? Non enim ex infinita linea et finita curva potest unum exoriri compositum, quod absque proportione esse equità. Proportionem vero inter infinitum et finitum cadere non posse nemo dubitat. Quomodo igitur capere potest intellectus esse linae curvae ab infinita recta esse, quae tamen ipsam non informat ut forma, sed ut causa et ratio? Quam quidem rationem non potest participare partem capiendo, cum sit infinita et indivisibilis; aut ut materia participat formam, ut Socrate set Plato humanitatem; aut ut totum participatur a partibus, sicut universum a suis partibus; nec ut plura specula eandem faciem diversi mode, cum non sit esse creaturae ante ab esse, cum sit ipsum, sicut speculum ante est speculum quam immagine faciei recipiat».

[437] Cf. K. Kremer, *Die Stellung des Nikolaus von Kues in der deutschen Philosophie*, in Id. *Praegustatio naturalis sapientiae. Gott suchen mit Nicholaus von Kues*, Aschendorff, Münster 2004, p. 527.

On the base of previous studies, Kremer has identified nine documents which are proof of such knowledge[438]:

1. The letter *Ad Octavii Pisani Lycurgum*, no. 31, from 1668-1670, in which *De concordantia catholica* is mentioned[439].
2. The notes Leibniz took between 1668 and 1669 from a handwritten copy of Bodin's *Colloquium heptaplomeres*, in which Cusanus is mentioned. It is a disapproving reference: the Cardinal is accused of applying the *petitio principii* device to the assumption that the real church is the Christian church[440].
3. The note *Cusanus egregie*, presumably from 1677[441].
4. *De vera proportione circuli ad quadratum circuscriptum in numeris rationalibus expressa*, from 1682, in which Cusanus is mentioned as a mathematician and with regard to the problem of the squaring of the circle[442].
5. *Ad Costitutionem Scientiae generalis* from 1682, cited by Kremer as *Contemplatio de historia literaria statuque presenti eruditionis*, in which Cusanus is listed among the Semi-geometers[443].
6. The exchange of letters between the English mathematican J. Wallis and Leibniz regarding the squaring of the circle and the cyloid. In particular, Cusanus is mentioned: in Wallis' letter to Leibniz from 01/11.12.1696[444], in Leibniz's letter to Wallis from 29/03/1697[445]; in Wallis' letter to Leibniz from 6/4/1697[446]; in Leibniz's letter to Wallis from 28/5/1697[447].
7. In Gerhard Wolter Molanus's letter to Leibniz from 1/2/1698, in which Cusanus is mentioned as a disciple of Raymond of Sabunde and his absurd rational demonstration of Trinitarian dogma[448].

438 Cf.*ibid.*, pp. 527-528

439 Where not otherwise specified, Leibniz citations refer to the critical edition G. W. Leibniz, *Sämtliche Schriften und Briefe*, hg. v. d. Deutschen Akademie der Wissenschaften, Akademie Verlag, Berlin, 1923ff, according to the following abbreviations: A for Akademie-Ausgabe, series number in Roman numerals,volume number in Arab numerals. Cf. A VI 2, p. 114.

440 Cf. A VI 2, p. 130.

441 Cf A VI 4 b, p. 1677.

442 Cf. G. W. Leibniz, *Mathematische Schriften*, 7 voll., hg. v. C. I. Gerhardt, Georg Olms, Hildesheim 1962, Bd. V, p. 119.

443 Cf. A VI 4, p. 487.

444 Cf. A III 7, p. 211.

445 Cf. A III, 7, p. 352.

446 Cfr. A III, 7, pp. 374-375.

447 Cf. A III, 7, p. 432.

448 Cf. A I 15, p. 295.

8. In G. W. Leibniz, *Mantissa codicis iuris gentium diplomaticis*, Hanover, 1700, 2. Teil, pp. 156-159, in which Cusanus' letter to the Bohemians from 27/6/1452 is mentioned[449].
9. In *Scriptores rerum Brunsvicensium illustrazioni inservientes*, II, Hanover, 1707 (414, 463, 945-946, 956, 962), which includes some documents and records by Cusanus originally published in J. Busch, *De reformatione monasterium quorundam Saxoniae*, liber 6[450].

Klaus Kremer's evidence can be implemented with four new documents, which raise the number to 13:

10. A note concerning *Pneumatica* from Otto von Guericke's *Experimenta Nova* from 1672, Chapter 15[451];
11. Leibniz's letter to Johann Gröning from 3/9/1701, once again concerning the cycloid, in which Cusanus is mentioned alongside Bovillus[452];
12. Eckhart's letter to Leibniz from 19/6/1700, in which there is a reference to Cusanus's *De conjectura de ultimus diebus*, a text used in the polemics between Catholics and Reformers[453];
13. The *Annotations sur l'Ecrit de Mons. l'Eveque de Meaux* added to the letter to Jacques-Bénigne Bousset from 5/2/1707, regarding some cosmological notes in which Cusanus is cited alongside Copernicus[454].

[449] Cf. G. W. Leibniz, *Mantissa codicis iuris gentium diplomaticis*, Freytag, Hannover, 1700, II, pp. 156-159.

[450] Cf. G. W. Leibniz, *Scriptores rerum Brunsvicensium illustrazioni inservientes*, II, Freytag,Hannover, 1707, pp. 414, 463, 945-946, 956, 962.

[451] Cf. A VIII 1, 276.

[452] Cf. A I 20, 411.

[453] Cf. A I 8 a, 163.

[454] Cf. A I 20, p. 755.

3.2. Cusanus, Forerunner of Leibniz: the nineteenth-century interpretation

As A.-L. Rey and F. Vengeon have argued, a systematic analysis of these philological data is yet to be conducted[455]. The relationship between the two philosophers has been the object of several studies since the middle of the nineteenth century, when Robert Zimmermann's *Cardinal Cusanus als Vorläufer Leibnitzens* was published, in 1852. Drawing parallels between the fundamental features of Cusanus and Leibniz's philosophies – though without any concrete evidence regarding the relation between the two – Zimmermann's work supports the view according to which Cusanus was "a spiritual Forerunner of Leibniz"[456]. Amongst others, the main themes dealt with are the idea of divine absoluteness or fullness, the vision of the universe as God's self-expression, the idea of monad and thus the monadic vision, the *quodlibet in quolibet*, the vision of individuality and the identity of indiscernibles, and cognitive idealism. According to the German scholar, even though any direct relations of Leibniz with Cusanus's work have not been found yet, it is most unlikely that Leibniz was unfamiliar with the contents of Cusanus' doctrine– even if through the mediation of other authors[457].

Franz Anton Scharpff in his *Cusa und Leibnitz* published in *Der Cardinal Nicolaus von Cusa als Reformator in Kirche,Reich und Philosophie des fünfzehnten Jahrhunderts* del 1871 – a work which he defends Cusanus from the accusations of pantheism lodged against him at the time by Albert Stöckl[458] – with regard to the relationship between the two thinkers one relies mainly on the work of

455 A.-L. Rey - F. Vengeon, *Présentation*, in *Nicolas de Cues et G. W. Leibniz: infini, expression et singularité*, Eds. A.-L. Rey – F. Vengeon, «Reveu de Métaphysique et de Morale», 2 (2011), p. 149.

456 Cf. R. Zimmermann, *Der Cardinal Nikolaus Cusanus als Vorläufer Leibnitzens*, In: Sitz. Ber. D. kaiserl. Akade. D. Wiss., Philos.-hist. Kl. Bd. 8, Staatsdrückerei, Wien 1852, 306-328. On the reading of Zimmermann and its context cf. H. Schwaetzer, *Cusanus, Leibniz, Herbart? Robert Zimmermanns Cusanus-Deutung im Kontext des 19. Jahrhunderts*, in A. Dall'Igna – D. Roberi, *Cusano e Leibniz. Prospettive filosofiche*, Mimesis, Milano 2013, pp. 169-182.

457 Cf. *ibidem*

458 Cf. A. Stöckl, *Geschichte der Philosophie des Mittelalters*, III, Kirchheim, Mainz 1966, pp. 59-67. We may recall that Stöckl is part, together with Michael Glossner, Edmond Vansteenberg, of that group of Neoscholastic Cusanus scholars who between the end of the nineteenth and the beginning of the twentieth century considerably criticised the doctrine of the *coincidentia oppositorum* for not being in keeping with scholastic thinking and dangerously tending towards pantheism. This line of interpretation is followed by a second generation, whose works are to be located in the second half of the twentieth century, which has seen in the *coincidentia* a conception which does not teach anything new with regard to the scholastic conception of the unity of God's attributes, being only a venturous version of the Aristotelian theory of the pure act as

Zimmermann in re-introducing the conclusions[459]. During the nineteenth century the thesis of Cusanus' being forerunner of Leibniz and of modern thought more generally is reproposed, especially on the gnosiological theme, by Richard Falckenberg and earlier by his maestro Rudolf Eucken[460]. At the beginning of the twentieth century again Edmond Vansteenberghe, in what may be considered historically as one of the classical studies on Cusanus, on the basis of Zimmermann's theses, expressed himslf in favour of there being a close relationship between the two philosophers[461].

3.3. The Debate in the Twentieth Century: Monadology and Mathematics

The affinities between Cusanus and Leibniz's philosophical thought have also been investigated by D. Manhke[462]. In *Leibnizens Synthese von Universalmathematik und Individualmetaphysik*, published in 1925, the German scholar observed how close the two authors' perspectives were regarding topics such as the vision of individuality as a monad being both contraction and mirror of the universe at the same time, the perspective vision of knowledge and of the creative nature of the human soul, and finally in their affiliation with the Mathematical Mystique[463]. According to Mahnke, not only do Cusanus and Leibniz broadly agree on the idea of monad, but he also asserts that Leibniz, in fact, took this term from Cusanus.

containing in itself all possible wealth and perfection (Paul Wilpert, Joseph Stallmach, Carlo Giacon).

459 Cf. F. A. Scharpff, *Cusa und Leibnitz*, in Id., *Der Cardinal Nicolaus von Cusa als Reformator in Kirche,Reich und Philosophie des fünfzehnten Jahrhunderts*, Laupp,Tübingen, 1871 [repr. Minerva, Frankfurt am Main, 1966].

460 Cf. R. Falckenberg, *Grundzüge der Philosophie des Nicolaus Cusanus mit besonderer Berücksichtigung der Lehre vom Erkennen*, Koebner, Breslau 1880; R. Eucken, *Untersuchungen zur Geschichte der älteren deutschen Philosophie*, in «Philosophische Monatshefte», XIV (1878), pp. 449-470. On the theme cf. K. Zeyer, *Cusanus als Vorläufer von Leibniz. Cusanus-Rezeption im 19. Jahrhundert mit besonderer Beücksichtigung von R. Eucken und R. Falckenberg*, in A. Dall'Igna – D. Roberi, *Cusano e Leibniz*, cit., pp. 227-239; Id., *Cusanus in Marburg*, cit., pp. 41-76, 77-126.

461 Cf. E. Vansteenberghe, *Le cardinal Nicolas de Cues (1401-1464)*, cit., [repr. Frankfurt am Main, Minerva, 1963], pp. 450-451

462 Cf. D. Mahnke, *Leibnizens Synthese von Universalmathematik und Individualmetaphysik*, Niemeyer, Halle 1925 [rist. Frommann, Stuttgart, 1964].

463 Cf. D. Mahnke, *Leibnizens Synthese von Universalmathematik und Individualmetaphysik*, cit., pp. 60-61, 76, 125, 134-135, 216.

However, the German scholar admits not having found any documents concerning Leibniz's possession of Cusanus' texts, apart from a work by Kymeus entitled *Das Babst Hercules wider die Deudschen,* which was published in 1538 and which contains some excerpts taken from Cusanus' works[464].

In his fortunate and important work of 1927 *Individuum und Kosmos in der Philosophie der Renaissance* Ernst Cassirer also recognized in Cusanus a forerunner of Leibniz's vision of monadology[465]. Together with Pico and Bovillus, with his reflection on the value of individuality and of the subject's role in the theory of knowledge, his doctrine of the *coincidentia oppositorum*, his vision of man as microcosm and in accordance with God, he was probably a forerunner of the concept of monad as living mirror of the universe and of Leibniz's cognitive theories. The historian and Neokantian philosopher reconstructs the threads of a historico-speculative development which from Cusanus' gnosiological and anthropological doctrines through Pico's *Oratio*, the edition of the Cusanian texts and the work of Jacques Lefèvre d'Etaples and the *De sapiente* of Charles de Bouelle arrives at the philosophical idealism of Leibniz[466].

In Italy the idea that a prelude to Leibniz is present in Cusanus, especially to his monadic conception of reality and of the principle of the indiscernibles is a thesis that was advanced in 1958 by Giovanni Santinello in his *Il pensiero di Nicolò Cusano nella sua prospettiva estetica*[467]. According to the Italian scholar in the vision of Cusanus' *contractio* the being is concentrated in so many unitary centres, each one autonomous and centred in itself participating in the unity of all, although not as a part extracted from all, but as an all in all: every being is the contracted all. For the Cardinal the participation of the being is not a fractioning, but a contraction of all being. Yet, precisely for this there cannot be two entities perfectly equal. According to Cusanus every individual entity is an active mirror which cannot be reduced to all the others and reflect all. Cusanus' universe therefore appears as a community of monads, each reflecting in a different and unrepeatable way the act of forming, which participates in all and in each one individually[468].

464 Cf. *ibid.*, pp. 251-252, note 84. Kymeus' text can now be read in the edition J. Kymeus, *Des Babst Hercules wider die Deutschen*, in *Cusanus-Studien*, cit. In fact the text has a purely polemical and controvesial tone and is included in the disputes between Catholics and Protestants of the day. Interestingly it contains the German translation of several extracts of Cusanus' works, especially of the *De pace fidei*, but also of the *De concordantia catholica*, and of the *De docta ignorantia*. Hence it would not be a great source of knowledge for Leibniz.

465 Cf E. Cassirer, *Individuum und Kosmos in der Philosophie der Renaissance*, in Id, *Gesammelte Werke. Hamburger Ausgabe*, cit., pp. 97ff., 137.

466 *Ibidem.*

467 Cf.G. Santinello, *Il pensiero di Nicolò Cusanonella sua prospettiva estetica*, Liviana, Padova 1958, pp. 111-118.

468 *Ibid.*, p. 126.

During his speech at the Brixen Conference commemorating the fifth centenary of the Cardinal's death, the German philosopher H.-G. Gadamer underlined the affinity of Cusanus' vision to that of Leibniz's monadology in that they pioneered the speculation of the future Idealism[469]. During the same meeting, G. Gawlick's *Zur Nachwirkung cusanischer Ideen im siebzehnten und achtehzenten Jahrhundert* claimed – in a way that seems too authoritative – that although there is no doubt that parallels between Cusanus's work and Leibniz's monadology can be drawn, "it is not possible to talk about a direct knowledge of Cusanus"[470].

F. Nagel, instead, focused on the Mathematical and Geometrical aspects of the topic in his *Nicolaus Cusanus und die Entstehung der Exakten Wissenschaften*, published in 1984. The German scholar closely analysed both Leibniz's mathematical works and the exchange of letters he had had with the English mathematician J. Wallis. Indeed, Nagel showed that they contained references to Cusanus and to the contents of his works regarding the quadrature of the circle, mathematics and geometry. The outcome of his study reveals that Leibniz did know about some of Cusanus's ideas, even though he had not read the texts himself. He had acquired his mathematical-geometric knowledge from a secondary source[471]. However, Nagel's references to the sources do not appear to be very clear and satisfactory.

One of the most prestigious experts on the matter, however, is not very positive about the relationship between the two authors. In fact Raymond Klibansky claims that although Leibniz cited Cusanus many times, he did not know him as a philosopher but only as a mathematician, an ambassador and a historical character. Therefore, he was not influenced by him in the elaboration of his own philosophical thought. Klibansky adds that the research done in 1984 does not provide any evidence of Leibniz making explicit use of Cusanus' philosophy[472].

T. P. Mc Tighe explicitly spoke against any parallelism between Cusanus and Leibniz in his *Nicholas of Cusa and Leibniz's principle of indiscernibility* (1965). The American scholar maintains that there is a radical opposition between Cusanus' and Leibniz's views on individuality. He argues that a modern-age counterpart to the Cusanian doctrine concerning the impossibility of equality among individuals is more likely to be closer to authors such as Hegel or Bradley, rather than to Leibniz. Mc Tighe is also mistrustful of other Cusanian views which are

469 Cf. H.-G. Gadamer, *Nikolaus von Kues im modernen Denken*, in *Nicolò Cusano agli inizi del mondo moderno*, cit., pp. 39-48, especially p. 45.

470 Cf. *Zur Nachwirkung cusanischer Ideen im siebzehnten und achtehzenten Jahrhundert*, in *Nicolò Cusano agli inizidel mondo moderno*, cit., 225-239, especially p. 225 note 1

471 Cr. F. Nagel, *Nicolaus Cusanus und die Entstehung der Exakten Wissenschaften*, Aschendorff, Münster 1984,pp. 135, 138.

472 Cf. R. Klibansky, *Die Wirkungsgeschichte des Dialogs De pace fidei*, cit.,pp. 113-125, 120.

considered to be the forerunners of Leibniz's thought, especially his views on matter, the universe and the monads[473].

J. Hopkins has spoken against Mc Tighe's interpretation in his work entitled *Cusa's Metaphysical Speculation*, of which an entire section is dedicated to the relationship between Cusanus and Leibniz[474]. In contrast to Mc Tighe, according to the American scholar Cusanus and Leibniz indeed had very similar views on the identity of indiscernibles[475]. Moreover, he identifies six more shared views in the two philosophers: the notion of monads, the idea that creatures are like mirrors, the harmonic vision of the universe, the principle of sufficient reason, the philosophy of innatism, and the problem of maximum and minimum and their proportionality or comparison. However, there does not seem to be a systematic-conceptual connection between these six views close enough to sustain the idea of Cusanus as "forerunner" of Leibniz; rather, he might be seen as a "catalyst of Leibniz"[476].

Die Präsenz des Vergessenen. Zur Rezeption der Philosophie des Nicolaus Cusanus vom 15. Bis zum 18. Jahrhundert, published in 1989, might be considered the most complete study on Cusanus's fortune in modern times. Its author, S. Meier-Oeser, argues that although Leibniz did not own any of Cusanus's works, it is possible to draw links between the two philosophers through the mediation of texts such as Johannes Kymeus's *Das Babst Hercules wider die Deudschen* (1538), which sharply criticised Cusanus's philosophy and which also contained some excerpts from his works, Comenius's polemic *De irenico irenicorum* and Giordano Bruno's dialogue *De l'infinito universo et Mondi*[477]. Meier-Oeser's contribution to the research aimed to identify the possible sources Leibniz drew on and therefore from which he derived Cusanus' paradigmatic diagram P, mentioned by Leibniz in his *Von der Allmacht und Allwissenheit Gottes und der Freiheit des Menschen* from 1670-1671[478]. Possible links between the two philosophers might have been Valentin Weigel, Athanasius Kircher and Robert Fludd[479].

Some important reflections on the relationship between Cusanus' conception of the *mens* and the vision of Leibniz's spiritual monad have been dealt with

473 Cf. Th. P. Mc Tighe, *Nicholas of Cusa and Leibniz' principle of indiscernibility*, in: «The Modern Schoolmann», 42 (1964), pp. 33-46, especially p. 46.

474 Cf. J. Hopkins, *Cusa's Metaphysical Speculation*, II, Minneapolis, Banning, 2000, pp. 139-144

475 Cf. *ibid.*, 139-140

476 Cf. *ibid.*, 139.

477 On Bruno's reception of Cusanus cf. T. Leinkauf, *Einleitung*, in G. Bruno, Über die Ursache, das Prinzip und das Eine, Meiner, Hamburg, 2007, pp. IX-CLIII.

478 Cf. A VI 1, 538. Cr. S. Meier-Oeser, *Die Präsenz des Vergessenen. Zur Rezeption der Philosophie des Nicolaus Cusanus vom 15. Bis zum 18. Jahrhundert*, Münster, Aschendorff, 1989, pp. 169-171.

479 Cf. S. Meier-Oeser, op. cit., pp. 169-170

by the German scholar Leinkauf in his study *Diversitas identitate compensata. Ein Grundtheoremen in Leibniz' Denken und seine Voraussetzungen in der frühen Neuzeit*[480], also with interesting references to the theories of Pico, Ficino, Bovillus and the encyclopaedist of Herbon, not forgetting Bruno[481]. In his analysis Leinkauf related Cusanus' reflection on the soul as *viva imago* Dei, that is living image of the divine Spirit and as active representation of all, microcosm, with the vision of Leibniz's spiritual monad as living mirror of the universe, showing that at the basis a change in perspective operates in the vision of the individual substance understood actively as force and of the monad or *mens* as movement of subjectivisation. In fact Cusanus and Leibniz seem to share a common dynamic and constructivist conception of the human mind even in their differences.

3.4. The Present State of Studies

Nowadays, the work which acts as a reference point in the study of the relationship between Cusanus and Leibniz is doubtlessly K. Kremer's *Die Stellung des Nikolaus von Kues in der deutschen Philosophie*[482]. According to Kremer, it is surprising that Cusanus and his works were mentioned by Leibniz both in his works and his letters from 1668-70 until 1707 – that is, for a period of almost forty years. According to the scholar, who also based his theories on former research, there are nine documents which can testify that the Hanoverian philosopher knew Cusanus (cf. K. Kremer, 2004, 527-528). However, Kremer also admits that there is no evidence of Leibniz's direct contact (*unmittelbar*) with Cusanus's works. In fact, he claims that there had been indirect contact (*mittelbar*) or, in his own words, that the knowledge Leibniz had gained was "mediated" (*vermittelter*) [483]. Kremer then

480 T. Leinkauf, «Diversitas identitate compensata. *Ein Grundtheoremen in Leibniz' Denken und seine Voraussetzungen in der frühen Neuzeit*, in «Studia leibnitiana», 1 (1996), pp. 58-83; Id., «Diversitas identitate compensata. Ein Grundtheoremen in Leibniz' Denken und seine Voraussetzungen in der frühen Neuzeit (II), in «Studia leibnitiana», 1 (1997), pp. 81-102. Both studies are now contained in Id., *Einheit, Natur, Geist. Beiträge zu metaphysischen Grundproblemen im Denken von Gottfried Wilhelm Leibniz*, Berlin, Trafo, 2012, pp. 15-65.

481 To Cusanus' influence on Athanasius Kircher are dedicated several interesting pages of the volume T. Leinkauf, *Mundus combinatus. Studien zur Struktur der barocken Universalwissenschaften am Beispiel Athanasius Kircher SJ (1602-1680)*, Akademie, Berlin 1993,20092, pp. 83ff., 86ff., 143-149, 170ff., 223 ff.. 320ff, 380ff.

482 The text originally published in «MFCG» 28(2003), pp. 27-63; is now contained, revised and extended in K. Kremer, *Praegustatio naturalis sapientiae. Gott suchen mit Nicholaus von Kues*, cit., pp. 515-553.

483 Cf. *ibid.*, 545-549

moves on to list all the potential parallels between Cusanus and Leibniz's schools of thought by drawing on Zimmermann's research among others, to which he adds extra information concerning the two philosophers' views on the theory of knowledge. Kremer, however, does not add anything new related to the potential sources which mediated the knowledge Leibniz had of Cusanus; he only mentions those which had already been referenced by Meier-Oeser and others.

A further contribution to the discussion, this time Italian, was the one made by Sandro Mancini who in a series of essays showed the closeness of Cusanus' teleological monadism to Leibniz's thought by stressing their difference with the cyclic modalism of Bruno, and *mutatis mutandis* of Spinoza[484]. Cusanus and Bruno apparently shared the same basic philosophical intuition, that is the vision of the One as infinite source of the expression contracting itself in the multiplicity of its manifestative figures thought of not as separate parts or fractions of the unity of the Principle, but as a plurality of centres, each being one and infinite. Yet they profoundly differ in their vision of the contraction: finalistic for the first and cyclic for the second. Bruno, as later Spinoza, thinks that all the complicated possibilities in the One must find implementation in its infinite explicative implementations and that between *complicatio* and *explicatio* there exists a perfect and necessary reversibility. In contrast for Cusanus and Leibniz there is no immediate continuity between *complicatio* and *explicatio*, the possible enfolding (complicatio) in God must not necessarily and exhaustively find unfolding (explicatio) in the world, but God creates the universe voluntarily and freely. Moreover while for Bruno the contingency of the single individuals is denied in the universal cyclicity of the world, for Cusanus and Leibniz singularity in its irriducibility and contingency is exalted to the highest degree. Hence the two different dialectics between the One and the many, God and the monadistic creatures: monadistic and finalistic the one of Cusanus' and Leibniz's, in which singularity is an individual centre which is not necessitated but free to return to the Principle which also constitutes the final cause of the process; modalistic and cyclic that of Bruno and Spinoza in which the world is only a different way of the divine being, fatalistically and cyclically necessitated. Not by chance does Mancini emphasise that Cusanus rejects the doctrine of the soul of the world (enthusiastically embraced, in contrast, by Nolano) in favour of the singularity of the exemplars or of the substantial forms, and supports the thesis that there are individuals that are in act.

One recent study relating to the subject are the records of a conference which took place at Université de Lille III on 18th March, 2010, later collected in the volume entitled *Nicolas de Cues et G. W. Leibniz: infini, expression et singularité*[485].

[484] S. Mancini, *Congetture su Dio*, cit., pp. 29-102, 201-252.

[485] Cf. *Nicolas de Cues et G. W. Leibniz: infini, expression et singularité*, cit.

According to the editors, there are close analogies between Cusanus and Leibniz's Metaphysics, analogies which cannot be thought of as accidental[486]. In particular, there is a fundamental question that haunts both authors' philosophies. It is the problem of infinity and its double-sided tension between an expressive Metaphysics of infinity and the value ascribed to the single, created individuality[487], a theme to which essays have been dedicated by Jean Celeyrette, Frédéric Vengeon and Anne-Lise Rey. While to an analysis of the idea of the best of Leibniz's possible worlds is dedicated that of Paul Rateau, to the vision of the mathematical infinite of Cusanus and Leibniz the one written by David Rabouin; and to the theory of the small perceptions the essay by Marc Parmentier. The identity of a historical relationship between the two authors is assigned to the essay by Pierre Magnard. Pierre Magnard's contribution, *Le chanson manquant*, identifies Bovillus as the missing part of the jigsaw, on the basis of the criticism aimed at Cassier's simplification in his reconstruction of the problem of knowledge – that is, a direct connection between Cusanus and Leibniz[488]. The paper analyses the ideas of the French philosopher in order to find in it the roots of modern subjective idealism. According to the French scholar, Bovillus is the missing link in the historical chain of Western Metaphysics and the unifying link between the Neoplatonic and Dionysian tradition and modern philosophy[489]. It is only towards the end of the paper that Magnard mentions Leibniz, arguing that he might have been introduced to Bovillus's Metaphysics through the Dutch philosopher Martin Shoock, editor and expert of the French philosopher's works, as well as Leibniz's correspondent[490]. However, the scholar does not provide any philological or historical evidence for his claims, but leaves the problem of Leibniz's reception of his and Cusanus's philosophy without solution. In fact, all the contributions which are present in the volume appear to be more focused on the analysis of single themes and facets of the two philosophers' thought, rather than on their actual links of transmission and reception.

Oriented towards analyzing certain theoretical affinities between the thoughts of the two philosophers more than towards ascertaining possible philological and historical links there also appears the most recent study available to date, namely

486 Cf A.-L. Rey - F. Vengeon, *Présentation*, in *Nicolas de Cues et G. W. Leibniz: infini, expression et singularité*, cit. p. 147.

487 Cf *Ibid.*, p. 148

488 Cf. P. Magnard, *Le chaînon manquant*, in A*Nicolas de Cues et G. W. Leibniz: infini, expression et singularité*, cit., p. 167. In fact as we have already seen Cassirer had underlined this mediation.

489 Cf. *ibid.*, p. 179

490 *Ibidem.*

the volume *Cusano e Leibniz. Prospettive filosofiche*[491]. The text brings together only some of the reports made at a conference held in Turin between 7 and 9 June 2012. One part of these are effectively dedicated to analyzing certain themes and problems in the two authors. As Gianluca Cuozzo writes in the first contribution to the volume, the philosophies of Cusanus and Leibniz' are two philosophies seemingly aspiring towards *panopticon*, for which perspectivism and the principle of the "right distance", using Leonardo da Vinci's language, represent elements that are dear to both authors[492]. To the common definition of Cusanus and Leibniz's systems such as transcendent, monadistic and finalistic idealism is dedicated the essay by Sandro Mancini. The Milanese scholar designs the two positions as transcendent idealism in that the contraction of the infinite and absolute Principle is seen as an unfathomable, contingent and gratuitous act of creation *ex nihilo*. It is a matter of a monadistic idealism since God, as *Monas monadium*, in contracting himself gives life to indivisible and indestructible individuality. He represents the singularity of every spiritual monad, albeit being beyond each one. Mancini speaks of finalistic idealism since in both authors final causality prevails over every other type of causality[493]. Jean Seidegart's contribution is aimed at exploring how the two thinkers conceive the connection between mathematics and philosophy regarding the question of the infinite, going so far as to discuss a "speculative mathematics" which would be common to both authors[494]. Christiane Bacher's essay is dedicated to investigating the theme of ancient origin, but present in both philosophers, of self-knowledge as intrinsic knowledge of God. For both authors self-awareness that is attainable by the *mens humana* represents a way of approaching God and his knowing. However if Cusanus's aim does not lie in rationality but in gaining access to the *docta ignorantia* and in arriving at the comprehension of the incomprehensibility of God, for Leibniz God, who is the highest rationality, can be reached by perfecting the human rationality itself[495]. To the theme of Christian ecumenism is dedicated the essay by the Director of the Istitut fuer Cusanus-Forschung of Trier, Walter Andreas Euler. If both thinkers have always promoted the reconciliation between the Christian churches and the return to the unity of the Christians: the ecumenical theme is closely examined by following two routes, namely the Cusanian one through the idea of the *religio*

491 Cf. A. Dall'Igna – D. Roberi (eds.), *Cusano e Leibniz. Prospettive filosofiche*, Mimesis, Milano 2013.

492 Cf. G. Cuozzo, *Arte e metafisica in Cusano e Leibniz: prospettive a confronto*, in *Cusano e Leibniz. Prospettive filosofiche*, cit., pp. 17-28.

493 Cf. S. Mancini, *L'idealismo trascendente tra Cusano e Leibniz*, in *Cusano e Leibniz. Prospettive filosofiche*, cit., pp. 29-44.

494 Cf. J. Seidengart, *L'infini chez Nicolas de Cues et Leibniz*, in *Cusano e Leibniz. Prospettive filosofiche*, cit., pp. 57-71.

495 Cf. C. Bacher, *Selbsterkenntnis als Gotteserkenntnis bei Cusanus und Leibniz*, in *Cusano e Leibniz. Prospettive filosofiche*, cit., pp. 89-100.

una in rituum varietate, a most profound affirmation contained in the *De pace fidei* of 1453, and the Leibnizian one examining the idea of *Omnia ad unum*, which may be considered as a carrying on of Cusanus' idea. For some interesting historiographical perspectives on the question of the historical and speculative relationships between Cusanus' thought and that of Leibniz' are focused the essays of Harald Schwaetzer and Kirstin Zeyer. Schwetzer analyses the interpretation offered by Robert Zimmermann locating it in the context of readings on Cusanus of the 19th century, more especially evidencing their relations with the letters of Franz Jacob Clemens and of Moriz Carrière, directed towards examining in depth the question of Cusanus as forerunner of idealism and his relationship with Giordano Bruno. Zimmermann's Cusanian hermeneutics were probably designed to interpret Cusanus as an forerunner of subjectivism, to which sceptical and nominalistic tracts are no strangers. According to Schwaeter this reading should be understood by starting from Zimmermann's idea which sees Leibniz as forerunner of Herbart; only by starting from this connection could his attempt be understood of creating a historico-philosophical trend linking Cusanus, Leibniz, and Herbart. To the reading of Cusanus as forerunner of Leibniz given by Eucken and by his pupil Falckenberg is dedicated the contribution made by Zeyer. This is of considerable importance in the history of the interpretation of Cusanus since the nineteenth-century neo-idealistic readings of Eucken and of Falckenberg would have influenced the subsequent twentieth-century Neokantian rediscovery of Hermann Cohen and of Ernst Cassirer. The task of closing the volume is entrusted to Enrico Pasini, who tackles the question of the opposites, their oneness and the contradiction, extending the investigation to include Erasmus. Of special interest is the stimulating approach of the idea of harmony as a result of the conveniences and the differences, of *unitas* and of *veritas*, of the entities, which is contained in the *Phosphorus Catholicus* of Johann Henrich Bisterfeld, important source of Leibniz', to that of Cusanus' *concordia discors*.

Bibliography

I. Primary Sources

A. The Critical edition of Cusanus' works

Apologia doctae ignorantiae, ed. R. Klibansky, in *Nicolai de Cusa Opera omnia*, iussu et auctoritate Academiae Litterarum Heidelbergensis ad codicum fidem edita, II, Meiner, Hamburg 1932 (2007²).

Compendium, ed. B. Decker - K. Bormann, in *Nicolai de Cusa Opera omnia*, cit, XI/3, Meiner, Hamburg 1964.

Cribratio Alkorani, ed. L. Hagemann, in *Nicolai de Cusa Opera omnia*, cit, VIII, Meiner, Hamburg 1986.

De aequalitate, ed. H. G. Senger, in *Nicolai de Cusa Opera omnia*, cit, X/1, Meiner, Hamburg 2001.

De apice theoriae, ed. R. Klibansky - H. G. Senger, in *Nicolai de Cusa Opera omnia*, cit, XII, Meiner, Hamburg 1982.

De beryllo, ed. H. G. Senger - K. Bormann, in *Nicolai de Cusa Opera omnia*, cit, XI/1, Hamburg 1988.

De concordantia catholica, ed. G. Kallen, in *Nicolai de Cusa Opera omnia*, cit, XIV/1-4, Meiner, Hamburg 1959-1968.

De coniecturis, ed. J. Koch - K. Bormann - G. H. Senger, in *Nicolai de Cusa Opera omnia*, cit, III, Meiner, Hamburg 1972.ww

De dato patris luminum, ed. P. Wilpert, in *Nicolai de Cusa Opera omnia*, cit, IV, Meiner, Hamburg 1959.

De Deo abscondito, ed. P. Wilpert, in *Nicolai de Cusa Opera omnia*, cit, IV, Meiner, Hamburg 1959.

De docta ignorantia, ed. E. Hoffmann - R. Klibansky, in *Nicolai de Cusa Opera omnia*, cit, I, Meiner, Leipzig 1932 (2014²).

De filiatione Dei, ed. P. Wilpert, in *Nicolai de Cusa Opera omnia*, cit, IV, Meiner, Hamburg 1959.

De genesi, ed. P. Wilpert, in *Nicolai de Cusa Opera omnia*, cit, IV, Meiner, Hamburg 1959.

De pace fidei, ed. R. Klibansky - H. Bascour, in *Nicolai de Cusa Opera omnia*, cit, VII, Meiner, Hamburg 1959 (1970²).

De possest, ed. R. Steiger, in *Nicolai de Cusa Opera omnia*, cit, XI/2, Meiner, Hamburg 1973.

Tu quis es, ed. K. Bormann - A. D. Riemann, in *Nicolai de Cusa Opera omnia*, cit, X/2b, Meiner, Hamburg 1994.

De quaerendo Deum, ed. P. Wilpert, in *Nicolai de Cusa Opera omnia*, cit, IV, Meiner, Hamburg 1959.

De theologicis complementis, ed. H. D. Riemann - K. Bormann, in *Nicolai de Cusa Opera omnia*, cit, X/2a, Meiner, Hamburg 1994.

De venatione sapientiae, ed. R. Klibansky - H. G. Senger, in *Nicolai de Cusa Opera omnia*, cit, XII, Meiner, Hamburg 1982.

De visione Dei, ed. A. D. Riemann, in *Nicolai de Cusa Opera omnia*, cit, VI, Meiner, Hamburg 2000.

DialogusDe ludo globi, ed. G. H. Senger, in *Nicolai de Cusa Opera omnia*, cit, IX, Meiner, Hamburg 1998.

Directio speculantis seu de non aliud, ed. L. Baur - P. Wilpert, in *Nicolai de Cusa Opera omnia*, cit, XIII, Meiner, Leipzig 1944.

Epistula ad Ioannem de Segobia, ed. R. Klibansky - H. Bascour, in *Nicolai de Cusa Opera omnia*, cit, VII, Meiner, Hamburg 1959.

Idiota de sapientia, ed. R. Steiger, in *Nicolai de Cusa Opera omnia*, cit, V, Meiner, Hamburg 1983.

Idiota de mente, ed. R. Steiger, in *Nicolai de Cusa Opera omnia*, cit, V, Meiner, Hamburg 1983.

Idiota de staticis experimentis, ed. L. Baur, in *Nicolai de Cusa Opera omnia*, cit, V, Meiner, Hamburg 1983.

Opuscula bohemica, ed. S. Nottelmann – H. G. Senger, in *Nicolai de Cusa Opera omnia*, cit, XV/1, Meiner, Hamburg 2014.

Opuscula ecclesiastica, ed. H. G. Senger, in *Nicolai de Cusa Opera omnia*, cit, XV/2, Meiner, Hamburg 2008.

Sermones I (1430-1441). Fasciculus 1: sermones I-IV, ed. R. Haubst - M. Bodewig - W. Krämer, in *Nicolai de Cusa Opera omnia*, cit, XVI/1, Meiner, Hamburg 1970.

Sermones I (1430-1441). Fasciculus 2: sermones V-X, ed. R. Haubst - M. Bodewig - W. Krämer, in *Nicolai de Cusa Opera omnia*, cit, XVI/2, Meiner, Hamburg 1973.

Sermones I (1430-1441). Fasciculus 3: sermones V-X, ed. R. Haubst - M. Bodewig, in *Nicolai de Cusa Opera omnia*, cit, XVI/3, Meiner, Hamburg 1977.

Sermones I (1430-1441), Fasciculus 4: sermones XI-XXI, ed. R. Haubst - M. Bodewig, in *Nicolai de Cusa Opera omnia*, cit, XVI/4, Meiner, Hamburg 1984.

Sermones II (1443-1452). Fasciculus 1: sermones XXVII-XXXIX, ed. R. Haubst - H. Schnarr, in *Nicolai de Cusa Opera omnia*, cit, XVII/1, Meiner, Hamburg 1983.

Sermones II (1443-1453). Fasciculus 2: sermones XL-XLVIII, ed. R. Haubst - H. Schnarr, in *Nicolai de Cusa Opera omnia*, cit, XVII/2, Meiner, Hamburg 1991.

Sermones II (1443-1452). Fasciculus 3: sermones XLIX-LVI, ed. R. Haubst - H. Schnarr, in *Nicolai de Cusa Opera omnia*, cit, XVII/3, Meiner, Hamburg 1996.

Sermones II (1443-1452). Fasciculus 4: sermones LVII-LXI, ed. H. Schnarr, in *Nicolai de Cusa Opera omnia*, cit, XVII/4, Meiner, Hamburg 2001.

Sermones II (1443-1452). Fasciculus 5: sermones LXII-LXXV, ed. M.-A. Aris - H. Hein - H. Schnarr, in *Nicolai de Cusa Opera omnia*, cit, XVII/5, Meiner, Hamburg 2006.

Sermones II (1443-1452). Fasciculus 6: sermones LXXXVI-CXXI, ed. H. Hein - H. Schnarr, in *Nicolai de Cusa Opera omnia*, cit, XVII/6, Meiner, Hamburg 2006.

Sermones III (1452-1455). Fasciculus 1: sermones CXXII-CXL, ed. R. Haubst - H. Pauli, in *Nicolai de Cusa Opera omnia*, cit, XVIII/1, Meiner, Hamburg 1995.

Sermones III (1452-1455). Fasciculus 2: CXLI-CLX, ed. H. Pauli, in *Nicolai de Cusa Opera omnia*, cit, XVIII/2, Meiner, Hamburg 2001.

Sermones III (1452-1455). Fasciculus 3: CLXI-CLXXV, ed. S. Donati - I. Mandrella - H. Schwaetzer, in *Nicolai de Cusa Opera omnia*, cit, XVIII/3, Meiner, Hamburg 2003.

Sermones III (1452-1455). Fasciculus 4: sermones CLXXVI-CXCII, ed. S. Donati - H. Schwaetzer – F.-B. Stammkötter, in *Nicolai de Cusa Opera omnia*, cit, XVIII/4, Meiner, Hamburg 2005.

Sermones III (1452-1455). Fasciculus 5: sermones CXCIII-CCIII, ed. S. Donati - I. Mandrella, in *Nicolai de Cusa Opera omnia*, cit, XVIII/5, Meiner, Hamburg 2005.

Sermones IV (1455-1463). Fasciculus 1: sermones CCIV-CCXVI, ed. K. Reinhardt - W. A. Euler, in *Nicolai de Cusa Opera omnia*, cit, XIX/1, Meiner, Hamburg 1996.

Sermones IV (1455-1463). Fasciculus 2: sermones CCXVII-CCXXXI, ed. M.-A. Aris, in *Nicolai de Cusa Opera omnia*, cit, XIX/2, Meiner, Hamburg 2001.

Sermones IV (1455-1463). Fasciculus 3: sermones CCXXXII-CCXLV, ed. W. A. Euler - H. Schwaetzer, in *Nicolai de Cusa Opera omnia*, cit, XIX/4, Meiner, Hamburg 2002.

Sermones IV (1455-1463). Fasciculus 4: sermones CCXLVI-CCLVII, ed. I. Mandrella - H. D. Riemann, in *Nicolai de Cusa Opera omnia*, cit, XIX/5, Meiner, Hamburg 2004.

Sermones IV (1455-1463). Fasciculus 5: sermones CCLVIII-CCLXVII, ed. H. D. Riemann - H. Schwaetzer - F.B. Stammkötter, in *Nicolai de Cusa Opera omnia*, cit, XIX/6, Meiner, Hamburg 2005.

Sermones IV (1455-1463). Fasciculus 6: sermones CCLXVIII-CCLXXXII, ed. H. D. Riemann, in *Nicolai de Cusa Opera omnia*, cit, XIX/6, Meiner, Hamburg 2005.

Sermones IV (1455-1463). Fasciculus 7: sermones CCLXXXIII-CCXCIII, ed. S. Donati - H. D. Riemann, in *Nicolai de Cusa Opera omnia*, cit, XIX/7, Meiner, Hamburg 2005.

Scripta mathematica, ed. M. Folkerts, in *Nicolai de Cusa Opera omnia*, cit, XX, Meiner, Hamburg 2010.

B. Texts of Nicholas of Cusa

Autour de la docte ignorance. Une controverse sur la Théologie Mystique au XVe Siècle, ed. E. Vansteenberghe, Aschendorff, Münster 1910.

Le "De ignota letteratura" de Jean Wenck de Herrenberg contre Nicolas de Cuse, ed. E.Vansteenberghe, Aschendorff, Münster 1910.

Vom Nichtanderen, ed. P. Wilpert, Meiner, Hamburg 1952.

Acerca de lo no-otro o de la definición que todo define. Nuevo texto crítico original, intr. and trans by J. M. Machetta, critical text and notes by C. D'Amico - M. D'Ascenso - A. Eisenkopf - J. G. Rios - J. M. Machetta - K. Reinhardt - C. Rusconi - H. Schwaetzer, Biblios, Buenos Aires 2008.

De non aliud. Nichts anderes, eds. K. Reinhardt, J. M. Machetta, H. Schwaetzer, Aschendorff, Münster 2010.

C. Marginalia

L. Baur, *Nicolaus Cusanus und Ps. Dionysius im Lichte der Zitate und Randbemerkungen des Cusanus*, Winter, Heidelberg 1941.

R. Haubst, *Die Thomas- und Proklos-Exzerpte des "Nicolaus Treverensis"in Codicillus Strassburg 84*, in «MFCG», 1 (1961), pp. 17-51.

J. Koch, *Kritisches Verzeichnis der Londoner Handschriften aus dem Besitz des Nikolaus von Kues*, in «MFCG», 3 (1963), pp. 16-100.

G. Santinello, *Glosse di mano del Cusano alla Repubblica di Platone*, in «Rinascimento», XX (1969), pp. 117-145.

P. Lucentini, *Le annnotazioni di Nicola Cusano alla* Clavis Physicae, in Id., *Platonismo medievale. Contributi per la storia dell'eriugenismo*, La Nuova Italia, Firenze 1980², pp. 77-109.

P. Lucentini, *Le glosse al libro I del* De divisione naturae *nel Codice Brit. Mus. Addit. 11035*, in Id., *Platonismo medievale. Contributi per la storia dell'eriugenismo*, La Nuova Italia, Firenze 1980², pp. 113-124.

R. Haubst, *Marginalien des Nikolaus von Kues zu Abelard*, in *Petrus Abaelardus (1079-1142). Person, Werk und Wirkung*, ed. R. Thomas, Paulinus, Trier 1980, pp. 287-296.

T. Pindl-Büchel, *Die Exzerpte und Randnoten des Nikolaus von Kues zu den Schriften des Raimundus Lullus*, Winter, Heidelberg 1990.

H. Boese, *Wilhelm von Moerbeke als Übersetzer der «Stoicheiosis theologike» des Proclus*, Bitsch, Heidelberg 1985.

H. G. Senger, *Die Exzerpte und Randnoten des Nikolaus von Kues zu den lateinischen Übersetzungen der Proclus-Schriften. Theologia Platonis – Elementatio theologica*, Winter, Heidelberg 1986.

K. Bormann, *Die Exzerpte und Randnoten des Nikolaus von Kues zu den lateinischen Übersetzungen der Proclus-Schriften. Expositio in Parmenidem Platonis*,Winter, Heidelberg 1986.

K. Bormann, *Die Randnoten des Nikolaus von Kues zur lateinischen Übersetzung des platonischen "Parmenides" in der Handschrift Volterra, Biblioteca Guarnacci 6021*, in J. Helmrath - H. Müller- H. Wolff, *Studien zum 15. Jahrhundert.Festschrift für E. Meuthen*, I, Oldenbourg, München 1994, pp. 331-340.

U. Roth, *Die Exzerptensammlung aus Schriften des Raimundus Lullus im Codex Cusanus 83*, Winter, Heidelberg 1999.

P. Arfè, *Apuleius. Hermes Trismegistus. Aus Codex Bruxellensis 10054-56*, Winter, Heidelberg 2004.

S. Frost, *Nikolaus von Kues und Meister Eckhart. Rezption im Spiegel der Marginalien zum Opus tripartitum Meister Eckharts*, Aschendorff, Münster 2006.

D. Ancient, Medieval and Early Modern Authors

Briefwechsel des Beatus Rhenanus, eds. T. Birt - A. Horawitz, Teubner, Leipzig, 1886 [repr. Georg Olms, Hildesheim 1966].

Commentaries on Boethius by Thierry of Chartres and his School, ed. N. M. Häring, Pontifical Institute of Mediaeval Studies, Toronto 1971.

La caduta di Costantinopoli, 2 voll., ed. A. Pertusi, Mondadori, Milano 1976.

Albertus Magnus, *Super Dionysium de divinis nominibus*, ed. P. Simon, in Id., *Opera omnia*, t. XXXVII, Pars I, Aschendorff, Münster 1972.

Anselmus Cantuariensis, *Monologion*, in Id., *Opera omnia*, ed. F. S. Schmitt, t. I, vol. II, Fromman-Holzboog, Stuttgart-Bad Cannstatt, 1968.

Aristoteles, *Opera*, 5 voll., ed. I. Bekker Reimer, Berlin 1831-1870 (II ed., ed. O. Gigon, De Gryter, Berlin 1960-1987).

Aurelius Augustinus, *De civitate Dei*, voll. 2, eds. B. Dombart – A. Kalb, Brepols, Turnhout 1955.

Aurelius Augustinus, *De anima et eius origine*, in PL 44, 476-548.

Giovanni Andrea de Bussi, *Prefazioni alle edizioni di Swynheym e Pannartz prototipografi romani*, a cura di M. Miglio, Il Polifilo, Milano 1978.

Gregorius Nazianzenus, *Epistula 101*, in PG 37, 175-190.

Honorius Augustodunensis, *Clavis Physicae*, ed. P. Lucentini, Edizioni di Storia e Letteratura, Roma 1974.

J. Kymeus, *Des Babst Hercules wider die Deudschen*, ed. O. Menzel, Winter, Heidelberg 1941.

Iohannes Scotus Eriugena, *Periphyseon (De divisione naturae)*, 5 voll., ed. É. Jeauneau, Brepols, Turnhout 1996-2003.

Iohannes Scotus Eriugena, *Homélie sur le Prologue de Jean*, ed. É. Jeauneau, Cerf, Paris 1969.

Iustinus, *Apologie pour les Chrétiens*, ed. C. Munier, Cerf, Paris 2006.

G. W. Leibniz, *Sämtliche Schriften und Briefe*, ed. Deutschen Akademie der Wissenschaften, Akademie Verlag, Berlin 1923ff.

G. W. Leibniz, *Mathematische Schriften*, 7 voll., ed. I. Gerhardt, Georg Olms, Hildesheim 1962.

G. W. Leibniz, *Mantissa codicis iuris gentium diplomaticis*, Freytag, Hannover, 1700.

G. W. Leibniz, *Scriptores rerum Brunsvicensium illustrazioni inservientes*, II, Freytag, Hannover, 1707.

Gotthold Ephraim Lessing, *Nathan der Weise*, in Id., *Sämtliche Werke. Unveränderter photomechanischer Abdruck der von Karl Lachmann und Franz Muncker 1886 bis 1924 herausgegebenen Ausgabe von Gotthold Ephraim Lessings sämtlichen Schriften*, vol. III, De Gruyter, Berlin 1979.

Gotthold Ephraim Lessing, *Die Erziehung des Menschengeschlechts*, in Id., *Sämtliche Werke. Unveränderter photomechanischer Abdruck der von Karl Lachmann und Franz Muncker 1886 bis 1924 herausgegebenen Ausgabe von Gotthold Ephraim Lessings sämtlichen Schriften*, vol. XIII De Gruyter, Berlin 1979.

Marius Victorinus, *Opera. Pars I: Opera theologica*, eds. P. Henry – P. Hadot, Hoelder, Wien 1986.

Meister Eckhart, *Prologi in Opus tripartitum*, in Id., *Die lateinischen Werke*, vol. I.1, ed. K. Weiss, Kohlhammer, Stuttgart 1965.

Meister Eckhart, *Expositio libri Genesis*, in Id., *Die lateinischen Werke*, vol. I.1, ed. K. Weiss, Kohlhammer, Stuttgart 1965.

Meister Eckhart, *Expositio libri Sapientiae*, in Id., *Die lateinischen Werke*, vol. II, eds. J. Koch - H. Fischer - K. Weiss, Kohlhammer, Stuttgart 1992.

Meister Eckhart, *Expositio libri Exodi*, Id., Id., *Die lateinischen Werke*, vol. II, eds. J. Koch - H. Fischer - K. Weiss, Kohlhammer, Stuttgart 1992.

Meister Eckhart, *Expositio sancti Evangelii secundum Iohannem*, in Id., *Die lateinischen Werke*, vol. III, eds. K. Christ - B. Decker - J. Koch - H. Fischer - A. Zimmermann, Kohlhammer, Stuttgart 1994.

Meister Eckhart, *Sermones*, in Id., *Die lateinischen Werke*, vol. IV, eds. E. Benz – B. Decker – J. Koch, Kohlhammer, Stuttgart 1956.

Pius II, Papa (Aeneas Sylvius Piccolomineus), *Epistola ad Mahumetem*, eds. R. Glei – M. Köhler, WVT, Trier 2001.

Plato, *Opera*, 5 voll., ed. J. Burnet, Clarendon, Oxford 1900-1907.

Plato, *Parmenides vel De ideis*, in *Il Platone latino. Il Parmenide: Giorgio di Trebisonda e il cardinale Cusano*, ed. I. Ruocco, Olschki, Firenze 2003.

Plato, *Meno, interprete Henrico Aristippo*, ed. V. Kourdeuter, Warburg Institute, London 1940.

Plotinus, *Opera*, 3 voll.,eds. P. Henry – H.-R. Schwyzer, Desceé de Brouwer, Paris 1951-1973.

Porphyrius, *In Platonis Parmenidem*, in P. Hadot, *Porphyre et Victorinus*, vol II, Études Augustiniennes, Paris 1968.

Proclus, *Commentaire sur le Parménide de Platon. Traduction de Guillaume de Moerbeke*, 2 tt., ed. C. Steel, Brill, Leiden 1982-1985.

Proclus, *Commentarium in Platonis Parmenidem*, in *Procli philosophi platonici opera inedita*, ed. V. Cousin, Eberhard, Paris 1820-1827 [rist. Minerva, Frankfurt am Main 1962], 617-1244.

Proclus,*In Platonis Parmenidem commentaria*, 3 voll., ed. C. Steel, Clarendon, Oxford 2007-2009.

Proclus, *Commentaire sur le Parménide de Platon*, 5 voll, eds. C. Luna - A.-Ph. Segonds, Les Belles Lettres, Paris 2007-2014.

Proclus, *Théologie Platonicienne*, 6 voll., ed. H. Saffrey – L.G. Westerink, Les Belles Lettres, Paris 1968-1997.

Ps. Dionysius Areopagita, *Corpus Dionysiacum*, vol. I, ed. B.R. Suchla, De Gruyter, Berlin 1990.

Ps. Dionysius Areopagita, *Corpus Dionysiacum*, vol. II, ed. G. Heil – A. M. Ritter, De Gruyter, Berlin 1991.

Dionysiaca. Recueil donnant l'ensemble des traductions latines des ouvrage attribués au Denis de l'Aréopage, ed. P. Chevallier, 2 voll., Desclée de Brouwer, Paris 1937-1950.

J. S. Semler, *Versuch eines fruchtbaren Auszugs der Kirchengeschichte*, 3 voll., Hemmerde, Halle 1173-1778.

Tertullianus, *Adversus Praxeam*, ed. A. Kroymann, in Id., *Opera montanistica*, eds. A Gerlo et alii, Brepols, Turnhout 1954.

Thomas Aquinas, *In duodecim libros Metaphysicorum Aristotelis expositio*, eds. M. R. Cathala – R. M. Spiazzi, Marietti, Torino 1950.

Thomas Aquinas, *Summa theologiae*, in Id., *Opera omnia iussu Leonis XIII P.M. edita, ed. cura et studio Fratrum Ordinis Praedicatorum*, IV-XII, Tip. Polyglotta, Roma 1888-1906.

Vespasiano da Bisticci, *Vite di uomini illustri del secolo XV*, riveduta sui manoscritti da Ludovico Frati, Romagnoli-Dell'Acqua, Bologna 1892.

Voltaire, *Lettres philosophiques*, ed. R. Pomeau, Garnier-Flammarion, Paris 1964.

Thomas Aquinas, *Dictionnaire philosophique*, 2 voll., ed. C. Mervaud, in *Les Oeuvres complètes de Voltaire*, XXXVI, Voltaire Foundation, Oxford 1994.

II. Secondary Literature

A. Nicolaus Cusanus

A. A. Akasoy, *Zur Toleranz gegenüber dem Islam bei Lullus und Cusanus*, in *Ramon Llull und Nikolaus von Kues: Eine Begegnung im Zeichen der Toleranz – Raimondo Lullo e Niccolò Cusano: un incontro nel segno della tolleranza*, eds. E. Bidese - A. Fidora - P. Renner, Brepols, Turnhout 2005, pp. 105-124.

D. Albertson, *Mathematical Theologies. Nicholas of Cusa and the Legacy of Thierry of Chartres*, Oxford University, Oxford 2014.

J. L. C. Alonso, *Teofanía y Concordia. Leyendo a Escoto Eriúgena y Nicolás de Cusa*, in *Coincidencia de Opuestos y Concordia. Los Caminos del Pensamiento en Nicolás de Cusa*, vol. II, eds. J. M. André - M. Álvarez-Gómez, Ed. Sociedad Castellano-Leonesa de Filosofia, Salamanca 2002, pp. 107-131.

M. Álvarez-Gómez, *Die verborgene Gegenwart des Unendlichen bei Nikolaus von Kues*, Anton Pustet, München.

A. Alvarez-Gomez, *Über die Bedingungen des Friedens im Glauben bei Johannes von Segovia und Nicolaus von Kues*, Paulinus, Trier 2003.

M. J. André, *Tolerância, Diálogo intercultural e globalização: A atualidade de Nicolau de Cusa*, in «Scintilla», 1 (2007), pp. 41-64.

M. J. André, 'Concordantia fidei' *y multiculturalismo*, in *Nicholás de Cusa, identidad y alteridad: Pensamiento y diálogo*, eds. J. M. Machetta - C. D'Amico, Biblos, Buenos Aires 2010, pp. 491-509.

M. L. Arduini, «Ad hanc supermirandam harmonicam pacem». *Riforma della chiesa ed ecumenismo religioso nel pensiero di Niccolò Cusano*: il De pace fidei, in «Rivista di Filosofia Neoscolastica», LXXII (1980), pp. 224-242.

C. Bacher, *Selbsterkenntnis als Gotteserkenntnis bei Cusanus und Leibniz*, in *Cusano e Leibniz. Prospettive filosofiche*, eds. A. Dall'Igna – D. Roberi, Mimesis, Milano 2013, pp. 89-100.

G. T. Bakos, *On faith, rationality, and the other in the late Middle Ages: A study of Nicholas of Cusa's manuductive approach to Islam*, Eugene, Oregon 2010.

O. F. Bauchwitz, *Nicolás de Cusa y Escoto Eriúgena: aportes para una metafísica más allá de la ontoteologîa*, in *El problema del conocimiento en Nicolás de Cusa: genealogía y proyección*, eds. J. M. Machetta - C. D'Amico, Biblos, Buenos Aires 2005, 41-48.

W. Beierwaltes, *Philosophische Marginalien zu Proklos-Texten*, «Philosophische Rundschau», 11 (1963), pp. 49-90.

W. Beierwaltes, *Deus oppositio oppositorum*, in «Salzburger Jahrbuch für Philosophie», 8 (1964), pp. 175-185.

W. Beierwaltes, *Cusanusund Proclus. Zum neuplatonischen Ursprung des non-aliud*, in *Nicolò Cusano agli inizi del mondo moderno*, ed. G. Santinello, Sansoni, Firenze 1970, pp. 138-140.

W. Beierwaltes, *Das Seiende Eine. Zur neuplatonischen Interpretation der zweiten Hypothesis des platonischen Parmenides: das Beispeiel Cusanus*, in Id., *Procliana. Spätantikes Denken und seine Spuren*, Klostermann, Frankfurt am Main 2007, pp. 215-222.

W. Beierwaltes, *Identität und Differenz als Prinzip des cusanischen Denkens*, in Id., *Identität und Differenz*, Klostermann, Frankfurt am Main 1980, pp. 105-143.

W. Beierwaltes, Visio absoluta *oder absolute Reflexion (Cusanus)*, in Id., *Identität und Differenz*, Klostermann, Frankfurt am Main 1980, pp. 144-175.

W. Beierwaltes, *Über die Cusanus-Ausgabe*, in M. Meiner, *Ceterum censeo... Bemerkungen zur Aufgabe und Tätigkeit eines philosophischen Verlegers (Festschrift für Richard Meiner zum 8.April 1983)*, Hamburg 1983, pp. 26-30.

W. Beierwaltes, *Einheit und Gleichheit. Eine Fragestellung im Platonismus von Chartres und ihre Rezeption durch Nicolaus Cusanus*, in Id., *Denken des Einen. Studien zum Neuplatonismus und ihrer Wirkungsgeschichte*, Klostermann, Frankfurt am Main 1985, pp. 368-384.

W. Beierwaltes, *Die Cusanus-Ausgabe. Nicolai de Cusa Opera Omnia iussu et auctoritate Academiae Litterarum Heidelbergensis ad codicum fidem edita*, in «Jahrbuch der Heidelberger Akademie der Wissenschaften», 1987, Heidelberg 1988, pp. 101-106.

W. Beierwaltes, *Visio facialis. Sehen ins Angesich. Zur Coincidenz des endlichen und unendlichen. Blicks bei Cusanus*, Beck, München 1988.

W. Beierwaltes, *Eriugena und Cusanus*, in Id., *Eriugena. Grundzüge seines Denkens*, Klostermann, Frankfurt am Main 1994, pp. 266-312.

W. Beierwaltes, *Der verborgene Gott. Cusanus und Dionysius*, in Id., *Platonismus im Christentum*, Klostermann, Frankfurt am Main 1998, pp. 130-171.

W. Beierwaltes, *Mystische Elemente im Denken des Cusanus*, in *Deutsche Mystik im abendländischen Zusammenhang. Neu erschlossene Texte, neue methodische Ansätze, neue theoretische Konzepte*, eds. W. Haug - W. Schneider-Lastin, Niemeyer, Tübingen 2000, 425-448.

W. Beierwaltes, *Das Verhältnis von Philosophie und Theologie bei Nicolaus Cusanus*, in «Philotheos», 1 (2001), pp. 150-176 [repr. in «MFCG», 28 (2003), pp. 65-102.

W. Beierwaltes, *Cusanus. Reflexión metafísica y Espiritualidad*, EUMS, Pamplona 2005.

W. Beierwaltes, *Hans Gerhard Senger. Ein Leben mit Cusanus*, in «Litterae Cusanae», 2 (2002), pp. 50-65.

W. Beierwaltes, *Visio dei. Die mystiche Theologie des Nicolaus Cusanus im Kontext benediktinischer Spiritualität*, in «Studien und Mittleitungen des Benediktinerordens und seiner Zweige», 117 (2006), pp. 81-96.

W. Beierwaltes, *Theophanie. Nicolaus Cusanus und Johannes Scottus Eriugena. Eine Retractatio*, in «Philotheos», 6 (2006), pp. 153-175 [rep. in *Nicolaus von Kues in der Geschichte des Platonismus*, eds. K. Reinhardt - H. Schwaetzer, Roderer, Regensburg 2006, pp. 103-134].

W. Beierwaltes, *Dank und Gedanken*, in *Nicolai de Cusa Opera Omnia. Symposium zum Abschluß der Heidelberger Akademie-Ausgabe. Heidelberg, 11. und 12. Februar 2005*, eds. W. Beierwaltes - H. G. Senger, Winter, Heidelberg 2006, pp. 9-19.

W. Beierwaltes, *"Centrum tocius vite". Zur Bedeutung von Proclos' "Theologia Platonis" im Denken des Cusanus*, in Id., *Procliana. Spätantikes Denken und seine Spuren*, Klostermann, Frankfurt am Main 2007, pp. 191-214.

W. Beierwaltes, *Nicolaus Cusanus: Innovation durch Einsicht aus der Überlieferung – paradigmatisch gezeigt an seinem Denken des Einen*, in Id., *Procliana. Spätantikes Denken und seine Spuren*, Klostermann, Frankfurt am Main 2007, pp. 165-190.

W. Beierwaltes, Venatio sapientiae. *Das Nicht-Andere und das Licht*, in «MFCG» 33 (2010), pp. 83-104.

W. Beierwaltes, Preface by D. Monaco, Deus Trinitas. *Dio come non altro nel pensiero di Nciolò Cusano*, Città Nuova, Roma 2010, pp. 9-14.

E. Bidese - A. Fidora - P. Renner (eds.), *Ramon Llull und Nikolaus von Kues: Eine Begegnung im Zeichen der Toleranz – Raimondo Lullo e Niccolò Cusano: un incontro nel segno della tolleranza*, Brepols, Turnhout 2005.

J. E. Biechler, *Nicholas of Cusa and Muhammad*, in «The Downside Review», 101 (1983), pp. 50-59.

J. E. Biechler, *Interreligious dialogue*, in *Introducing Nicholas of Cusa: a guide to a renaissance man*, eds. C. M. Bellitto - T. M. Izbicki - G. Christianson, Paulist, New York 2004, pp. 270-296.

N. Bisava, *'New Barbarian' or Worthy Adversary? Humanist Constructs of the Ottoman Turks in Fifteenth-Century Italy*, in *Western Views of Islam in Medieval and Early Modern Europe. Perception of Other*, eds. D. R. Blanks - M. Frassetto, Hampshire - London 1999, pp. 185-205.

P. R. Blum, *Nikolaus von Kues und die italienische Renaissance*, Paulinus, Trier 2015.

I. Bocken, *Toleranz und Wahrheit bei Nikolaus von Kues*, in «Philosophisches Jahrbuch», 105 (1998), pp. 241-266.

I. Bocken (ed.), *Conflict and Reconciliation. Perspectives on Nicholas of Cusa*, Brill, Leiden 2004.

P. Bolberitz, *Philosophischer Gottesbegriff bei Nicolaus Cusanus in seinem Werk* De non aliud, Benno, Leipzig 1989.

A. Bonetti, *La ricerca metafisica nel pensiero di Nicolò Cusano*, Paideia, Brescia 1973.

A. Bonetti, *La filosofia dell'unità nel pensiero di Nicolò Cusano*, in *L'Uno e i molti*, Vita e Pensiero, Milano 1990, pp. 283-318.

K. Bormann, *Affirmation und Negation. Der Parmenides-Kommentar des Proklos in Nikolaus von Kues' Schrift Tu quis es*, in «Theologische Quartalschrift», 181 (2001), pp. 84-96.

K. Bormann, *Der Mensch als zweiter Gott*, Paulinus, Trier 1999.

G. F. von Bredow, *Der Geist als lebendiges Bild Gottes (Mens viva dei imago)*, in «MFCG», 13 (1978), pp. 58-67.

G. von Bredow, *Nachdenken mit Nikolaus von Kues über das Wesen der Freiheit*, in En kai plēthos*: Einheit und Vielheit. Festschrift für Karl Bormann zum 65. Geburtstag*, eds. L. Hagemann – R. Glei, Würzburg 1993, pp. 56-76.

G. F. von Bredow, *Gott der Nichtandere*, in «Philosophisches Jahrbuch», 1 (1965), pp. 15-24 [rep. in Ead., *Im Gespräch mit Nikolaus von Kues. Gesammelte Aufsätze 1948-1993*, ed. H. Schnarr, Aschendorff, Münster 1995].

E. Brient, *Meister Eckhart's Influence on Nicholas of Cusa: A Survey of the Literature*, in *A Companion to Meister Eckhart*, ed. J. M. Hackett, Brill, Leiden 2013, pp. 553-586.

M. Brösch - W.A. Euler - A. Geissler - V. Ranff (eds.), *Handbuch Nikolaus von Kues, Leben und Werk*, WBG, Darmstadt 2014.

A. Brüntrup, *Können und Sein. Der Zusammenhang der Spätschriften des Nikolaus von Kues*, Anton Pustet, München 1973.

M. Cacciari, *Sul presupposto*, in «aut aut», 211-212 (1986), pp. 43-65.

M. Cacciari, *Dell'Inizio*, Adelphi, Milano 1990.

M. Cacciari, *Geofilosofia dell'Europa*, Adelphi, Milano 1994.

M. Cacciari, *Filosofia e Teologia*, in *La filosofia*, vol. II, ed. P. Rossi, Utet, Torino 1995, pp. 365-421.

M. Cacciari, *Della cosa ultima*, Adelphi, Milano 2004.

S. Caramella, *Il problema di una logica trascendente nell'ultima fase del pensiero di Nicola Cusano*, in *Niccolò Cusano agli inizi del mondo moderno*, ed. G. Santinello, Sansoni, Firenze 1970, pp. 367-373.

S. Caramella, *Unità ideale e coincidenza reale degli opposti nel pensiero di Nicolò da Cusa*, in *Nicolò da Cusa. Relazioni tenute al Convegno Interuniversitario di Bressanone nel 1960*, ed. G. Flores D'Arcais, Sansoni, Firenze 1962, pp. 17-25.

P. J. Casarella, *Nicholas of Cusa and the Power of the Possible*, in «The American Catholic Philosophical Quarterly», 1 (1990), pp. 7-34.

P. Casarella, *Cusanus on Dionysius*, in *Re-thinking Dionysius the Areopagite*, eds. S. Coakley – C.M. Stang, Blackwell, Chichester 2009 pp. 137-148.

E. Cassirer, *Das Erkenntnisproblem in der Philosophie und Wissenschaft der neueren Zeit*, I, ed. T. Berben, in Id., *Gesammelte Werke. Hamburger Ausgabe*, II, Meiner, Hamburg 1999.

E. Cassirer, *Individuum und Kosmosin der Philosophie der Renaissance*, eds. F. Plaga - C. Rosenkranz, in Id., *Gesammelte Werke. Hamburger Ausgabe*, XIV, Meiner, Hamburg 2002, pp. 1-220.

C. Catà, *La Croce e l'Inconcepibile. Il pensiero di Nicola Cusano tra filosofia e predicazione*, Eum, Macerata 2009.

J.-M. Counet, *Mathématiques et dialectique chez Nicolas de Cues*, Vrin, Paris 2000.

F. J. Clemens, *Giordano Bruno und Nikolaus von Cues*, Wittmann, Bonn 1847.

M. Costigliolo, *Islam e cristianesimo: modi di differenze nel Medioevo. Il dialogo con l'Islam nell'opera di Nicola da Cusa*, Genova University, Genova 2012.

F. E. Cranz, *The Late Works of Nicholas of Cusa*, in *Nicholas of Cusa in search of God and Wisdom*, eds. G. Christianson - T. M. Izbicki, Brill, Leiden 1991, pp. 140-160.

F. E. Cranz, *Nicholas of Cusa and the Renaissance*, ed. T. M. Izbicki – G. Christianson, Ashgate, Aldershot 2000.

R. Crowley, *The Holy War for Constantinople and the Clash of the West*, Hachette Books, New York 2005.

C. M. Cubillos, *Los múltiples nombres del Dios innombrable: una aproximación a la metafísica de Nicolás de Cusa desde la perspectiva de sus nombres divinos*, Eunsa, Navarra 2013.

C. M. Cubillos, *Für eine Systematisierung der cusanischen Gottesnamen*, in *Der Bildbegriff bei Meister Eckhart und Nikolaus von Kues*, eds. H. Schwaetzer – M.A. Vannier, Aschendorff, Münster 2015, pp. 179-199.

G. Cuozzo, Mystice videre. *Esperienza religiosa e pensiero speculativo in Cusano*, Trauben, Torino 2002.

G. Cuozzo, *Arte e metafisica in Cusano e Leibniz: prospettive a confronto*, in *Cusano e Leibniz. Prospettive filosofiche*, eds. A. Dall'Igna – D. Roberi, Mimesis, Milano 2013, pp. 17-28.

D. Cürsgen, *Die Logik der Unendlichkeit. Die Philosophie des Absoluten im Spätwerk des Nicolaus von Kues*, Peter Lang, Frankfurt am Main 2007.

D. Cürsgen, *Die Metaphysik der Negativität und Identität bei Nikolaus von Kues*, in «Freiburger Zeitschrift für Philosophie und Theologie», 2 (2009), pp. 341-369.

A. Dall'Igna – D. Roberi (eds.), *Cusano e Leibniz. Prospettive filosofiche*, Mimesis, Milano 2013.

M.-T. D'Alverny, *Le cosmos symbolique du XIIe siècle*, in «Archives *d*'Histoire Doctrinale et Littéraire du Moyen Age», 20 (1953), pp. 31-81.

C. D'Amico, *La docta ignorancia y la tiniebla del inconoscimiento: Nicolás de Cusa y Pseudo Dionisio Areopagita*, in *Memoria y silencio en la filosofía medieval*, ed. C. Ruta, Jorge Baudino, Buenos Aires 2006, pp. 225-235.

C. D'Amico, *Nicolaus von Kues als Leser von Proklos*, in *Nicolaus von Kues in der Geschichte des Platonismus*, eds. K. Reinhardt - H. Schwaetzer, Roderer, Regensburg 2006, pp. 33-64.

C. D'Amico, *Proclo*, in Nicolás de Cusa, *Acerca de lo no-otro o de la definición que todo define. Nuevo texto crítico original*, intr. and trans by J. M. Machetta, critical text and notes by C. D'Amico - M. D'Ascenso - A. Eisenkopf - J. G. Rios - J. M. Machetta - K. Reinhardt - C. Rusconi - H. Schwaetzer, Biblos, Buenos Aires 2008, pp. 359-369.

S. Dangelmayr, *Gotteserkenntnis und Gottesbegriff in den philosophischen Schriften des Nikolaus von Kues*, Hain, Meisenheim am Glan 1969.

P. David, *Lichtblick des Friedens. Grundlinien einer sapientialen Theologie der Religionen im Anschluss an Nikolaus von Kues*, Lit, Berlin 2006.

B. Decker, *Nikolaus von Kues und der Friede unter Religionen*, in *Humanismus, Mystik und Kunst in der Welt des Mittelalter*, ed. J. Koch, Brill, Leiden 1953, pp. 94-121.

B. Decker, *Die Toleranzidee bei Nikolaus von Kues und in der Neuzeit*, in *Nicolò da Cusa. Relazioni tenute al Convegno Interuniversitario di Bressanone nel 1960*, cit., pp. 197-213.

J. Decorte, *Tolerance and Trinity*, in *Conflict and Reconciliation. Perspectives on Nicholas of Cusa*, ed. I. Bocken, Brill, Leiden 2004, pp. 107-117.

Ó. De la Cruz Palma, *Alcuni argomenti della polemica antiislamica in Raimondo Lullo e Niccolò Cusano*, in *Ramon Llull und Nikolaus von Kues: Eine Begegnung im Zeichen der Toleranz – Raimondo Lullo e Niccolò Cusano: un incontro nel segno della tolleranza*, eds. E. Bidese - A. Fidora - P. Renner, Brepols, Turnhout 2005, pp. 25-40.

M. De Gandillac, *Genèses de la modernité*, Cerf, Paris 1992.

M. De Gandillac, *Der cusanische Friedensbegriff*, in «Zeitschrift für philosophische Forschung», 9 (1955), pp. 186-196.

M. De Gandillac, *Nikolaus von Kues zwischen Platon und Hegel*, in «MFCG», XI (1975), pp. 21-38.

M. De Gandillac, *Das Ziel der* una religio in varietate rituum, in «MFCG», 16 (1984), pp. 192-213.

R. O. Diéz, *Fides una, ritus diversus*, in*El problema del conocimiento en Nicolás de Cusa: genealogía y proyección*,eds. J. M. Machetta - C. D'Amico, Biblos, Buenos Aires 2005, eds. J. M. Machetta - C. D'Amico, Biblos, Buenos Aires 2005, pp. 333-342.

G. d'Onofrio, Vera philosophia. *Studies in Late Antique, Early Medieval and Renaissance Christian Thought*, Brepols, Turnhout 2008.

F. D. Duclow, *Masters of Learned Ignorance: Eriugena, Eckhart, Cusanus*, Ashgate, Aldershot 2006

D. F. Duclow, *Pseudo Dionusius, John Scotus Eriugena, Nicholas of Cusa. An Approach to the Hermeneutic of Divine Names*, in «International Philosophical Quarterly», XII (1972), pp. 260-278.

D. F. Duclow, *Coinciding in the Margins: Cusanus Glosses Eriugena*, in *Eriugena – Cusanus*, eds. A. Kijewska - R. Majeran - H. Schwaetzer, KUL, Lublin 2011, pp. 83-103.

L. Dupré, *A passage to Modernity. An Essay in the Hermneutics of Nature and Culture*, Yale University, New Haven 1993.

L. Dupré, *The Mystical Theology of Cusanus's De visione dei*, in *"videre et videri coincidunt". Theorien des Sehens in der ersten Hälfte des 15. Jahrhunderts*, eds. W. C. Schneider – H. Schwaetzer – M. de Mey - I. Bocken, Aschendorff, Münster 2011, pp. 45-66.

L. Dupré, *The question of pantheism from Eckhart to Cusanus*, in *Cusanus. The legacy of learned ignorance*, ed. P. J. Casarella, The Catholic University of America Press, Washington 2006, pp. 74-88.

W. Dupré, *Die non-aliud Lehre des Nikolaus von Kues*, (Dissertation) Wien 1963.

W. Dupré, *Der Mensch als Mikrokosmos im Denken des Nikolaus von Kues*, «MFCG», 13 (1978), pp. 68-87.

W. Dupré, *Implicit religion and inter-faith Dialogue: a Philosophical perspective*, in «Implicit Religion», 1 (1998), pp. 29-39.

W. Dupré, *Spirit, Mind and Freedom*, in *Conflict and Reconciliation. Perspectives on Nicholas of Cusa*, ed. I. Bocken, Brill, Leiden 2004, pp. 207-221.

W. Dupré, *Weg und Wege der Wahrheit. Zur Bedeutung der Wahrheitsfrage bei Nikolaus von Kues*, Paulinus, Trier 2005.

W. Dupré, *Religious Plurality and Dialogue in the Sermons of Nicholas of Cusa*, in «Studies in Interreligious Dialogue», 1 (2005), pp. 76-85.

J. B. Elpert, Loqui est revelare – verbum ostensio mentis. *Die Sprachephilosophischen Jagdzüge des Nikolaus Cusanus*, Peter Lang, Frankfurt am Main 2002.

R. Eucken, *Untersuchungen zur Geschichte der älteren deutschen Philosophie*, in «Philosophische Monatshefte», XIV (1878), pp. 449-470.

W. A. Euler, *Die beiden Schriften* De pace Fidei *und* De visione Dei *aus dem Jahre 1453*, in «MFCG», 22 (1995), pp. 187-203.

W. A. Euler, *Unitas und Pax. Religionsvergleich bei Raimond Lullus und Nikolaus von Kues*, Echter, Würzburg 1995[2].

W.A. Euler, *'Pia philosophia' et 'docta religio'. Theologie und Religion bei Marsilio Ficino und Giovanni Pico della Mirandola*, Fink, München 1998.

W. A. Euler, *Cusanus' Verständnis der negativen Theologie und seine Auseinandersetzung mit nichtchristlichen Religionen in De pace fidei und Cribratio Alkorani*, in «Theologische Quartalschrift», 181 (2001), pp. 132-142.

W. A. Euler, *Der Friede unter den Religionen nach Nikolaus von Kues*, in «Konferenzblatt für Theologie und Seelsorge», 112 (2001), pp. 147-158.

W. A. Euler, *Die Schrift 'De pace fidei' des Nikolaus von Kues*, «Edith Stein Jahrbuch», 7 (2001), pp. 165-173.

W. A. Euler, Una religio in rituum varietate. *Die Begegnung der Religionen bei Nikolaus von Kues*, «Zeitschrift für Missionswissenschaft und Religionswissenschaft», 85 (2001), pp. 243-257.

W. A. Euler, *Konkordanz der Religionen bei Ramon Llull und Nikolaus von Kues*, in *Coincidentia dos Opostos e Concórdia*, vol. 1, eds. J. M. André - M. Álavarez-Gómez, FL, Coimbra 2002, pp. 119-140.

W. A. Euler, *Nikolaus von Kues als Wegbereiter des interreligiösen Dialogs und der Theologie der Religionen*, in «MFCG», 28 (2003), pp. 211-231.

W.A. Euler, *Il De pace fidei di Nicolò Cusano e la parabola dell'anello di Lessing*, in *Cusanus*,ed. D. Monaco, «Il Pensiero»,1-2 (2009), pp. 59-74.

W. A. Euler – F.-B. Stammkötter, *Johannes von Segovia und Nikolaus von Kues im Gespräch mit dem Islam*, in *Cusanus und der Islam*, eds. W. A. Euler – T. Kerger, Paulinus, Trier 2010, pp. 49-64.

W. A. Euler – T. Kerger (eds.), *Cusanus und der Islam*, Paulinus, Trier 2010.

W. A. Euler, *Religionsfriede und Ringparabel. Die religionstheologischen Ideen von Cusanus und Lessing*, in «Cusanus Jahrbuch» 4 (2012), pp. 3-24.

W. A. Euler, *L'image de l'Islam à la fin du Moyen âge: La correspondance entre Jean de Ségovie et Nicolas de Cues*, in *Nicolas de Cues et l'Islam*, ed. H. Pasqua, Peeters, Leuven 2013, pp. 9-20.

W. A. Euler, *Der christliche Ökumenismus von Cusanus und Leibniz*, in *Cusano e Leibniz. Prospettive filosofiche*, eds. A. Dall'Igna – D. Roberi, Mimesis, Milano 2013, pp. 153-166.

W. A. Euler, *Cusanus' Auseinandersetzung mit dem Islam*, in «Das Mittelalter», 1 (2014), pp. 72-85.

C. Fabro, *Partecipazione e causalità secondo s. Tommaso*, Edivi, Segni 2010.

R. Falckenberg, *Grundzüge der Philosophie des Nicolaus Cusanus mit besonderer Berücksichtigung der Lehre vom Erkennen*, Koebner, Breslau 1880.

R. Falkenberg, *Aufgabe und Wesen der Erkenntnis bei Nikolaus von Kues*, Koebner, Breslau 1880 [rist. Minerva, Frankfurt am Main 1968].

F. Fiorentino, *Il risorgimento filosofico nel Quattrocento*, Tipografia della Regia Università, Napoli 1885.

K. Flasch, *Nikolaus von Kues und Pico della Mirandola*, in «MFCG», 14 (1980), pp. 113-120.

K. Flasch, *Die Metaphysik des Einen bei Nikolaus von Kues. Problemgeschichtliche Stellung und systematische Bedeutung*, Brill, Leiden 1973.

K. Flasch, *Nicolaus von Kues. Geschichte einer Entwicklung*, Klostermann, Frankfurt am Main 1998.

K. Flasch, *Cusano e gli intellettuali del Quattrocento*, in *Le filosofie del Rinascimento*, ed. C. Vasoli, Bruno Mondadori, Milano 2002, pp. 175-192.

P. Floss, *Cusanus und Comenius*, in «MFCG», 10 (1973), pp. 172-190.

A. Franz, *Möglichkeit und Wirklichkeit als Grundprinzipien neuzeitlichen Wirklichkeitverständnisses bei Nikolaus von Kues und F. W. J. Schelling*, in *Nicolaus Cusanus und der deutsche Idealismus*, eds. K. Reinhardt - H. Schwaetzer, Roderer, Regensburg 2007, pp. 41-58.

S. Frost, *Nikolaus von Kues und Meister Eckhart. Rezeption im Spiegel der Marginalien zum Opus Tripartitum Meister Eckharts*, Aschendorff, Münster 2006.

E. Fräntzki, *Nikolaus von Kues und das Problem der absoluten Subjektivität*, Hain, Meisenheim am Glan, 1972.

P. Gaia, *Introduzione*, in N. Cusano, *Opere religiose*, Utet, Torino 1993, pp. 9-66.

P. Gaia, *L'ecumenismo religioso di Niccolò Cusano nel* De pace Fidei, in *Vangelo, Religioni, Culture*, ed. R. Penna, Edizioni San Paolo, Cinisiello Balsamo 1993, pp. 233-261.

H.-G. Gadamer, *Nicolás de Cusa y la filosofía del presente*, in «Folia Humanistica», 23 (1964), pp. 929-937.

H.-G. Gadamer, *Nikolaus von Kues im modernen Denken*, in *Nicolò Cusano agli inizi del mondo moderno*, ed. G. Santinelli, Sansoni, Firenze 1970, pp. 39-48.

E. Garin, *Ricerche sulle traduzioni di Platone nella prima metà del sec. XV*, in *Medioevo e Rinascimento. Studi in onore di B. Nardi*, Sansoni, Firenze 1955, pp. 339-347.

E. Garin, *Cusano e i platonici del Quattrocento*, in *Nicolò da Cusa. Relazioni tenute al Convegno Interuniversitario di Bressanone nel 1960*, cit., pp. 75-96.

G. Gawlick, *Zur Nachwirkung cusanischer Ideen im siebzehnten und achtehzenten Jahrhundert*, in *Nicolò Cusano agli inizi del mondo moderno*, cit., 225-239.

C. Giacon, *Il "possest" del Cusano e le dottrine aritotelico-tomistiche dell'atto e potenza e dell'essenza ed esistenza*, in *Nicolò Cusano agli inizi del mondo moderno*, cit., pp. 375-384.

E. Gilson, *Les métamorphoses de la cité de Dieu*, Vrin, Paris 1952.

G. Gobillot, *La singulière clairvoyance de Nicolas de Cues à l'égard du Coran*, in *Nicolas de Cues et l'Islam*, ed. H. Pasqua, Peeters, Leuven 2013, pp. 35-86.

S. Gottlöber, *Das Prinzip der Relationalität: Grundzüge cusanischen Denkens als Parameter für Toleranz und interreligiösen Diskurs*, Thelem, Dresden 2013.

S. Grotz, *Negationes des Absoluten: Meister Eckhart, Cusanus, Hegel*, Meiner, Hamburg 2009.

E. Gutwenger, *Das „Nichtandere" bei Nikolaus von Kues*, in *Nikolaus Cusanus Gedächtnisschrift*, ed. N. Grass, Wagner, Innsbruck 1970, pp. 17-22.

S. Grotz, *Über den Zusammenhang von Name und Negation bei Nicolaus Cusanus*, in *Der Bildbegriff bei Meister Eckhard und Nikolaus von Kues*, eds. H. Schwaetzer – M.A. Vannier, Aschendorff, Münster 2015, pp. 201-213.

L. Hagemann, *Der Ḳur'ān in Verständnis und Kritik bei Nikolaus von Kues*, Knecht, Frankfurt am Main 1976.

K. Harries, *Infinity and perspective*, Mit, Cambridge Massachusetts 2001.

R. Haubst, *Das Bild des Einen und Dreienen Gottes in der Welt nach Nikolaus von Kues*, Paulinus, Trier 1952.

R. Haubst, *Die Christologie des Nikolaus von Kues*, Herder, Freiburg im Breisgau 1956.

R. Haubst, *Nikolaus von Kues auf Spuren sed Thomas von Aquin*, in «MFCG», 5 (1965), pp. 15-62.

R. Haubst, *Nikolaus von Kues als Interpreter und Verteidiger Meister Eckharts*, in *Freiheit und Gelassenheit: Meister Eckhart heute*, ed. U. Kern, Kaiser, München 1980, pp. 75-96.

R. Haubst, *Streifzüge in die cusanische Theologie,* Aschendorff, Münster 1991.

N. Herold, *Menschliche Perspektive und Wahrheit. Zur Deutung der Subjektivität in den philosophischen Schriften des Nikolaus von Kues*, Aschendorff, Münster 1975.

J. Hirschberger, *Das Platon-Bild bei Nicolaus von Kues*, in *Niccolò Cusano agli inizi del mondo moderno*, ed. G. Santinello, Sansoni, Firenze 1970, pp. 113-135.

J. Hirschberger, *Die Stellung des Nikolaus von Kues in der Entwicklung der deutschen Philosophie*, in «Sitzungsberichte der wissenschaftlichen Gesellschaft an der Johann Wolfgang Goethe-Universität Frankfurt am Main», Bd. XV, n. 3, Weisbaden 1978, pp. 119-137.

J. Hochstafl, *Die negative Theologie des Dionysius vom Areopag und die wissende Unwissenheit des Nikolaus von Kues*, in *Gottes Weisheit im Mysterium. Vergessene Wege christlicher Spiritualität*, ed. A. Schilson, Matthias-Grünewald, Mainz 1989, pp. 117-141.

W. J. Hoye, *Die mystische Theologie des Nicolaus Cusanus*, Herder, Freiburg 2004.

W. J. Hoye, *Die Grenze des Wissens. Nikolaus von Kues in Auseinandersetzung mit der mystischen Theologie des Dionysius Areopagita*, in K. Reinhardt - H. Schwaetzer (eds.), *Nicolaus von Kues in der Geschichte des Platonismus*, Roderer, Regensburg 2006, pp. 87-101.

W. Hoye, *The Idea of Truth as the Basis for Religious Tollerance According to Nicholas of Cusa with Comparisons to Thomas Aquinas*, in *Conflict and Reconciliation. Perspectives on Nicholas of Cusa*, ed. I. Bocken, Brill, Leiden 2004, pp. 161-176.

E. Hoffmann, *Gottesschau bei Meister Eckhart und Nikolaus von Kues*, in *Festschrift Heinrich Zangger*, 2 voll. ed. J. Dettling, Rascher, Zürich 1935, vol. II, pp. 1033-1045.

J. Hopkins, *Introduction*, in Nicholas of Cusa, *On God as Non-other*, Banning Press, Minneapolis 1979 [II ed. 1983], pp. 3-23.

J. Hopkins, *Nicholas of Cusa's Metaphysic of Contraction,* Arthur J. Banning, Minneapolis 1983.

J. Hopkins, *The Role of* Pia Interpretatio *in Nicholas of Cusa's Hermeneutical Approach to the Koran*, in *Concordia discors. Studi su Niccolò Cusano e l'umanesimo europeo offerti a Giovanni Santinello*, ed. G. Piaia, Antenore, Padova 1993, pp. 251-273.

J. Hopkins, *Cusa's Metaphysical Speculation*, 2 voll., Minneapolis, Banning, 1998-2000.

C. Horn, *Cusanus über Platon und dessen Pythagoreismus*, in *Nicolaus von Kues in der Geschichte des Platonismus*, eds. K. Reinhardt - H. Schwaetzer, Roderer, Regensburg 2006, pp. 9-31.

A.Hubert, *Influencia del Pseudo Dionisio en Nicolás de Cusa*, in «Teología y Vida», 4 (2007), pp. 425-438.

K. Jacobi, *Die Methode der cusanischen Philosophie*, Alber, Freiburg 1969.

K. Jaspers, *Nikolaus von Kues*, Piper, München 1964.

K.-M. Kandler, *Nikolaus von Kues als testis veritatis. Beitrag eines evangelisch-lutherischen Theologen zur Wirkungsgeschichte von De pace fidei*, in: «MFCG», 17 (1986), pp. 223-234.

T. Kerger, *Pia interpretatio. Vier christliche Theologen im Gespräch mit dem Islam*, Paulinus, Trier 2010.

T. Kerger, *La* Cribratio Alkorani: *un project de dialogue avec l'Islam*, in *Nicolas de Cues et l'Islam*, ed. H. Pasqua, Peeters, Leuven 2013, pp. 21-34.

A. Kijewska, *Divine Non-Being in Eriugena and Cusanus*, «Philotheos», 2 (2002), pp. 155-167.

A. Kijewska, *Conception of Intellect in Eriugena and Cusanus*, in *Nicolaus Cusanus: ein bewundernswerter historischer Brennpunkt. Philosophische Tradition und wissenschaftliche Rezeption*, Eds. K. Reinhardt – H. Schwaetzer, Roderer, Regensburg 2008, pp. 11-20.

A. Kijewska - R. Majeran - H. Schwaetzer (eds.), *Eriugena – Cusanus*, KUL, Lublin 2011.

R. Klibansky, *Ein Proklos-Fund und seine Bedeutung*, Winter, Heidelberg 1929.

R. Klibansky, *The continuity of the Platonic Tradition during the Middle Ages: outlines of a corpus platonicum medii aevi*, Warburg Institute, London 1939 [new ext. ed. Kraus, München 1982].

R. Klibansky, *Plato's Parmenides in the Middle Age and the Renaissance*, in «Medieval and Renaissance Studies», 1 (1943), pp. 281-330 [new ext. ed. in Id., *The continuity of the Platonic Tradition*, Kraus, München 1981].

R. Klibansky, *Die Wirkungsgeschichte des Dialogs De pace fidei*, in «MFCG», 16 (1984), pp. 113-125.

W. Knoch, *Die historische und systematische Bedeutung der cusanischen Trinitätsspekulation*, in «MFCG», 33 (2012), pp. 19-36.

J. Koch, *Nikolaus von Kues und Meister Eckhart. Randbemerkungen zu zwei in der Schrift «de coniecturis» gegebenen Problem*, in «MFCG», 4 (1964), pp. 164-173.

K. Kremer, *Gott – in allem alles, in nichts nichts. Bedeutung und Herkunft dieser Lehrer des Nikolaus von Kues*, in «MFCG», 17 (1986), pp. 188-219.

K. Kremer, *Praegustatio naturalis sapientiae. Gott suchen mit Nicholaus von Kues*, Aschendorff, Münster 2004.

J. Kreuzer, *Der Geist als imago Dei — Augustinus und Cusanus*, in K. Reinhardt - H. Schwaetzer (eds.), *Nicolaus von Kues in der Geschichte des Platonismus*, Roderer, Regensburg 2006, pp. 65-86.

J. Kreuzer, *Der Geist als lebendiger Spiegel. Zur Theorie des Intellekts bei Meister Eckhart und Nikolaus von Kues*, in «Meister-Eckhart-Jahrbuch», 4 (2011), pp. 49-66.

P. O. Kristeller, *A Latin Translation of Gemisto Plethon's De Fato by Johannes Sophianos dedicated to Nicholas of Cusa*, in *Niccolò Cusano agli inizi del mondo moderno*, cit., pp. 175-193.

T. Leinkauf, *Die Bestimmung des Einzelseienden durch die Begriff Contractio, Singularitas und Aequalitas bei Nicolaus Cusanus*, in Id., *Cusanus, Ficino, Patrizi. Formen platonischen Denkens in Renaissance*, Trafo, Berlin 2014, pp. 25-58.

T. Leinkauf, *Nicolaus Cusanus und Bonaventura. Zum Hintergrund von Cusanus' Gottesname «Possest»*, in T. Leinkauf, *Cusanus, Ficino, Patrizi. Formen platonischen Denkens in Renaissance*, Trafo, Berlin 2014, pp. 59-77.

T. Leinkauf, *Nicolaus Cusanus. Eine Einführung*, Aschendorff, Münster 2006.

T. Leinkauf, *Einleitung*, in G. Bruno, *Über die Ursache, das Prinzip und das Eine*, ed. T. Leinkauf, Meiner, Hamburg, 2007, pp. IX-CLIII.

T. Leinkauf, «Diversitas identitate compensata. *Ein Grundtheoremen in Leibniz' Denken und seine Voraussetzungen in der frühen Neuzeit*, in Id., *Einheit, Natur, Geist. Beiträge zu metaphysischen Grundproblemen im Denken von Gottfried Wilhelm Leibniz*, Trafo, Berlin 2012, 15-42 [I ed. in «Studia leibnitiana», 1 (1996), pp. 58-83].

T. Leinkauf, «Diversitas identitate compensata. *Ein Grundtheoremen in Leibniz' Denken und seine Voraussetzungen in der frühen Neuzeit (II)*, in Id., *Einheit, Natur, Geist. Beiträge zu metaphysischen*

Grundproblemen im Denken von Gottfried Wilhelm Leibniz, Trafo, Berlin 2012, 43-66 [I ed. in «Studia leibnitiana», 1 (1997), pp. 81-102].

T. Leinkauf, *Renovatio und unitas. Nicolaus Cusanus zwischen Tradition und Innovation. Die 'Reformation' des Möglichkeitsbegriff*, in *Id.*, *Cusanus, Ficino, Patrizi. Formen platonischen Denkens in Renaissance*, Trafo, Berlin 2014, pp. 105-122.

T. Leinkauf, *Cusanus, Ficino, Patrizi. Formen platonischen Denkens in Renaissance*, Trafo, Berlin 2014.

I. Levy – R. George-Tvrtkovi – D. Duclow (eds.), *Nicholas of Cusa and Islam. Polemic and Dialogue in the Late Middle Ages*, Brill, Leiden 2014.

J. M. Machetta, *La negación en cuanto principio prímero de la metafísica cusana*, in *El problema del conocimiento en Nicolás de Cusa: genealogía y proyección*, eds. J. M. Machetta - C. D'Amico, Biblos, Buenos Aires 2005, pp. 165-181.

D. Mahnke, *Leibnizens Synthese von Universalmathematik und Individualmetaphysik*, Niemeyer,Halle 1925 [repr. Frommann, Stuttgart 1964].

D. Mahnke, *Unendliche Sphär und Allmittelpunkt. Beiträge zur Genealogie der mathematischen Mystik*, Niemeyer, Halle 1937.

S. Mancini, *L'estrema soglia della riflessione trascendentale di Cusano: nient'altro che nome divino*, in *La persona e i nomi dell'essere*, 2 voll., eds. F. Botturi - F. Totaro - C. Vigna, Vita e Pensiero, Milano 2001, pp. 871-881.

S. Mancini, *L'idealismo trascendente tra Cusano e Leibniz*, in *Cusano e Leibniz. Prospettive filosofiche*, eds. A. Dall'Igna – D. Roberi, Mimesis, Milano 2013, pp. 29-44.

S. Mancini, *Congetture su Dio. Singolarità, finalismo, potenza nella teologia razionale di Nicola Cusano*, Mimesis, Milano 2015.

L. Martínez-Gómez, *From the Names of God to the Name of God: Nicholas of Cusa*, in «International Philosophical Quarterly», 1 (1965).

J. Marx, *Verzeichnis der Handschriften-Sammlung des Hospital zu Cues bei Bernkastel a./Mosel*,Schaar & Dathe, Trier 1905.

M. Maurizi, *La nostalgia del totalmente* non *altro. Cusano e la genesi della modernità*, Rubbettino, Soveria Mannelli 2008.

Th. P. Mc Tighe, *Nicholas of Cusa and Leibniz' principle of indiscernibility*, in: «The Modern Schoolmann», 42 (1964), pp. 33-46.

T. Mc Tighe, *'Nicholas of Cusa's Unity-Metaphysics and the Formula* religio una in rituum varietate*'*, in *Nicholas of Cusa in search of God and Wisdom*, eds. G. Christianson - T. Izbicki, Brill, Leiden 1991, pp. 161-172.

M. H. van der Meer, *Divus Dionysius: Jean Gerson, Nicholas of Cusa, and the Interpretation of Pseudo-Dionysius's Mystical Theology*, in «Viator», 2 (2013), 323-342.

S. Meier-Oeser, *Die Präsenz des Vergessenen. Zur Rezeption der Philosophie des Nicolaus Cusanus vom 15. Bis zum 18. Jahrhundert*, Aschendorff, Münster 1989.

S. Meier-Oeser, *J. A. Comenius und die Theorie der* coincidentia oppositorum *in der Philosophie der frühen Neuzeit*, in *Comenius und die Genese des modernen Europa. Internationales Comenius-Kolloquium*, eds. J. Lásek - N. Kotowski, Flacius, Fürth 1992, pp. 138-149.

S. Meier-Oeser, *Die Cusanus-Rezeption im deutschen Renaissancehumanismus des 16. Jahrhunderts*, in *Nicolaus Cusanus zwischen Deutschland und Italien*, ed. M. Thurner, Akademie, Berlin 2002, pp. 617-632.

H. Meinhardt, *Konjekturale Erkenntnis und Religiöse Toleranz*, in «MFCG», 16 (1984), pp. 325-342.

M. Merlo, *Introduzione*, in N. Cusano, *Congetture di pace. Scritti irenici*, a c. di M. Merlo, Edizioni del Cerro, Tirrenia 2003, pp. XXI-LXXXII.

E. Meuthen, *Die universalpolitischen Ideen des Nikolaus von Kues in seiner Erfahrung der politischen Wirklicheit*, in «Quellen und Forschungen aus italienischen Archiven und Biblioteken», 37 (1957), pp. 192-221.

E. Meuthen, *Die letzten Jahre des Nikolaus von Kues. Biographische Untersuchungen nach neuen Quellen*, Westdeutscher Verlag, Köln 1958.

E. Meuthen, *Der Fall von Konstantinopel und der Lateinische Westen*, in «MFCG», 16 (1984), pp. 35-60.

C. L. Miller, *Not Other Than Divine*, in Id., *Readings Cusanus*, The Catholic University of America Press, Washington 2003, pp. 180-205.

P. Moffitt Watts, *Nicolaus Cusanus. A fifteenth-century vision of man*, Brill, Leiden 1982.

B. Mojsisch, *Nichts und Negation. Meister Eckhart und Nikolaus von Kues*, in *Historia Philosophiae Medii Aevi. Studien zur Geschichte der Philosophie des Mittelalters*, eds. B. Mojsisch - O. Pluta,John Benjamins, Amsterdam-Philadelphia 1991, vol. II, pp. 675-693.

B. Mojsisch, *Die Andersheit Gottes als Koinzidenz. Negation und Nicht-Andersheit bei Nikolaus von Kues: Explication und Kritik*, in «Documenti e studi sulla tradizione filosofica medievale», 7 (1996), pp. 437-454.

D. Monaco, *Dialogo interreligioso, intrareligioso e identità cristiana nel De pace fidei di Niccolò Cusano. Una prospettiva ermeneutica*, in «Filosofia e Teologia», 2 (2007), pp. 323-335.

D. Monaco, *La visione di Dio e la pace nella fede*, in *Universalität der Vernunft und Pluralität der Erkenntnis bei Nikolaus Cusanus*, eds. K. Reinhardt - H. Schwaetzer, Roderer, Regensburg 2008, pp. 21-30.

D. Monaco, *Dalla* coincidentia oppositorum *al non aliud: la caccia cusaniana all'infinito*, in *A caccia dell'Infinito. L'Umano e il Divino nell'opera di Nicola Cusano*, ed. C. Catà, Aracne, Roma 2010, 103-116.

D. Monaco, Deus Trinitas. *Dio come* non altro *nel pensiero di Nicolò Cusano*, praeface by Werner Beierwaltes, Città Nuova, Roma 2010.

D. Monaco, *Cusano e la pace della fede*, praeface by Francesco Tomatis, Città Nuova, Roma 2013.

D. Monaco, *Dalla* coincidentia oppositorum *al non aliud: la caccia cusaniana all'infinito* in *A caccia dell'Infinito. L'Umano e il Divino nell'opera di Nicola Cusano*, ed. C. Catà, Aracne, Roma 2010, 103-116.

D. Monaco, *Monadologia, prospettivismo e centralità dell'uomo in Cusano*, in «Giornale critico di storia delle idee», 10 (2014).

D. Monaco, *Il Dio nascosto e la pluralità delle religioni: il* De pace fidei *di Nicolò Cusano*, in Dialogus. *Il dialogo filosofico tra le religioni nel pensiero tardo-antico, medievale e umanistico*, ed. M. Coppola - G. Fernicola - L. Pappalardo, Città Nuova, Roma 2014, pp. 415-428.

D. Moran, *Pantheism from John Scottus Eriugena to Nicholas of Cusa*, in «American Catholic Philosophical Quarterly», 1 (1990), pp. 131-152.

D. Moran, *Nicholas of Cusa (1401-1464) Platonism at the Dawn of Modernity*," in *Platonism at the Origins of Modernity: Studies on Platonism and Early Modern Philosophy*, eds. Douglas Hedley - Sarah Hutton, Springer, Dordrecht 2007, pp. 9-29.

D. Moran, *Cusanus and Modern Philosophy*, in *The Cambridge Companion to Renaissance Philosophy*. Ed. J. Hankins, Cambridge University, Cambridge 2007, pp. 173-192.

A. Moritz, *Die Andersheit des Anderen – noch einmal zum Problem der Toleranz in Nicolaus von Kues' Dialog De pace fidei*, in «Litterae Cusanae», 1 (2006), pp. 1-17.

F. Nagel, *Nicolaus Cusanus uns die Entstehung der exakten Wissenschaften*, Aschendorff, Münster 1984.

S. Otto, *Language dialectique et silence hiérophanique. L'horizon de la métaphysique chez Proclus, Cusanus et Hegel*, in «Archivio di Filosofia», 1 (1975), pp. 105-114.

E. Pasini, *Ex oppositis quid. Cusano, Erasmo, Leibniz*, in *Cusano e Leibniz*, eds. A. Dall'Igna – D. Roberi, Mimesis, Milano 2013, pp. 249-269.

H. Pasqua, *Le* De non-aliud*: un oeuvre de la maturite*, in *Nicolas de Cues. Les Méthodes d'une Pensée*, Éditions de l'Institut Supérieur de Philosophié, Lovain-La-Neuve 2005, pp. 33-46.

H. Pasqua, *Préface*,in Nicolas de Cues, *Du non-Autre*, Cerf, Paris 2002, pp. 5-27.

H. Pasqua (ed.), *Nicolas de Cues et l'Islam*, Peeters, Leuven 2013.

H. Pasqua, *Nicolas de Cues et l'Islam*, in *Nicolas de Cues et l'Islam*, ed. H. Pasqua, Peeters, Leuven 2013, pp. 1-7.

D. Pätzold, *Einheit und Andersheit: die Bedeutung kategorialer Neubildungen in der Philosophie des Nicolaus Cusanus*, Pahl-Rugenstein, Köln 1981.

M. von Perger, *Nichts Anderes – Ein Fund des Cusanus auf der Namenssuche für das erste Prinzip aller Dinge*, in «Internationale Zeitschrift für Philosophie», 2 (2004), pp. 114-139.

G. Piaia (ed.), *Concordia discors. Studi su Niccolò Cusano e l'umanesimo europeo offerti a Giovanni Santinello*, Antenore, Padova 1993.

G. Piaia, *Nicolò Cusano vescovo filosofo e il castello di Andraz*, Livinallongo del Col di Lana, Belluno 2007.

G. Piaia, *Pericolo turco, universalità del vero e pluralità delle filosofie nel De pace fidei di Nicolò Cusano*, in *Universalität der Vernunft und Pluralität der Erkenntnis bei Nikolaus Cusanus*, eds. K. Reinhardt - H. Schwaetzer, Roderer, Regensburg 2008, pp. 31-44.

V. Ranff, *Mystische Theologie und Gottes-Gedanke bei Pseudo-Dionysius und Nikolaus von Kues*, in «MFCG», 33 (2012), pp. 19-36.

V. Ranff, *Mit Dionysius gegen Wenck*, in *Die Modernitäten des Nikolaus von Kues*, T. Müller – M. Vollet (eds.), Transcript, Bielefeld 2013, pp. 43-56.

E. Reinhardt, *Gemeinsamkeiten und Unterschiede in der trinitarischen Terminologie bei Thierry von*

Chartres und Nikolaus von Kues, in*Eriugena – Cusanus*, eds. A. Kijewska - R. Majeran - H. Schwaetzer, KUL, Lublin 2011, pp. 231-248.

K. Reinhardt, *"Eine bisher unbekannte Handschrift mit Werken des Nikolaus von Kues in der Kapitelsbibliotek von Toledo"*, in «MFCG», 17 (1986), pp. 96-141.

K. Reinhardt, *El nacimento de Dios en el alma según Nicolás de Cusa*, in *Memoria y silencio en la filosofía medieval*, ed. C. Ruta, Jorge Baudino, Buenos Aires 2006, pp. pp. 181-190.

K. Reinhardt, *Die cusanische Idee vom Frieden im Glauben nach der Interpretation von Raymond Klibansky (1905-2005)*, in «Litterae Cusanae», 1 (2006), pp. 18-24.

K. Reinhardt, *Das cusanische Verständnis der Einheit der Religionen im Spiegel hermetischer, platonischer und averroistischer Traditionen*, in *Universalität der Vernunft und Pluralität der Erkenntnis bei Nikolaus Cusanus*, eds. K. Reinhardt - H. Schwaetzer, Roderer, Regensburg 2008, pp. 45-66.

K. Reinhardt - H. Schwaetzer (eds.), *Nicolaus Cusanus und der deutsche Idealismus*, Roderer, Regensburg 2007.

K. Reinhardt, *Die Auslegung des Johannesprologs bei Johannes Scottus Eriugena und Nikolaus von Kues*, in *Eriugena – Cusanus*, eds. A. Kijewska - R. Majeran - H. Schwaetzer, KUL, Lublin 2011, pp. 104-116.

A.-L. Rey – F. Vengeon (eds.), *Nicolas de Cues et G. W. Leibniz: infini, expression et singularité*, «Revue de Métaphysique et de Morale», 2 (2011).

F. Resch, *Triunitas. Die Trinitätspeculation de Nikolaus von Kues*, Aschendorff, Münster 2014.

C. Riccati, *Eriugena e Cusano: due concezioni del mondo come esplicazione della natura intellettuale*, in «Memorie dell'Accademia delle scienze di Torino», I (1976-77), pp. 85-161.

C. Riccati, *«Processio» et «Explicatio»: la doctrine de la création chez Jean Scote et Nicolas de Cues*, Bibliopolis, Napoli 1983.

C. Riccati, *La presenza di Proclo tra neoplatonismo arabizzante e tradizione dionisiana (Bertoldo di Moosburg e Niccolò Cusano)*, in *Concordia discors. Studi su Niccolò Cusano e l'Umanesimo europeo offerti a Giovanni Santinello*, ed. G. Piaia, Antenore, Padova 1993, pp. 23-38.

M. Riedenauer, *Geschichtliche und kulturelle Relativierung der Religion bei Nikolaus Cusanus*, in *Nicolaus Cusanus*, in *Perspektiven seiner Geistphilosophie*, eds. K. Reinhardt - H. Schwaetzer, Roderer, Regensburg 2003, pp. 35-50.

M. Riedenauer, *Logik, Rationalität und religiöse Rede nach Nikolaus Cusanus*, in *Juden, Christen und Muslime. Religionsdialoge im Mittelalter*, ed. M. Lutz-Bachmann - A. Fidora, WBG, Darmstadt 2004.

M. Riedenauer, *Religiöse und kulturelle Pluralität als Konfliktursache bei Nikolaus Cusanus*, in *Conflict and Reconciliation. Perspectives on Nicholas of Cusa*, ed. I. Bocken, Brill, Leiden 2004, pp. 131-159.

M. Riedenauer, *Pluralità di prospettive finite nell'orizzonte dell'infinito. Conseguenze della epistemologia nuova di Cusano*, in *El problema del conocimiento en Nicolás de Cusa: genealogía y proyección*, eds. J. M. Machetta - C. D'Amico, Biblos, Buenos Aires 2005, pp. 281-290.

M. Riedenauer, *Pluralität und Rationalität. Die Herausforderung der Vernunft durch religiöse und kulturelle Vielfalt nach Nikolaus Cusanus*, Kohlhammer, Stuttgart 2007.

M. Riedenauer, *Aufgeklärte Religion als Bedingung interreligiösen Diskurses nach Nikolaus Cusanus*, in «Polylog», 21 (2009), pp. 21-34.

J. G. Ríos, *Dionisio Areopagita*, in Nicolás de Cusa, *Acerca de lo no-otro o de la definición que todo define. Nuevo texto crítico original*, intr. and trans by J. M. Machetta, critical text and notes by C. D'Amico - M. D'Ascenso - A. Eisenkopf - J. G. Rios - J. M. Machetta - K. Reinhardt - C. Rusconi - H. Schwaetzer, Biblos, Buenos Aires 2008, pp. 347-358.

J. G. Ríos, *La fuerza significativa de "Lo no-otro" como enigma de lo-no-otro mismo*, in *El problema del conocimiento en Nicolás de Cusa: genealogía y proyección*, eds. J. M. Machetta - C. D'Amico, Biblos, Buenos Aires 2005, pp. 219-226.

J. G. Ríos, *Metafísica de la Palabra,* Biblos, Buenos Aires 2014.

G. Ríos, *Possest, non aliud, posse ipsum. Los nombres enigmáticos como manuductiones en el pensamiento cusano de senectud*, in *Manuductiones. Festschrift zu Ehren von J M. Machetta und C. D'Amico*, eds. C. Rusconi, Aschendorff, Münster 2014, pp. 169-190.

F. Rohstock, *Rezension von Davide Monaco, 2010, Deus Trinitas. Dio come non altro nel pensiero di Nicolò Cusano, prefazione di Werner Beierwaltes, Roma, Città Nuova*, in «Bochumer philosophisches Jahrbuch für Antike und Mittelalter» 15 (2012), pp. 298-300.

M. Rohstock, *Der negative Selbstbezug des Absoluten: Untersuchungen zu Nicolaus Cusanus' Konzept des Nicht-Anderen*, De Gruyter, Berlin 2014.

C. M. Rusconi, *Cusanus und Thierry von Chartres. Die Einteilung der spekulativen Wissenschaften und der Begriff forma essendi in „De possest" und im Kommentar „Librum hunc"*, in *Das europäische Erbe im Denken des Nikolaus von Kues. Geistesgeschichte als Geistesgegenwart*, eds. H. Schwaetzer - K. Zeyer, Aschendorff, Münster 2008, pp. 285-302.

C. M. Rusconi, *Commentator Boethii* De Trinitate[...] ingenio clarissimus. *Die Kommentare des Thierry von Chartres zu De Trinitate des Boethius als Quellen des Cusanus*, in «MFCG», 33 (2012), pp. 247-290.

G. Saitta, *Niccolò Cusano e l'umanesimo italiano*, Tamari, Bologna 1957.

G. Santinello, *Il pensiero di Nicolò Cusanonella sua prospettiva estetica*, Liviana, Padova 1958.

G. Santinello, *Proclo nel pensiero del Cusano,* in Id., *Saggi sull'umanesimo di Proclo*, Pàtron, Bologna 1966, pp. 15-50.

G. Santinello, *Riflessioni sul concetto di analogia nel pensiero moderno*, in *Metafore dell'invisibile. Ricerche sull'analogia*, ed. G. Santinello, Brescia, Morcelliana, 1984, pp. 34-58.

G. Santinello, *Nicolò Cusano e l'utopia dell'unità culturale e religiosa nel Quattrocento*, in «Archivio di filosofia», 53 (1985), pp. 381-391.

G. Santinello, *L'uomo «ad imaginem et similitudinem» nel Cusano*, in «Doctor Seraphicus», XXXVII (1990), pp. 85-97.

G. Santinello, *Novità nel pensiero del tardo Cusano*, in En kai plēthos*: Einheit und Vielheit. Festschrift für Karl Bormann zum 65. Geburtstag,* eds. L. Hagemann – R. Glei, Würzburg 1993, pp. 161-173.

R. P. Scharlemann, *God as Not-Other: Nicholas of Cusa's* De li Non Aliud, in Id. (ed.), *Naming God*, Paragon Hause, New York 1985, pp. 116-132.

F. A. Scharpff, *Cusa und Leibnitz*, in Id., *Der Cardinal Nicolaus von Cusa als Reformator in Kirche, Reich und Philosophie des Fünfzehnten Jahrhunderts*, Laupp, Tübingen 1871 [repr. Minerva, Frankfurt am Main 1966].

H. Schnarr, *Fruhe Beziehungen des Nikolaus von Kues zu italienischen Humanisten*, in M. Thurner (ed.), *Nicolaus Cusanus zwischen Deutschland und Italien*, Akademie, Berlin 2002, pp. 187-213.

G. Schneider, *Gott – das Nichtandere*, Aschendorff, Münster 1970.

W. Schulze, *Zahl, Proportion, Analogie*, Aschendorff, Münster 1978.

T. Schumacher, *Trinität. Zur Interpretation eines Strukturelements Cusanischen Denkens*, Herbert Utz, München 1997.

H. Schwaetzer, *"Mens" y "Memoria". El maestro Eckhart en el espejo del Cusano*, in *Memoria y silencio en la filosofía medieval*, ed. C. Ruta, Jorge Baudino, Buenos Aires 2006, pp. 171-180.

H. Schwaetzer, *Aequalitas*, Georg Olms, Hildesheim 2000.

H. Schwaetzer, *Zur Cusanus-Rezeption im Deutschen Idealismus*, in «Litterae Cusanae», 3 (2003), pp. 24-26.

H. Schwaetzer, *Die intellektuelle Anschauung als methodisches Prinzip einer naturwissenschaftlichen "scientia aenigmatica": Anmerkungen zur Konzeption von Wissenschaft bei Cusanus und im Deutschen Idealismus*, in «MFCG», 29 (2005), pp. 247-261.

H. Schwaetzer, Viva imago dei: *Überlegungen zum Ursprung eines anthropologischen Grundprinzips bei Nicolaus Cusanus*, in *Spiegel und Porträt. Zur Bedeutung zweier zentraler Bilder im Denken des Nicolaus Cusanus*, eds. I. Bocken - H. Schwaetzer, Uitgeverij Shaker, Maastricht 2005, pp. 113-132.

H. Schwaetzer, *"Visio intellectualis" – Cusanus und Schelling. Eine systematische Annäherung*, in *Nicolaus Cusanus und der deutsche Idealismus*, eds. K. Reinhardt - H. Schwaetzer, Roderer, Regensburg 2007, pp. 87-102.

H. Schwaetzer, *"visio intellectualis" – Cusanus und Schelling. Eine systematische Annäherung*, in, *Nicolaus Cusanus und der deutsche Idealismus*, eds. K. Reinhardt - H. Schwaetzer, Roderer, Regensburg 2007, pp. 87-102.

H. Schwaetzer, *Ein unbekannter Bekannter – Die Rezeption des Nikolaus von Kues bei Schelling*, in *Nicolaus Cusanus: ein bewundernswerter historischer Brennpunkt. Philosophische Tradition und wissenschaftliche Rezeption*, Eds. K. Reinhardt – H. Schwaetzer, Roderer, Regensburg 2008, pp. 167-188.

H. Schwaetzer, *"Non-autre" comme la Trinité*, in *La Trinité chez Eckhart et Nicolas de Cues*, ed. M.A. Vannier, Cerf, Paris 2009, pp. 145-153.

H. Schwaetzer – G. Steer (eds.), *Meister Eckhart und Nikolaus von Kues*, Kohlhammer, Stuttgart 2011.

H. Schwaetzer – M. A. Vannier (eds.), *Zum Subjektbegriff bei Meister Eckhart und Niklaus von Kues*, Aschendorff, Münster 2011.

H. Schwaetzer – M.A. Vannier (eds.), *Zum Intellektverständnis bei Meister Eckhart und Nikolaus*, Aschendorff, Münster 2012.

H. Schwaetzer, *Cusanus, Leibniz, Herbart? Robert Zimmermanns Cusanus-Deutung im Kontext des 19. Jahrhunderts*, in *Cusano e Leibniz. Prospettive filosofiche*, eds. A. Dall'Igna – D. Roberi, Mimesis, Milano 2013, pp. 169-182.

H. Schwaetzer – M.A. Vannier (eds.), *Der Bildbegriff bei Meister Eckhard und Nikolaus von Kues*, Aschendorff, Münster 2015.

H. Schwaetzer, *Nichts anderes als Spiegel*, in *Der Bildbegriff bei Meister Eckhard und Nikolaus von Kues*, eds. H. Schwaetzer – M.A. Vannier, Aschendorff, Münster 2015, pp. 155-166.

W. Schwarz, *Das Problem der Seinsvermittlung bei Nikolaus von Cues*, Brill, Leiden 1970.

J. Seidengart, *L'infini chez Nicolas de Cues et Leibniz*, in *Cusano e Leibniz. Prospettive filosofiche*, eds. A. Dall'Igna – D. Roberi, Mimesis, Milano 2013, pp. 57-71.

M. Seidlmayer, *'Una religio in rituum varietate'. Zur Religionsauffassung des Nicolaus von Kues*, in «Archiv für Kultergeschichte», 2 (1954), pp. 145-207.

M. Seidlmayer, *Nicolaus von Cues und der Humanism*, in *Humanismus, Mystik und Kunst in der Welt des Mittelalters*, by J. Koch, Brill, Leiden 1959, pp. 1-38.

H. G. Senger, *Ludus sapientiae. Studien zum Werk und zur Wirkungsgeschichte des Nikolaus von Kues*, Brill, Leiden 2002.

E. Sonderegger, *Cusanus: Definitio als Selbstbestimmung*, in «Bochumer Philosophisches Jahrbuch für Antike und Mittelalter», 4 (1999), pp. 153-177.

A. Speer, *Zwei Versuche, Gott zu denken: Meister Eckhart und Nicolaus Cusanus*, in «MFCG», 33 (2012), pp. 169-194.

R. Stadelmann, *Vom Geist des Ausgehenden Mittelalters*, Niemeyer, Tübingen 1929.

J. Stallmach, *Das Nichtandere als Begriff des Absoluten*, in *Universitas. Dienst an Wahrheit und Leben. Festschrift für Bischof Dr. Albert Stohr*, vol. I, ed. Ludwig Lenhart, Matthias-Grünewald, Meinz 1960, pp. 329-335 [repr. in J. Stallmach, *Ineinsfall der Gegensätze und Weisheit des Nichtwissens. Grundzüge der Philosophie des Nikolaus von Kues*, Aschendorff, Münster 1989].

J. Stallmach, *Immanenz und Transzendenz im Denken des Cusanus*, in *Transzendenz. Zu einem Grundwort der klassischen Metaphysik*, eds. L. Honnefelder - W. Schüssler, Schöningh, München 1992, pp. 183-192.

J. Stallmach, *Sein und das Können-selbst bei Nikolaus von Kues*, in *Parusia. Studien zur Philosophie Platons und zur Problemgeschichte des Platonismus. Festgabe für J. Hirschberger*, ed. K. Flasch, Minerva, Frankfurt am Main 1965, pp. 407-421.

J. Stallmach, *Einheit der Religionen - Friede unter den Religionen*, in «MFCG», 16 (1984), pp. 61-81.

G. Steer, *Die Predigten des Nikolaus von Kues im Vergleich mit dem Predigtenwerk von Meister Eckhart*, in «MFCG», 30 (2005), pp. 145-169.

M. O. Stephan, *Potentia vs Possibilitas? Posse! Zur cusanischen Konzeption der Möglichkeit*, in *Potentialität und Possibilität. Modalaussagen in der Geschichte der Metaphysik*, ed. T. Bucheim, Frommann-Holzboog, Stuttgart 2001, pp. 237-253.

A. Stöckl, *Geschichte der Philosophie des Mittelalters*, III, Kirchheim, Mainz 1966.

M. Stünkel, *Una sit religio. Religionsbegriffe und Begriff Topologien bei Cusanus, Llull und Maimonides*, Königshausen, Würzburg 2013.

M. Thurner, *Die Philosophie der Gabe bei Meister Eckhart und Nikolaus Cusanus*, in *Nicolaus Cusanus zwischen Deutschland und Italien*, ed. M. Thurner, Akademie, Berlin 2002, pp. 153-184.

M. Thurner, *Explication der Welt und mystische Verinnerlichung. Die hermetische Definition des Menschen als "secundus deus" bei Cusanus*, in *Hermetism from the Antiquity to Humanism. La tradizione ermetica dal mondo tardo-antico all'Umanesimo*, ed. P. Lucentini -I. Parri - V. Perrone Compagni, Brepols, Turnhout 2003.

F. Tomatis, *Inizio e parola di Dio*, in *Vernunft und Glauben. Ein philosophischer Dialog der Moderne mit dem Christentum*, ed. G. F. Frigo, Akademie, Berlin 2006, pp. 55-61 [repr. in P. Coda – M. Donà, *Dio-Trinità tra filosofi e teologi*, Bompiani, Milano 2007, pp. 95-108].

F. Tomatis, *Ipseità, diversità e dia-ferenza*, in «Teoria», 1 (2006), pp. 31-35.

F. Tomatis, *Libertà di sapere. Università e dialogo interculturale*, Bompiani, Milano 2009.

F. Tomatis, *Cusano e l'ultimo Schelling*, in *Cusano*, ed. D. Monaco, «Il Pensiero», 1-2 (2009), pp. 75-114.

J. Übinger, *Die Gotteslehre des Nicolaus Cusanus*, Schöningh, Paderborn 1888.

P. Valkenberg, *Sifting the Qur' an: Two Forms of Interreligious Hermeneutics in Nicholas of Cusa*, in *Interreligious Hermeneutics in Pluralistic Europe*, eds. D. Cheetham – U. Winkler – O. Leirvik – J. Gruber, Rodopi, Amsterdam 2011, pp. 27-48.

M.-A. Vannier (ed.), *La naissance de Dieu dans l'âme chez Eckhart et Nicolas de Cues*, Cerf, Paris 2006.

P. Valkenberg, Una religio in Rituum Varietate: *Religious Pluralism, the Qur'an, and Nichols of Cusa*, in *Nicholas of Cusa and Islam Polemic and Dialogue in the Middle Ages*, eds. I.C. Levy – R. George-Turtkovíc – D. F. Duclow, Brill, Leiden 2014, pp. 30-48.

M.-A. Vannier, *Hat Nikolaus von Kues die Predigten 101 bis 104 von Eckhart gelesen?*, in *Das europäische Erbe im Denken des Nikolaus von Kues*, eds. H. Schwaetzer – K. Zeyer, Aschendorff, Münster 2008, pp. 303-314.

M.A. Vannier(ed.), *La Trinité chez Eckhart et Nicolas de Cues*, Cerf, Paris 2009.

M.A. Vannier(ed.), *Encyclopédie des mystiques rhénans d'Eckhart à Nicolas de Cues et leur reception*, Cerf, Paris 2011.

M.-A. Vannier (ed.), *La création et l'anthropologie chez Eckhart et Nicolas de Cues*, Cerf, Paris, 2011.

E. Vansteenberghe, *Le cardinal Nicolas de Cues (1401-1464). L'action – la pensée*, Champion, Paris 1920 [repr. Minerva, Frankfurt am Main 1963].

E. Vansteenberghe, *Quelques lectures de jeunesse de Nicolas de Cues d'après un manuscrit inconnu de sa bibliothèque*, in *«Archives d'Histoire Doctrinale et Littéraire du Moyen Âge»*, 3 (1928), pp. 275-284.

C. Vasoli, *L'ecumenismo di Niccolò Cusano*, in *Cusano e Galileo*, CEDAM, Padova 1964, pp. 9-51.

C. Vasoli, *De Nicolas de Kues et Jean Pic de la Mirandole à Jean Bodin: trois «colloques»*, in *Jean Bodin. Actes du Colloque Interdisciplinaire d'Angers*, 2 voll., Universitè d'Angers,Angers 1985, I, pp. 253-275.

C. Vasoli, *Niccolò Cusano e la cultura umanistica fiorentina, Nicolaus Cusanus zwischen Deutschland und Italien*, ed. M. Thurner, Akademie, Berlin 2002, pp. 75-90.

F. Vengeon, *Mathématiques, création et humanisme chez Nicolas de Cues*, in «Reveu d'histoire des sciences», 59 (2006), 219-244.

F. Vengeon, *Nicolas de Cues, le monde humain, métaphysique de l'infini et anthropologie*, Jérôme Millon, Grenoble 2011.

G. M. Verd, *Ser y nombre de dios en Nicolás de Cusa*, in «Miscelánea Comillas», 52 (1969), pp. 29-59.

V. Vitiello, *De Possest*, in *Cusanus*, ed. D. Monaco, «Il Pensiero», 1-2 (2009), pp. 129-139.

M. Watanabe, *Nicholas of Cusa and the idea of tollerance*, in *Niccolò Cusano agli inizi del mondo moderno*, ed. G. Santinello, Sansoni, Firenze 1970, pp. 409-418.

M. Watanabe, *Cusanus, Islam and Religious Tolerance*, in *Nicholas of Cusa and Islam Polemic and Dialogue in the Middle Ages*, eds. I.C. Levy – R. George-Turtkovíc – D. F. Duclow, Brill, Leiden 2014, pp. 14-16.

G. Wenz, *De pace fidei. Nicolaus von Kues als theoretiker eines christlichen Oekumenismus*, in «MFCG», 28 (2003), pp. 189-210.

P. Wilpert, *Einführung*, in Nicolaus von Kues, *Vom Nichtandere*, Meiner Hamburg 1952, pp. V-XXVIII.

E. A. Wyller, *Zum Begriff "non aliud" bei Cusanus*, in *Niccolò Cusano agli inizi del mondo moderno*, ed. G. Santinello, Sansoni, Firenze 1970, pp. 419-443.

E. A. Wyller, *Einheit/Andersheit – Dialektik oder Henologie*, in *Einheitskonzepte in der idealistischen und in der gegenwärtigen Philosophie*, eds. K. Gloy - D. Schmidig, Lang, Bern 1987, pp. 231-260.

E. A. Wyller, *Identität und Kontradiktion. Ein Weg zu Cusanus' Unendlichkeitsidee*, in «MFCG», 15 (1982), pp. 104-120 [ext. vers. in E. A. Wyller, *Henologische Perspective. Platon, Johannes, Cusanus*, Rodopi, Amsterdam 1995].

E. A. Wyller, *Nicolaus Cusanus "De non aliud" und Platons dialog "Parmenides"*, in *Studia Platonica*, eds. K. Döring - W. Kullmann, John Benjamins, Amsterdam 1974, pp. 239-251.

K. Yamaki, Imago Dei. *Über "anthropozentrische" Bezeichnungen in der cusanischen Imago-Dei-Lehre*, in *Manuductiones. Festschrift zu Ehren von J M. Machetta und C. D'Amico*, eds. C. Rusconi, Aschendorff, Münster 2014, pp. 124-136.

G. Zedania, *Von Einheit zu Pluralität. Nikolaus von Kues als Interpret der Schriften des Dionysius Pseudo-Areopagita*, Suedwestdeutscher Verlag für Hochschulschriften, Saarbrücken 2009.

K. Zeyer, *Neuplatonismusrezeption im Umfeld der deutschen Idealisten. Eine Recherche mit Blick auf Schelling und Cusanus*, in «Verbum» 14 (2012), pp. 61-81.

K. Zeyer, *Cusanus als Vorläufer von Leibniz. Cusanus-Rezeption im 19. Jahrhundert mit besonderer Beücksichtigung von R. Eucken und R. Falckenberg*, in *Cusano e Leibniz*, eds. A. Dall'Igna – D. Roberi, Mimesis, Milano 2013, pp. 227-239.

P. Zerbi, *Medioevo: tolleranza o intolleranza?*, in *La tolleranza religiosa. Indagini storiche e riflessioni filosofiche*, ed. M. Sina, Vita e Pensiero, Milano 1991, pp. 13-26.

P. Ziche, *"der Punkt sey der Kreis in seinem Chaos". Cusanische Kreisbildlichkeit und Schellingsche Möglichkeitsstrukturen &Spuren von Cusanus im Idealismus*, in *Nicolaus Cusanus und der deutsche Idealismus*, eds. K. Reinhardt - H. Schwaetzer, Roderer, Regensburg 2007, pp. 59-86.

R. Zimmermann, *Der Cardinal Nikolaus Cusanus als Vorläufer Leibnitzens*, in «Sitzungsberichte der Philos.-Histor. Classe der Kais. Akademie der Wissenschaften», Bd. 8, Staatsdruckerei, Wien 1852, pp. 306-328.

B. Other texts referred to

M. Abbate, *Il divino tra unità e molteplicità: saggio sulla Teologia Platonica di Proclo*, Edizioni dell'Orso, Alessandria 2008.

F. Bacchelli, *Giovanni Pico e Pierleone da Spoleto. Tra filosofia dell'amore e tradizione cabalistica*, Olschki, Firenze 2001.

W. Beierwaltes, *Proklos. Grundzüge seiner Metaphysik*, Klostermann, Frankfurt am Main 1965.

W. Beierwaltes, *Platonismus und Idealismus*, Klostermann, Frankfurt am Main 1972 [II. ed. 2004].

W. Beierwaltes, *Subjektivität, Schöpfertum, Freiheit. Die philosophie der Renaissance zwischen Tradition und neuzeitlichem Bewusstsein*, in *Der Übergang zur Neuzeit und die Wirkung von Traditionen*, Vandenhoeck & Ruprecht, Göttingen 1978, pp. 15-31.

W. Beierwaltes, *Identität und Differenz*, Klostermann, Frankfurt am Main 1980.

W. Beierwaltes, *Denken des Einen. Studien zum Neuplatonismus und dessen Wirkungsgeschichte*, Klostermann, Frankfurt am Main 1985.

W. Beierwaltes, *Eriugena. Grundzüge seines Denkens*, Klostermann, Frankfurt am Main 1994.

W. Beierwaltes *Procliana. Spätantikes Denken und seine Spuren*, Klostermann, Frankfurt am Main 2007.

W. Beierwaltes, *Platonismus in Christentum*, Klostermann, Frankfurt am Main 1998.

W. Beierwaltes *Das wahre Selbst. Studien zu Plotins Begriff des Geistes und des Einen*, Klostermann, Frankfurt am Main 2001.

W. Beierwaltes, *Fussnoten zu Plato*, Klostermann, Frankfurt am Main 2010.

E. Bellini, *Introduzione alla lettura del corpus dionisiano*, in D. Areopagita, *Tutte le opere*, eds. P Scazzoso and E. Bellini, Rusconi, Milano 1981, pp. 23-38.

M. Cacciari, *La maschera della tolleranza*, in *La maschera della tolleranza*, Bur, Milano 2006, 111-148.

R. Celada Ballanti, *Pensiero religioso liberale. Lineamenti, figure, prospettive*, Morcelliana, Brescia 2009.

C. Ciancio, *Introduzione al convegno*, in «Annuario Filosofico, 20 (2004), pp. 33-37.

C. Ciancio, *Libertà e dono dell'essere*, Marietti, Torino 2009.

P. Coda, *Evento pasquale. Trinità e storia*, Città Nuova, Roma 1984.

P. Coda, *Il negativo e la Trinità. Ipotesi su Hegel*, Città Nuova, Roma 1994.

P. Coda, *L'agape come grazia e libertà*, Città Nuova, Roma 1994.

P. Coda, *Teo-logia. La parola di Dio nelle mani dell'uomo*, Mursia, Milano 1997.

P. Coda, *L'altro di Dio. Rivelazione e kenosi in Sergej Bulgakov*, Città Nuova, Roma 2003.

P. Coda, *Teo-logia. La parola di Dio nelle mani dell'uomo*, Milano 1997.

P. Coda - A. Tapken (eds.), *La Trinità e il pensare. Figure, percorsi prospettive*, , Città Nuova, Roma 1997.

P. Coda - L. Zák (eds.), *Abitando la Trinità. Per un rinnovamento dell'ontologia*, Città Nuova, Roma 1998

P. Coda, *Il logos e il nulla. Trinità religioni mistica*, Città Nuova, Roma 2003.

Dio-Trinità, eds. P. Coda - M. Donà, Bompiani, Milano 2007.

P. Coda, *Sul luogo della Trinità*, Città Nuova, Roma 2008.

M. Coppola - G. Fernicola - L. Pappalardo (eds.), Dialogus. *Il dialogo filosofico tra le religioni nel pensiero tardo-antico, medievale e umanistico*, Città Nuova, Roma 2014.

E. Corsini, *Il trattato* De divinis nominibus *dello Pseudo Dionigi Areopagitae i commenti neoplatonici al Parmenide*, Giappichelli, Torino 1962.

L. D'Ascia, *Il Corano e la Tiara. L'epistola a Maometto II di Enea Silvio Piccolomini (papa Pio II)*, Pendragon, Bologna 2001.

H. Denifle, *Das Cusanische Exemplar lateinischer Schriften Eckharts in Cues*, in «Archiv für Literatur- und Kirchengeschichte des Mittelalters», 2 (1986), pp. 673-687.

G. d'Onofrio (dir.), *Storia della Teologia nel Medioevo*, 3 voll, Piemme, Casale Monferrato 1996.

G. d'Onofrio,*History of Theology*. II. *The Middle Ages*, eng. trans. M. J. O'Connell, Liturgical Press, Collegeville (Minnesota) 2008.

G. d'Onofrio (ed.),*History of Theology*. III. *The Renaissance*, eng. trans. M. J. O'Connell, Liturgical Press, Collegeville (Minnesota) 2008.

G. d'Onofrio, *Storia del pensiero medievale*, Città Nuova, Roma 2013[2].

G. d'Onofrio, *Pensiero medievale e dialogo tra le religioni*, in Dialogus. *Il dialogo filosofico tra le religioni nel pensiero tardo-antico, medievale e umanistico*, eds. M. Coppola - G. Fernicola - L. Pappalardo, Città Nuova, Roma 2014, pp. 11-58.

F. Ferrari, *L'enigma del Parmenide*, in Platone, *Parmenide*, Bur, Milano 2004, pp. 9-161.

E. C. Fontana, *Fabro all'Angelicum*, Edivi, Segni 2007;

E. C. Fontana, *Fabro e l'esistenzialismo*, Edivi, Segni 2008;

E. C. Fontana, *Metafisica della partecipazione. Genesi e significato della scoperta fabriana*, Edivi, Segni 2011.

E. Garin, *Erasmo*, Cultura della Pace, S. Domenico di Fiesole, 1988.

E. Garin, *Medioevo e Rinascimento. Studi e ricerche*, Laterza, Roma-Bari 1954[1], 2005.

R. Glei, *Pius Aeneas und der Islam. Der Brief des Papstes an den Eroberer Konstantinopels*, in *Religiöse Kommunikation - Formen und Praxis vor der Neuzeit*, eds. G. Binder - K. Ehlich, WVT, Trier 1997, pp. 301-325.

P. Hadot, *Porphyre et Victorinus*, 2 voll., Études Augustiniennes, Paris 1968.

J. Hankins, *Plato in the Italian Renaissance*, Brill, Leiden 1991[2].

J. Helmrath, *Wege des Humanismus,* Mohr, Tübingen 2013.

T. Khobusch, *Negative theologie als praktische Metaphysik*, in *Théologie négative*, ed. M.M. Olivetti, CEDAM, Padova 2002, pp. 185-200.

P. O. Kristeller, *Studies in Renaissance Thought and Letters*, I, Edizioni di Storia e Letteratura, Roma 1956.

K.-J. Kuschel, *"Jud, Christ und Muselmann vereinigt"? Lessings "Nathan der Weise"*, Patmos, Düsseldorf 2004.

M. L. Lanzillo, *Voltaire. La politica della tolleranza*, Roma 2000.

M.L. Lanzillo, *Tolleranza*, Bologna 2001.

S. Lilla, *Dionigi Areopagita e il platonismo cristiano*, Morcelliana, Brescia 2005.

T. Leinkauf, *Mundus combinatus. Studien zur Struktur der barocken Universalwissenschaften am Beispiel Athanasius Kircher SJ (1602-1680)*, Akademie, Berlin 1993, 2009[2].

T. Leinkauf, *Einheit, Natur, Geist. Beiträge zu metaphysischen Grundproblemen im Denken von Gottfried Wilhelm Leibniz*, Berlin, Trafo, 2012.

S. Mancini, *Beierwaltes e la trascendalità del pensiero*, in «Giornale di Metafisica», 1 (2007), pp. 191-210.

S. Mancini, *Beierwaltes nella corrente dell'eriugenismo: la duplex theoria e lo statuto trascendentale della manifestazione*, «Annuario Filosofico», 22 (2006), pp. 117-134.

F. Lo Monaco, *Tolleranza*, Guida, Napoli 2005.

G. Mazzotta, *Stupore della ragione*, Edizioni Ligea, Lamezia Terme 1986.

G. Mazzotta, *Ipotesi su Fabro*, in «Euntes Docete», 50 (1997), 213-231.

G. Mazzotta, *Teologia aristotelica e metafisica dell'essere. Ermeneutica tomista di Metafisica Lambda*, UUP, Città del Vaticano 2000.

M. Migliori, *Dialettica e verità. Commentario filosofico al "Parmenide" di Platone*, Vita e Pensiero, Milano 1990.

J. Monfasani, *George of Trebizond: a bibliography and a study of his Rhetoric and Logic*, Leiden, Brill 1976.

D. Moran, *The philosophy of Johannes Scottus Eriugena. A Study on Idealism in the Middle Ages*, Cambridge University Press, Cambridge 1989.

C. J. Nederman – J. Ch. Laursen (eds.), *Different and Dissent: Theories of Toleration in Early Modern Europa*, Rowman, Lanham 1996.

F. Niewöhner, *Veritas sive Varietas. Lessings Toleranzparabel und das Buch Von den drei Betrügern*, Schneider, Heidelberg 1988.

M. Pagano, *Ermeneutica e interculturalità*, in «Annuario filosofico», 26 (2010), pp. 135-148.

M. Pangallo, *L'essere come atto nel tomismo essenziale di Cornelio Fabro*, Libreria Editrice Vaticana, Città del Vaticano 1987.

M. Pangallo, *Il principio di causalità nella metafisica di s. Tommaso. Saggio di ontologia tomista alla luce dell'interpretazione di Cornelio Fabro*, Libreria Editrice Vaticana, Città del Vaticano 1991.

L. Pareyson, *Verità e interpretazione*, Mursia, Milano 1971.

L. Pareyson, *Ontologia della libertà. Il male e la sofferenza*, Einaudi, Torino 1995.

F. Piro, *Varietas identitate compensata: studio sulla formazione della metafisica di Leibniz*, Bibliopolis, Napoli 1990.

F. Piro, *Spontaneità e ragion sufficiente: determinismo e filosofia dell'azione in Leibniz*, Edizioni di Storia e letteratura, Roma 2002.

F. Piro, *Species infima: definibilità e indefinibilità dell'individuo*, in *Monadi e monadologie: il mondo degli individui tra Bruno, Leibniz e Husserl*, eds. B. M. D'Ippolito - A. Montano - F. Piro, Rubbettino, Soveria Mannelli 2005, pp. 83-113.

G. Riconda, *Tradizione e avventura*, SEI, Torino 2001.

G. Riconda, *Tradizione e pensiero*, Edizioni dell'Orso, Torino 2009.

M. Rotzoll, *Pierleone da Spoleto. Vita e opere di un medico del Rinascimento*, Olschki, Firenze 2000.

L. Sileo, *L'esordio della teologia universitaria: I maestri secolari della prima metà del Duecento*, in *Storia della Teologia nel Medioevo*, 3 voll, dir. G. d'Onofrio, Piemme, Casale Monferrato 1996, II, pp. 603-644.

C. Steel, *Beyond the Principle of contradiction? Proclus' Parmenides and the Origin of Negative Theologie*, in *Die Logik der Transzendentalen. Festschrift für Jan A. Aertsen zum 65. Geburtstag*, ed. Martin Pickavé, de Gruyter, Berlin 2003, pp. 581-599.

F. Tomatis, *Kenosis del logos. Ragione e rivelazione nell'ultimo Schelling*, Città Nuova, Roma 1994.

F. Tomatis, *Ontologia del male. L'ermeneutica di Pareyson*, Città Nuova, Roma 1995.

F. Tomatis, *L'argomento ontologico. L'esistenza di Dio da Anselmo a Schelling*, Città Nuova, Roma 1997.

F. Tomatis, *Schelling: mysterium Trinitatis* in *La Trinità e il pensare. Figure percorsi prospettive*, eds. P. Coda – A. Tapken, Città Nuova, Roma 1997, pp. 45-64.

F. Tomatis, *Trinità e inizio in Schelling*, in *Abitando la Trinità*, eds. P. Coda - L. Zak, Città Nuova, Roma 1998.

F. Tomatis, *Escatologia della negazione*, Città Nuova, Roma 1999.

F. Tomatis, *«Kénōsis» del Figlio e mistero trinitario*, in *Cristo nella filosofia contemporanea*, ed. S. Zucal, vol I, San Paolo, Cinisello Balsamo 2000, pp. 171-187.

F. Tomatis, *Inizio e scelta*, in *Il pensiero di Luigi Pareyson nella filosofia contemporanea*, Trauben, Torino 2000, pp. 115-124.

F. Tomatis, *Dialogo dei principi con Gesù Socrate Lao Tzu*, Bompiani, Milano 2007.

F. Tomatis, *Pensiero rivelativo e dialogo ermeneutico*, in *L'esistenza e il logos. Filosofia, esperienza religiosa, Rivelazione*, eds. P. D. Bubbio - P. Coda, Città Nuova, Roma 2009, pp. 224-236.

A. Tura, *Un incunabolo Grimani e due codici pichensi nella Bibliothèque Nationale di Parigi*, in «La Bibliofilia», 99 (1997), pp. 181-189.

C. A. Viano, *Introduzione*, in J. Locke, *Lettera sulla tolleranza*, a c. di C. A. Viano, Roma - Bari 1994.

V. Vitiello, *Cristianesimo senza redenzione*, Laterza, Roma-Bari 1995.

V. Vitiello, *Il Dio possibile. Esperienze di cristianesimo*, Città Nuova, Roma 2002.

V. Vitiello, *Dire Dio in segreto*, Città Nuova, Roma 2005.

Index